Calabashes and Kings

Calabashes

and Kings,

An Introduction to

HAWAII

Stanley D. Porteus

CHARLES E. TUTTLE CO.: PUBLISHERS
Rutland, Vermont & Tokyo, Japan

Representatives
Continental Europe: BOXERBOOKS, INC., *Zurich*
British Isles: PRENTICE-HALL INTERNATIONAL, INC., *London*
Australasia: PAUL FLESCH & CO., PTY. LTD., *Melbourne*
Canada: M. G. HURTIG LTD., *Edmonton*

Published by the Charles E. Tuttle Company, Inc.
of Rutland, Vermont & Tokyo, Japan
with editorial offices at
Suido 1-chome, 2-6, Bunkyo-ku, Tokyo, Japan

Copyright in Japan, 1970 by Charles E. Tuttle Co., Inc.

Library of Congress Catalog Card No. 70-116485

Standard Book No. 8048 0908-9

First Tuttle edition published 1970

Table of Contents

Publisher's Foreword

"ANOTHER BOOK about Hawaii?" the reader might be tempted to ask. The answer: Not just another book, but an excellent and highly interesting study of the many aspects of this important crossroads of the Pacific—an exposition based upon the observations of historians, missionaries, and writers such as Stevenson, Twain, and Jack London and upon the author's deep interest in and affection for Hawaii.

A pleasant subject was one of the "excuses" for this work, which has already gone into three printings. But, the author says candidly, "those of us who live here and love the place are fully conscious that the islands and their racial, social, and economic conditions are subject to criticism, mostly on the basis of misunderstanding. Some of these misconceptions lie at our own door, he says. We have been too busy building up our Hawaiian complex, that is as glamorous and unsubstantial as a pin-up girl. The intelligent visitor is entitled to an account which shall be independent and unbiased." A great part of this popular book's charm lies in its candor.

Introduction: Books on Hawaii

THE ROMANS called it *scribendi cacoëthes,* the itch for writing. In Hawaii it appears in a most contagious form. It seems that almost everyone who has lived or visited here is either inspired or irritated, with the result that Hawaii is one of the most written about places on earth. No phase of its past, its problems, paradoxes, scandals, and scenic features has been neglected by authors. Libraries list no fewer than ninety books in which the word "Hawaii" appears in either title or subtitle, though strangely enough, there is none in which the name stands alone. It is Hawaii, plus offshore territory, restless rampart, rainbow land, isles of enchantment, or else it is the history, people, kingdom, revolutions, legends, tales, string figures, folklore, marriages, feather cloaks, pioneer days of Hawaii. Besides all this mass of literature, the word "Hawaiian" is included on the title pages of another sixty books.

Why there should be added another book on Hawaii is a matter for the reader to determine. This is one situation where the proof of the pudding is clearly in the eating. There was, however, one personal reason: this book was undertaken somewhat as relaxation; the writer's last publication, being devoted to the effects of certain brain operations on the insane, bore a title that is perfectly appalling from the standpoint of reader-interest, namely, "Mental Changes After Bilateral Prefrontal Lobotomy." The next literary effort will be devoted to "Primitive Mentality." Between such dry crusts of daily bread the Sandwich Isles have been sandwiched. It is quite a pleasure to turn from psychotics and savages and follow the star which Kepelini, the old Hawaiian chronicler, declared rose over Hawaii and guided the weary mariners to these shores. For these ancient Polynesian sea adventurers, plying their double canoes with matting sail and hau tree paddles, also saw their star in the East and followed it. Hoku-loa was the name of this star and became the symbol of their quest and, I hope, of the islands' future.

Thus a pleasant subject to write about was one of the excuses for this book; it does not, however, provide any compelling reason why it should be read. That perhaps may be found in its more serious purpose. Those of us who live here and love the place are fully conscious that the islands and their racial, social, and economic conditions come under a great deal of criticism, mostly on the basis of misunderstanding. Some of these misconceptions lie at our own door. We have been too busy in building up our Hawaiian paradise complex, that is as glamorous and as unsubstantial as a pin-up girl. There is, unfortunately, no perfection here; the beaches, particularly Waikiki, are by no means the best in the world, though the swimming they afford may well be; the weather, as is the way with weather, has its unpleasant moods and petulances; the social conditions are so far from ideal that the visitor, impressed by half-truths and superficial contacts, may even regard them as unfavorable. And half-truths cannot be brushed aside, experience having shown that they are frequently much more dangerous than whole-truths. It seems to me that the intelligent visitor is entitled to an account of these islands, which shall be as independent and unbiased as may be, free also of evasion of troublesome and controversial issues. In matters of criticism an ounce of admission is worth a ton of discovery, and I have no fear of providing our enemies with some ammunition provided they fire it away vainly.

Whatever bias this book contains—and nothing that is written from conviction can be wholly free from bias—is the bias of affection. It stems from recognition of the fact that nowhere in the world, within the narrow compass of three degrees of latitude, will you find variety of interest and beauty such as Hawaii affords. That statement is, of course, only a variation of an old theme—where every prospect pleases and only man is human.

As mentioned above, the writer in penning this account of the islands is only one of a hundred and fifty others, perhaps even more earnest in presenting their impressions or experiences here. By way of acknowledgment of indebtedness to some of these, a brief survey of the literature will be useful.

Our early authors were transients. Among those who first looked on these shores and then hastened to put down their impressions were the great navigators, Cook and Vancouver, and the various naturalists or other scientists who accompanied their voyages of discovery. Cook, of course, finally laid down his pen in Hawaii, but the work was carried on to completion by James King, his former lieutenant and successor in command of the Discovery, the three volumes being published under the names of both Cook and King with the title *A Voyage to the Pacific Ocean (1784)*.

It is remarkable how contagious this Hawaiian form of the writer's itch is. Even a corporal of marines under Cook, John Ledyard, was infected, so that he wrote his *Journal of Captain Cook's Last Voyage to the Pacific Ocean,* from which is frequently quoted the account of the great navigator's death. The disease affected sailors, supercargoes, and passengers. Delano, the seaman,[1] contributed his narrative of voyages and travels in 1817, and Peter Corney, the supercargo, recorded his impressions about the same time. In 1809–10, Alexander Campbell stopped off thirteen months in the islands and included many shrewd observations of Hawaiian life in his *A Voyage Round the World*. Vancouver's lieutenant, Peter Puget, also was infected by the disease, and in his "Log of the Chatham" (MS. 1793) made the notable prediction that the "large and luxurious growth" of sugar cane would become the basis of Hawaiian commerce.

This occupational complaint was so virulent that merely touching at, or trading with, the islands was sufficient to inspire people to write about the place. Meares, Portlock, Dixon, Kotzebue, Turnbull are just a few of the ships' captains turned authors, who have added their accounts of things to be seen in Hawaii.

Then came another group, mainly missionaries, who stayed much longer, and wrote much more. Among these the most notable

[1] Second officer of the Massachusetts.

contributor was probably Ellis, who, in his *Narrative of a Tour Through Hawaii, or Owhyhee* (1826), was probably the first to use the word Hawaii on a title page. The designation Sandwich Isles had been common hitherto, and persisted for some time. Ellis was an English missionary who left Tahiti to assist for several years in the efforts of the American missionaries to christianize these islands. His book was notable for its keen observations of the activities of the volcano at Kilauea. He also described a hula dance in which the women performers "were crowned with garlands of flowers, having also wreaths of the sweet-scented *gardenia* on their necks, and branches of the fragrant *mairi* (another native plant), bound round their ancles." Thus the custom of wearing leis has a century and a quarter of historical precedent. The gardenia was not, however, native, but had been imported from China.

The missionaries, in the intervals of their labors, wrote freely. There is Bingham's large volume, supplemented by the contributions of Dibble, Coan, Chamberlain, Thurston, Bishop, Judd, etc. Other clergymen, not missionaries, such as Cheever and Anderson, wrote books on Hawaii, while the noted historian, James Jackson Jarves, was a nephew of the Rev. Reuben Tinker, another missionary. After the Hawaiians had been taught to write, some of them caught the itch also, and books by Malo, Kamalau, and Kepelini resulted. Students of native life and customs could wish that more of the Hawaiians, and perhaps fewer of the missionaries, had been infected.

Incidentally, in these missionary accounts, the unfavorable appearance of many parts of the islands, with the exception of Lahaina, is commented upon. Kailua on Hawaii, and Honolulu on Oahu were particularly unattractive. Sereno Bishop, writing of Hawaii in the 'thirties, called Honolulu "a hard old camp" with scarcely a tree in town and no grass visible, the Bermuda variety or *manienie* not having then obtained a footing. In 1836 some Pride of India trees were imported, but the place was still desolate, with not a single house or tree between Punahou and the town.

After the missionaries, came visitors to Hawaii whose trade was writing. Having been infected elsewhere, however, they wrote comparatively little about the islands. Robert Louis Stevenson was impressed by the magnificent scenery of the windward side of Molokai, but his imagination was saddened by the tragedy of the lepers at the settlement at Kalaupapa. He was a man who, for most of his life, had been himself in ill health. He expected to find his grave in the South Seas, but the wide expansiveness of the blue Pacific, and his carefree wanderings around its beauteous islands lifted the load from his spirit. To him the lepers seemed condemned not only to death, but to imprisonment in this "prison fortified by nature." What life was left to him was as unfettered as air, and so he felt the plight of these poor captives keenly.

Hence it was with the grimness of the scene that he was most concerned. Looking from the sea on what he called "the vast cathedral front of the island," he wrote that never before had he seen "scenery so formidable as the island front of Molokai from Pelekunu to Wailau." Nevertheless, his poetic and unerring descriptive powers seized hold of the viridescent mountains, with their hanging forests, and their cascades like attenuated grey mares' tails, and, below, tilted islands, bursting surges, and the clamor of the seas. These were his phrases, but over whatever he remembered of beauty in the scene lay the shadow of the sights he had beheld at the leper settlement; otherwise, as he admits, the outlook would have been grateful to a Northerner "like one of his minor native tunes." But in contrast to what he had looked on at Kalaupapa he could only think of "the cleanness of the antiseptic ocean." It is a pity that he could not have written more happily, because, as he points out, the leper settlement occupies much less than a twentieth of the island of Molokai.

Oddly enough, it is Mark Twain, the professional humorist, whose serious descriptions of Hawaii are quoted rather than those of R. L. S. or other writers. His recollections of the islands—which begin, "No alien land in all the world has any deep strong charm for me but that one," and end, "in my nostrils still lives the breath of flowers that perished twenty years ago"—are justly famous. Jack London was another literary visitor who found an Hawaiian peg upon which to hang his stories.

By this time the islands had been discovered long enough to produce *kamaainas,* people who were born here or had lived here so long that they called the place home. It was too much to expect that these individuals should escape the urge to write about Hawaii. Some, like Alexander, Restarick, or Kuykendall, were concerned with the historical facts and marshaled them in scholarly fashion. Among the most modern writers, Blake Clark has recorded the events of December 7, 1941, from close at hand.

Others have seen Hawaiian life and events unrolled like a South Seas tapa, made of beaten mulberry bark, and impressed with strange designs in primitive colors. Mrs. Withington's book *Hawaiian Tapestry* reflects this idea with a delicate, if somewhat fragile charm. If her book is lavender and old lace, then Clifford Gessler, in his *Hawaii: Isles of Enchantment* and *Tropic Landfall,* adds a touch of arsenic and the salt of the sea. Among the authors of fiction, Miss Von Tempski has written of ranch life in Hawaii against an authentic background of red dust, lava, and prickly pear.

Professional globe trotters are, of course, represented fully among those who would describe Hawaii. The marvel is that these people make such short stays, tell so much, and perpetrate as few blunders as they do. Like cats that make a habit of licking the cream, they have developed quite a facility for skimming the surface. Though superficial, their accounts of Hawaii make entertaining reading.

If the visitor is concerned with the natural history of the islands, he will find it comprehensively treated under that title by William Alanson Bryan. The botanists, Hillebrand, Degener, St. John, have been very busy, while the identification of trees and flowers is made easy by Neal and Metzger, or Kuck and Tongg. Perhaps the brilliantly colored fish that swim around our reefs interest him; then he will find David Starr Jordan's book or the check list of Hawaiian fishes by Spencer Tinker useful. The offshore and inshore birds of the islands are pictured and described by Munro, while nature notes of general interest have been compiled by E. N. Bryan. Various local fields of science have been written about by the men of the Bishop Museum, such as Cooke and Edmondson, while Brigham, Stokes, Buck, Handy, and Emory have dealt most faithfully with aspects of Polynesian anthropology. Then, too, for thirty years Professor Jaggar has sat at Pele's bedside at Kilauea recording all the fluctuations of her temperature and temperament. Besides his many contributions to the "Volcano Letter," there is his latest book *Volcanoes Declare War*.

These are but a few of the names of the most notable patients who have suffered from *pruritus scribendi Hawaiiensis*. It has even been carried to California, a notable case being that of H. W. Bradley, who has written most exhaustively of a period of Hawaiian history under the title *The American Frontier in Hawaii*.

Latterly there has been an outbreak of a particularly virulent and irritating nature which has attacked some transient visitors to our shores. They came, they saw, they criticized, and then went away and wrote about us, most uncheerfully. The charm of Hawaii is, it seems, nothing but a mockery. If you peep under the *holoku*, or Mother Hubbard gown which the missionaries brought with them to foist on the natives, you will find nothing but lies and unlovely nakedness. They have discovered revolt and piracy and oppression in paradise, and seem glad of it. Though these books are written with malice towards most, they are decidedly readable, and may be recommended in small doses as anti-paradisiacs. The latest to appear takes many a tilt at sugar-coated windmills.

You will remember that Milton wrote about another paradise lost, in which he pictured Lucifer, sitting at Eve's ear distilling drops of venom as she slept, until "Ithuriel with his spear touched lightly." There is no denying the fact that Hawaii presents the usual blend of the lovely and the unlovely, and is no more perfect than any other place. Some things are plainly here for anyone to see. Bits of history, when this place was not a crossroads but a

one-way street to happy adventure in the South Seas; a background
of the Polynesian sort, so easy-going and laughter-provoking on
the surface, so tragic in its end; green valleys barred with rainbows,
and windswept *palis,* unscalable but never grim; little quiet beaches,
with flashes of bright beauty around each headland; strange rumblings and volcanic fires, with fern and forest hastening to cover up
the scars; a welter of all the world's human problems thrown carelessly down and left to time, tolerance, and good-humor for solution—all these should appear in the *palapala,* the writing of Hawaii.
But, to my notion, nothing—whether history, romance, beauty,
peoples, or perplexities—should be underscored. The pen, like
Ithuriel's spear, should touch lightly, if it is to show us as we
really are. Perhaps you will find a little of all these things, thus
treated, in this book.[2]

[2]Having drawn on them freely for material, the writer is indebted to all the authors
mentioned in this preface. In addition, personal acknowledgments are due R. J. Baker for
illustrations taken from his published collections of extremely fine photography of Hawaii.
Others have been generously contributed by Dr. T. A. Jaggar, the Hawaiian Airlines, and
the Army Air Forces.

List of Illustrations

PART ONE

CHAPTER I

Popularizing the Pacific

HAWAIIAN HISTORY, except for oral traditions, goes back to that eighteenth day of January 1778, when the natives of Waimea on the island of Kauai awoke to see Cook's ships standing off shore. To men accustomed to canoes with no more than a couple of feet of freeboard, the bulk of the vessels seemed so huge that they promptly dubbed them *moku,* islands, which was thereafter adopted as the Hawaiian name for ships. Later when the Discovery ranged itself alongside the Resolution, and the natives saw the masts and cross-spars and rigging, they cried out to one another, "These are forests that have drifted out to sea." It was a fateful day, both for the discoverers and the discovered.

It is possible for us to turn back a few pages of history and trace the events which reached their culmination in Cook's most important discovery, a discovery which opened up a great and as yet unfinished chapter in Pacific and world history. In its beginning in the sixteenth century, it is a strange tale of tiny ships, ill-found and scarcely seaworthy, battling their way through the stormiest entrance to any ocean, of crews emaciated and scurvy-ridden, of quarreling pilots and captains and mutinous men, of fabulous destinations and will-o'-the-wisp discoveries, of ships' companies bursting into Te Deums or slitting one another's throats—a compound of avarice and high-mindedness, of courage and cowardice, of treachery and devotion. Such was the early story of the Pacific.

It all began on September 15, 1513, when Vasco Núñez de Balboa, having first viewed the vast expanse of ocean from a peak in Darien, waded into its waters and claimed it and all its lands and islands on behalf of the King of Spain. The Pope had granted the eastern half of the world to Portugal, the western half to Spain, and the dividing

3

line ran through Brazil. All that seamen knew of what lay to the south was an unending coastline extending south into the regions of bitter cold and tremendous storms. Some of the Spanish in that day even talked of digging a canal through Panama to give ships access to their ocean. Others were sure that somewhere to the south a strait existed.

It remained for Magellan, a Portuguese mariner who entered the service of Spain, to find the passage. His fleet of five small ships sailed south into intense cold, sighting on their way such strange things as penguins and "sea-wolves," or seals. Three of the ships' captains revolted. One was stabbed, two cast into chains, and a broadside was fired into one of the ships before the mutiny was quelled. After some months and the wreck of another ship, Magellan rounded a headland which he called the Cape of the Eleven Thousand Virgins. This tribute to virginity *en masse* must have brought the seamen luck, because they eventually discovered a strait which, after 32 days of struggle, they managed to traverse, and finally reached the open ocean. Ninety-eight more days of starvation, thirst, and scurvy brought them to the Ladrones or Thievish Islands, later known as the Marianas. In the Philippines, Magellan visited Samar and then Cebu, where he was killed in a battle undertaken by him to exhibit the power of Spanish arms. He lost his life, but he had crossed the Pacific.

Another forerunner of Cook in Pacific discovery was Mendana. Marco Polo, who visited China in the latter half of the thirteenth century, described a land to the south, probably Siam or Cambodia, filled with gold, elephants, porcelain shells, and precious timbers. He called it Locach. The name was distorted into Beach and the country expanded to the dimensions of a huge southern continent. To find this golden province of Beach, Mendana set out from Peru in 1567. He did not reach the lost continent, but on the island of Guadalcanal some miners in the ship's company washed sand from the mouths of streams and found signs of gold. Once again rumor took hold and magnified this circumstance into rivers of gold, so that, though the group was lost to view for nearly two centuries, it was thereafter known as the isles of Solomon. Now, 375 years later, Malaita, Guadalcanal, Guam, Tinian, and Samar are again in the news.

The promise of great wealth to be picked up in these golden isles persuaded the Viceroy of Peru to send Mendana out again to the Solomons, but unfortunately the latter was scarcely seaman enough to find his way back through this chartless ocean. Accompanied by de Quiros, he did, however, discover high islands which he named after his friend the Viceroy, Las Marquesas de Mendoza. After Mendana's death, de Quiros sailed back to Peru and finally was able to equip a third expedition to seek the lost continent. With Torres as "admiral" and Balboa as chief pilot, he came upon the New Hebrides, where three large islands lying in echelon gave him the notion that the land was of continental proportions. He named it Austrialia del Esperitu Santo—the furthest land of the Holy Spirit. The ships' commanders became separated, Torres to sail on and discover Torres Strait and to disappear from view in the Philippines, de Quiros to return to Peru and spend the rest of his life extolling to a skeptical world the marvels of the new continent.

It is strange to record that in Cook's day, the second half of the eighteenth century, this matter of a huge southern continent—Terra Australis Incognita—was still in doubt. Mercator's argument that the earth would topple over in space, if there were not some great land mass in the south to balance Europe and Asia, still carried weight. No one knew whether de Quiros' Esperitu Santo was part of New Holland (Australia) nor whether to the southeast another continent existed. Perhaps the whole matter was too visionary to have justified Cook's voyages except for another circumstance.

In 1769 European astronomers were all agog with excitement over Halley's prediction that the planet Venus would pass across the sun's disc in that year. If this transit could be accurately observed from widely separated places on the earth's surface, the distance of the sun from the earth could be calculated; also longitude, then a matter of difficult and uncertain calculation, could be checked. The neighborhood of Mendana's 1595 discovery, the Marquesas, was at first suggested as one suitable for observing the transit. Captain Wallis on the H.M.S. Dolphin, two years before, had sailed out in search of the southern continent, crossed the Pacific and found himself at Tahiti among the Society Islands, while just the year before, Bougainville, the French navigator, had also visited there and then sailed north to cut across the track of de Quiros' voyages. Tahiti was therefore selected as another suitable observation point. Hence, Cook would be able to combine two purposes, observe the transit of Venus on Tahiti, and then sail south to settle, once for all, the question of Terra Australis Incognita.

He was accordingly put in command of the Endeavour, a converted collier of 308 tons and 105 feet over-all length, a very slow but sturdy craft. With over eighty people on board, Cook set out for Tahiti. The ship's company included scientists who were evidently gentlemen in those days, as that is how they were always referred to, distinguishing them from the men belonging to the ship. Banks, the famous botanist, afterwards Sir Joseph, was the most distinguished of the scientific party. They reached Tahiti in time for the transit, which, according to Halley's prediction (made prior to his death, 28 years previously), was to occur on June 3, 1769, and then not again for 105 years.

Incidentally, the primary purpose of the expedition was nearly ruined by the thievish dexterity of the Tahitians who stole Cook's stockings from under his head though he maintained that he had not been asleep. Banks' snuff box, a sentry's musket, and finally the quadrant for taking the astronomical observations also disappeared. Thanks to the courage and enterprise of Banks and Green, the astronomer, the quadrant was recovered with, however, some parts broken, which had to be repaired.

The transit having been duly observed, Cook set forth on those three voyages which more than any other served to popularize the Pacific and to open a new chapter of Polynesian history. Andrew Kippis, who chronicled Cook's expeditions in 1788, raises an interesting question. "While we are considering," he says, "the advantages the discoverers have derived from the late navigations, a question naturally occurs, which is, what benefits have accrued to the discovered?"

The answer is, unfortunately, not a very happy one. The new chapter makes, in many places, extremely sad reading. While it would be idle to pretend that the original state of the native Pacific peoples was peaceful and idyllic, we must admit that the blessings of civilization came wrapped up in violence, disease, and exploitation, which to some groups brought near-extinction. However, the worst pages were by no means written in Hawaii. To illustrate this point, some experiences of other native groups may be cited.

For the discovered, things began badly. The men on both the Wallis and the Bougainville expeditions found the Tahitian women most generous with their favors. In return, no gift was more acceptable than a nail or other scrap of iron. As a consequence, if the navigators' ships had not got away quickly, they would have fallen apart for want of nails to hold them together. As reward, the hospitable Tahitians suffered the introduction of venereal disease. For this Cook has been blamed, probably without justice, as the fact that half his ship's company were soon infected by the native women pointed to the earlier transplantation of the disease. However, there is no point in discussing which of the three navigators should carry the blame of this first gift to the discovered, when undoubtedly each expedition contributed. Nothing is more certain than that, if Wallis' or Bougainville's men had not brought the disease to Tahiti, Cook's company would have done so.

Another point of criticism of Cook which has been made by highminded missionaries is that he obtained all kinds of valuable objects in return for nails and rusty iron. It should be remembered, however, that the Polynesians were great craftsmen, particularly adept in woodcarving, and appreciated to the full the opportunity to substitute iron for the shark's tooth, the broken shell, or the stone adze as a cutting instrument; nor were they ignorant of the advantage of nailing planks together instead of lashing them with sennit braid. Iron was more valuable to the natives than gold.

Cook headed southward from Tahiti and soon the high snow-covered mountains of New Zealand, discovered first by Tasman 127 years earlier, were sighted. The "gentlemen" on board were inclined to agree with Tasman's conclusion that this land was indeed part of the great southern continent, but Cook, with that genius for being right that he displayed up to his last fatal error, held that these were merely islands. Six months' circumnavigation proved his point.

Perhaps the best index of what was in store for newly discovered peoples, even at the hands of such an ordinarily humane and tolerant man as James Cook, is to be found in the story of his dealings with the Maoris. "Being desirous of conversing with some natives," he crossed a river with a party of marines to investigate some huts, leaving four midshipmen to guard the boat. Though invited by Tupia, a Tahitian whom Cook had brought with him to act as interpreter, the Maoris seemed averse to conversation and retreated inland until four of them saw a chance to cut off the boat. A midshipman fired a shot over their heads, but as no ill effects followed the noise of the thunderstick, they continued to advance. As one native raised his spear to throw, he was shot dead. The others then fled, dragging the body of their companion for some distance before they finally left him. Thus ended the first attempt to hold converse with the Maoris, who apparently would rather die than talk.

Cook next landed three boatloads of marines and sailors and on his assurances of safety, Tupia induced some of the Maoris to cross the river. Strangely enough, when offered glass beads in exchange for their polished cleavers of greenstone or New Zealand jade— worth a ton of civilized gewgaws—they refused to trade, though they were willing to barter them for the magic fire sticks which could kill men afar off.

Presently, one of the natives seized a hangar or cutlass from an officer, and received in exchange a charge of small shot in the legs from a distance of fifteen feet. With incredible hardihood, the savage refused to drop the weapon and insolently waved it around his head. Mr. Monkhouse, the surgeon, was compelled to fire with ball which effectively settled both the dispute and the Maori. Three or four other natives were wounded. Thus as the narrator remarks, Cook "unhappily experienced that nothing could be done with these people"; nothing, that is, except shoot them. It was rather an unhappy experience for the Maoris also.

But Cook was determined that these natives should not misunderstand his good intentions, so when he observed two canoes approaching Poverty Bay, in which his ships were anchored, he disposed his boats to intercept them. The men in one canoe outpaddled their pursuers and reached the shore. The other canoe, however, sailed right into the midst of the waiting boats before the Maoris, realizing the situation, dropped their sail and took to their paddles. Seeing that these men were also likely to escape, Cook ordered a musket shot fired over their heads. The result was unexpected. Instead of being properly intimidated, these ignorant "Indians" decided that if the white strangers wanted to fight instead of competing in a harmless boat race they would oblige them. When a boat approached they attacked with spirit, using stones and paddles. "They carried it with so much vigor and violence," wrote Kippis, "that the English thought themselves obliged to fire upon them in their own defence; the consequence of which was that four were unhappily killed."

Cook himself deplored this occurrence, but justified his actions on the ground that it was the only method possible to convince the natives that he intended them no harm. In other words, these Maoris were shot in the friendliest spirit, for their own good, and the advancement of civilization. To prove this point, the other three Maoris in the canoe who tried to swim to land were captured, taken aboard the ship, treated well, and in the morning, having been loaded with presents, were set ashore. Nevertheless, Banks referred to the tragic events in his journal as "a day of horror." What the Maoris thought of the whole performance is, of course, not recorded.

Perhaps Cook, on his side, had reason to distrust the friendly spirit of the Maoris, having in mind Tasman's first experiences with them. They managed to ram a cockboat carrying messages between

Tasman's two ships and of the seven men it contained, three were killed and one mortally wounded. To commemorate the event, Tasman called the place Murderer's Bay. But on this later occasion the aggressiveness seemed to be entirely on the side of the whites. There were several other incidents in which trigger-happy marines figured. These latter required restraint for, as Cook admits, his men, perhaps because of the previous bad example, "showed as much impatience to destroy the Indians, as a sportsman to kill his game." This was an altogether new and very exciting kind of hunting.

In justice to Cook, it should be said that his treatment of the Polynesians was most tolerant in comparison with what Pacific peoples suffered at the hands of other visitors, both before and after his time. When Mendana discovered the Solomon Islands, bloody clashes took place with the natives at every landing place, mainly because of the explorers' demands for food sufficient to feed two ships' companies. On his second voyage, when the Marquesas were discovered, seven or eight natives were shot on the first day of contact. The second day brought another massacre, canoes being fired upon for the offense of crowding too close about the boat, while on the third day a large number of natives were killed for the theft of four jars at a time when fruit and water were being delivered to a ship's party. This brutality was shown mainly at the instance of the Camp Master, who declared it his "diligence to kill, because he liked to kill." Bloody forays, kidnapings, and murder also accompanied the Esperitu Santo discoveries, but the high object of the expedition was attained. As the ship's poet, Belmonte Bermudez, wrote:

> "Those are regions now made known
> Pressed by the feet of Christian men."

It is little wonder that Christians were traditionally held in low repute in those regions. Against this Spanish record, Cook's voyages were merely slightly blood-stained. In comparison also with other Pacific lands, the impact of civilization on Hawaii was quite gentle.

From New Zealand, Cook struck west, his intention being to

follow up the east coast of New Holland, as Australia was then called. Having determined that there was certainly no continent southeast of Australia, another question of geographical importance remained. Was Esperitu Santo part of the continental mainland or were the whole New Hebrides merely a group of islands? It was on this voyage of discovery that an event occurred upon which Hawaii's future turned. Perhaps all history hangs by threads, but it is only rarely that the individual strand is plainly visible.

Plymouth Rock, since 1620, has been justly famous, but only because someone marked the spot where the Pilgrim Fathers stood. But there is a piece of rock off Australia, quite unmarked and almost forgotten, upon which the whole history of this Pacific area hinged. If Plymouth Rock had not been where it is, another would have served, but this rock was itself essential. It played a vital if not dramatic role and was a point on which history actually depended. Without it, Hawaii would most probably have had a different name and flag, and Australia would have been a French possession. Certainly this book would not have been written and you who read may never have sailed or flown over the Pacific. Because of this fragment, we have joined Cook's company, his story has become linked with our own experiences.

It was a clear moonlit night on the 10th of June 1770 and Cook's little ship, the Endeavour, had been standing on and off shore all day. Suddenly, about nine o'clock, the water shoaled, causing a general alarm. Then it deepened again, and the danger apparently past, "the gentlemen left the deck in great tranquillity and went to bed." Then at eleven p.m. the ship struck violently on a coral reef. The waves lifted her into a hollow where she at once began to tear her heart out on the jagged points of coral. "To complete the scene of distress," says Kippis, "it appeared from the light of the moon that the sheathing boards from the bottom of the ship were floating away all round her, and at last, her false keel."

Then began a long struggle for the life of the ship and the safety of her company, whose anxiety can well be imagined. Here they were, over fifty miles away from an unknown coast, inhabited bv a people who had shown no friendliness, and what was more surprising, no interest in their distinguished visitors. Cook had not boats enough to convey even half his people to land, and those who did reach it would find it almost barren of any means of sustenance, civilized or otherwise. Whether the survivors would be able to defend themselves for any length of time against hostile natives was problematical. Certainly there was no chance of rescue, for no one would have any notion of their situation. How desperate their plight looked may be judged from the fact that in all this time of struggle the men forgot to swear.

First of all, the ship must be lightened in the hope that she might float off into the deep water astern, where if the leak were sufficiently great, she would founder immediately. But that chance must be taken. Cook ordered six cannon, all that were on deck, to be thrown overboard, together with what stone and iron ballast could be carried up from below. But since the tide was going out, all this was of no avail; the ship settled more firmly on the rocks. Perhaps the next full tide, due at eleven in the morning, would suffice to float her. This was, however, lower than the previous tide, and their only chance remaining was at midnight. Jettisoning fifty tons of cargo from the ship gave her eighteen inches floating depth. Anchors were put out astern and the lines "hove tort," as Cook puts it.

But in the meantime with the rising tide the leak gained, so that two pumps could not keep the water in check. At last, about nine o'clock, by hauling on the five anchors, the ship was pulled off. The last pump that would work was manned and the struggle to keep afloat became desperately critical.

By this time after 24 hours' incessant exertion, everyone, gentlemen and all, were nearing complete exhaustion. "None of them," says the narrator, "could work at the pumps above five or six minutes together, after which, being totally exhausted, they threw themselves down on the deck, though a stream of water, three or four inches deep, was running over it from the pumps. When those who had succeeded them had worked their time, and in their turn were exhausted, they threw themselves down in the same manner, and the others started up again to renew their labor."

But still the leak gained until a midshipman named Jonathan Monkhouse suggested a plan that he had seen worked successfully on a previous voyage. Quantities of wool and oakum, "smeared with the dung of the sheep and other filth" were stitched lightly to the surface of a sail, which was then hauled with ropes under the hull of the ship. The inrush of water carried the wool and oakum together and plugged the hole. This is called "fothering" the ship, and once again the trick worked, so that one pump held the inflow of water. The spare masts that were floating about were recovered, and three days later a little river was discovered, where with the utmost pains the ship was hauled ashore and careened on the beach.

Then the circumstance that really saved the ship was discovered. The gap in the hull was so large that three times the number of pumps available could not have kept the Endeavour from sinking, except that a large piece of coral rock had broken off and was stuck in the hole. Probably no fragment of rock was ever of more fateful historical significance. If it could only be found again in its resting place at the mouth of the Endeavour River, it could well be Australia's most significant monument. Just as appropriately it could be laid at the base of the Cook monument at Kealakekua Bay in Hawaii. It would serve then as a double commemoration, first of the place where the great navigator's life was saved and secondly, where he lost it.

In his dealings with the Polynesians, Captain Cook made two tragic errors. On each occasion he was greatly mistaken with regard to the psychology of the natives. He thought that they would recognize and bow to the superiority of the white man's lethal weapons, and that all that was necessary to overawe these Polynesian warriors was to fire his guns and if necessary kill a man or two. Cook's first mistake of this kind was in Poverty Bay, New Zealand, where, as we have seen, contrary to all that was expected of them, the Maoris turned and fought. However, that was just a small canoeful of seven men, four of whom received a final lesson in the white man's superior might. The second mistake was made at Kealakekua Bay in Hawaii. Hawaiians were shot and killed, but Cook reckoned without the unbreakable loyalty of these simple warriors to their aged king. The mistake cost Cook his life. This was one time when the blow of a savage club, like the shot at Concord bridge, was heard around the world.

After discovering Christmas Island on Christmas Eve, 1777,[1] the great explorer continued his way northward, and on January 18, 1778, land was again sighted, first the island of Oahu away to port, then Kauai and Niihau lying ahead. On the first contact with the whites, the natives showed the most eager curiosity and a desire to possess themselves by theft or otherwise of the strangers' possessions. This latter tendency, however, was effectually checked by the shooting to death of one man. It was on Kauai that Cook first received royal honors, the people prostrating themselves as he passed. Was not his mere word sufficient to guide the great canoes, or to loose off the thundersticks? The navigator's ear for native sounds was none too good, and he called the island Atooi and the smaller one Oneowhow. The natives really called them Tauai and Niihau, the o being the form used in beginning an answer to the question, "What lands are these?" and the a being merely a conjunction, so that A Tauai meant "and Kauai." At that time k had not replaced t in the language, so that Kamehameha was at one time spelled Tameameah.

It is worth noting that both Cook and Vancouver, supported later by Ellis, Dibble, and others agree in distinguishing the w sound in Hawaii, calling the island Owhyhee, though many Hawaiian-born people now give it the v sound, probably believing this to be more correct. It is true that the v and w sounds are sometimes interchangeable in certain words, such as Ewa, but in the case of Hawaii the w sound seems to have been general.

After a brief visit to Kauai, Cook sailed on to the north in his

[1] A note on a map issued by the National Geographic Society in Washington in 1941, credits Cook with visiting and renaming Christmas Island, south of Sunda Strait near Java, in December 1777. He could hardly have been in the Pacific and Indian Oceans at the same time.

search for a northwest passage to Europe, noting in his journal the pleasant disposition of the island people and their neatness and ingenuity in the manufacture of articles such as fishhooks. It was not until he had failed to get through the Alaskan ice that the explorer again turned south and sighted the islands he calls Mowee (Maui). On the 30th of November he came to Owhyhee (Hawaii) and coasted along its shores.

The natives of Kauai had sent to Oahu the most startling accounts of the mysterious beings who had appeared and disappeared in their floating islands, and these stories were carried to the other islands by a man named Moho, a native of the island of Hawaii, then residing on Oahu. These people, he said, were white, with loose and folding skin—"fire and smoke issue from their mouths; they have openings in the sides of their bodies into which they thrust their hands, and draw out iron, beads, nails, and other treasures; and their speech is unintelligible." As instances of their queer lingo, he cited words such as "oolaki" and "walawalalaki." These were probably native spellings of some of the rude sailors' comments when they saw the native belles. "Oh, lookee!" "Well, well, lookee!" and the like. This supposition is founded, however, on knowledge of sailors, not the language.

The people in the other islands naturally put down the men of Kauai as fearful liars, but when the news spread that the *haoles* or strangers had come back to the islands, everyone who could beg, borrow, or steal a canoe came to see for himself. And when the Hawaiians saw smoke coming from the mouths of the sailors and watched them eat Monterey watermelons, which from a distance looked like raw human flesh, the reputation of Kauai folk for veracity reached a new high. They viewed with terror the ships' portholes, for it was from these, so the Kauai folk said, that smoke and fire belched with a noise like thunder. On January 16th the two ships, Resolution and Discovery, were surrounded by a fleet of canoes estimated at well over a thousand. This curious multitude caused Cook to over-estimate the population of the islands. He did not reckon on the Hawaiians' readiness to travel miles to see a good show.

Next day, Cook anchored his ships in Kealakekua Bay and, no doubt being impressed by the great concourse of people both afloat and on shore, he recorded in his diary his satisfaction with his failure to find a Northwest Passage, since it had enabled him "to enrich our voyage with a discovery, which, though the last, seemed in many respects to be the most important that had hitherto been made by Europeans throughout the extent of the Pacific Ocean." This may seem to many to have been a too optimistic view, considering that Australia and New Zealand were included in this area. But, in any case, the Hawaiian Islands were, in time to come, to form the most important link in the chain uniting those great land masses with the rest of the world; so important indeed was that link that had it been broken at the battle of Midway in 1942, the defense of those countries might have been indeed a desperate problem. Cook, of course, could not foresee such a trend in world events, nor could he envisage the establishment of a great commonwealth in Australia; but no one should grudge him his hour of triumph. Those were the last words of his journal.

The events that led up to the final tragedy gave no hint of its imminence. Relations with the Hawaiians had been most friendly, the old king Kalaniopuu having given Cook a beautiful featherwork cape, and in return was invested with a linen shirt and the Captain's own sword. Kippis remarks that instances of kindness and civility on the part of the natives were too numerous to mention. The priests were particularly cordial and sent the ships endless supplies of hogs and vegetables without any expectation of return.

About this time Cook submitted at two of the *heiaus* to those ceremonies which some forty years later were to be so irefully denounced by the missionaries in Hawaii as idolatrous worship. They maintained that he should have embraced the opportunity to do a little missionary work of his own on behalf of true religion. Some of them, particularly the Rev. Sheldon Dibble, did not like Cook under any circumstances. The navigator was blamed on the

Except for nails, cotton malos and diving glasses,
100 per cent Hawaiian

Photo by Tai Sing Loo

The explosive eruption of 1924 was similar to that which
destroyed Keoua's army in 1790

one hand for showing disrespect to heathen religion by his use of a *heiau* fence and some of its idols as firewood, and on the other hand for accepting this heathen "adoration." "In view of this fact," says Dibble, "and of the death of Captain Cook, which speedily ensued, who can fail being admonished to give to God at all times and even among barbarous tribes, the glory which is his due." In short, all that happened was a judgment upon Cook.

So generous were the natives that the countryside was becoming depleted of food, prompting a polite inquiry from the king as to when his guests planned to depart. When the date was announced, an astonishing quantity of tapa, hogs, and vegetables were gathered as farewell gifts.

Unfortunately, a gale three days later sprung the Resolution's foremast and both ships had to turn back. On February 10th Kamehameha, then a young chief, visited Cook's ship and exchanged his feather cloak for nine iron daggers. Relations on both sides continued extremely amicable.

Samwell, surgeon of the Resolution, gives the most reasonable account of the events that quickly followed. An Hawaiian stole a blacksmith's tongs and chisel and dived overboard with them. Pareah (Palea), a chief, at once went ashore and returned not only the stolen articles but the lid of a watercask as well, which had not been missed. Not satisfied with this restitution, an officer who had gone ashore with a boat decided to seize a canoe as additional punishment for the theft. Pareah objected, since it was his canoe, and a scuffle, with some stone-throwing, ensued. The chief, notwithstanding the fact that he had been struck by a sailor, quieted his men and afterwards paddled out to return a midshipman's cap which had been lost in the struggle.

The next night one of the Discovery's cutters was stolen for the nails it contained, and Cook determined to make the king a hostage on board the Discovery. "In the meantime," according to Dibble's account, "was acted the consummate folly and outrageous tyranny of placing a blockade upon a heathen bay." Cook, attended by nine marines, a lieutenant, and the crew of the pinnace, went to the king's house and demanded that Kalaniopuu accompany him to the ship. Cook took the king by the hand and was leading him to the shore when a crowd gathered, showing every sign of hostility. As they neared the beach the king's wife and his chiefs interfered and the old man sat down. Just then news came to the crowd that a chief had been shot and killed while entering the bay.

Cook still thought that a show of force would be sufficient to overawe the crowd, which had become very threatening. A chief named Koho was seen to be edging nearer as if to attack and was given a charge of small shot. Cook turned to order the men to embark and as he did so was struck on the head with a stone. According to Ledyard, who viewed the affair from a distance, Cook shot his assailant dead. The men in the boats opened fire and Cook's men joined in with a volley. By all the rules of native behavior the Hawaiians should have fled, but as Cook turned, either to order the men in the boat to cease fire, or to wave them ashore, the crowd rushed to the attack.

From this point on, accounts of the battle differ. Samwell describes Cook being left alone after four marines had been struck down, while the rest, some of whom were wounded, attempted to board the boat. Then the captain walked towards the pinnace, protecting the back of his head from stones with his hand. Samwell says that the first blow was struck with a heavy club and that Cook then staggered a few paces, dropped his musket, and at that moment was stabbed in the back. He fell into knee-deep water and was at once set upon by the natives who pushed him under, until, struggling violently, he "got his head up, and casting his look towards the pinnace, seemed to solicit assistance." Apparently the men in the boat could not keep up an effective fire. Cook was clinging to a rock when he received his death blow from a club in the hands of one of the chiefs.

Samwell was most indignant because Cook's body was not recovered but lay exposed on the beach which was deserted by the natives. Ledyard says that the men in the boats kept up a hot fire which "made great havoc among the Indians, particularly among the chiefs," who stood foremost in the crowd and were most exposed. He thinks, however, that their bravery was the valor of ignorance. He says that the chiefs thought it was the flash of the gun that killed and they accordingly protected themselves by dipping their thick mats and cloaks in sea water. However, the gaps in the ranks made by those who fell were at once filled, and it was not till the Resolution fired two cannon into the crowd that they retreated. Thus ended the battle of Kealakekua Bay in which four chiefs were killed and six wounded, not counting twenty-five of the common people who were also slain.

The bodies of Cook and the four marines who had fallen were carried inland. Some of Cook's bones were afterwards brought back to the ship. Several accounts agree in saying that his death was due to "his mistaken confidence in the power of his firearms, of which the Hawaiians were entirely ignorant." The whole occurrence was a tragedy of misunderstanding.

Dibble's account was based on *Ka Mooolelo Hawaii,* "the narrative of Hawaii," as written by some of his native students at the missionary seminary at Lahainaluna, Maui. These students included among them the native historian David Malo, and under Dibble's direction they "sifted" the oral traditions concerning these early events in Hawaiian history. This sifting naturally reflected a strong missionary bias and did much to undermine the high esteem in which for forty years after his death the Hawaiians held the memory of Captain Cook. But Dibble's criticism of the great navigator was mild compared to that of Bingham, who wrote:

"How vain, rebellious, and at the same time contemptible, for a worm to presume to receive homage and sacrifices from the stupid and polluted worshippers of demons and of the vilest visible objects of creation . . . . without one note of remonstrance on account of the dishonor cast on the Almighty Creator."

Mixed with this wholesale condemnation of the great navigator who "was left to infatuation and died by the visitation of God," was another antipathy. American missionaries were somewhat afraid of the pro-British leanings of the Hawaiian rulers. Thus they killed two birds with the one stone, holding up to scorn a notable and much-admired Englishman, and at the same time the heathen adoration which he accepted.

This is at least one bitterness that time has assuaged. When you see the monument to Captain Cook that stands near the scene of his death, it may be well to reflect that all the courage was not on one side. Men with iron daggers, wooden clubs, and spears pitted themselves against muskets, swords, and cannon and did not come out badly in the trial. But they have no monument, though they, too, died for king and country.

This popularizing of the Pacific which Cook began with his promise of "coasts to survey, countries to explore, inhabitants to describe and perhaps render more happy," was to have effects on the people of Australia and on many an island population. Those who have written about the exploitation of labor on behalf of the sugar industry in Hawaii should take a glance at the records of blackbirding, by which kanakas were obtained for the Queensland sugar growers. It is a tale of brazen kidnaping, unmitigated brutality, and frequent wholesale murder. So long as ship captains could get fifteen to twenty-seven pounds sterling a head for natives, they were not going to be at all particular as to how the men were "recruited." There was competition between the chief blackbirders, each man trying to make things difficult and dangerous for the next ship that came along. The natives themselves participated in the trade, the chiefs selling their young men in exchange for firearms—one gun per head. Armed with these the natives attempted reprisals, but with only moderate success. They thought that by elevating the sights of the rifles the guns could shoot harder. Others shut both eyes when they shot, while the men of one tribe, to improve the technique of aiming, each wore a black patch over one eye, thus advertising their evil intentions.

The tricks of the trade were amusing as well as tragic. All kinds of devices were used to lure the natives on board. One captain would astonish the natives by sticking a knife into his wooden leg until one day a native in the spirit of experiment thrust a penknife into the seat of the captain's pants. Another blackbirder had a glass eye and threatened that if the inhabitants of an island did not supply him with a shipload of laborers, he would cause an eye to drop from the head of every person, illustrating his power by removing his own. These were the more innocent and facetious methods.

A Dr. Murray, a pioneer on Epi, one of the middle islands of the New Hebrides group, owned the blackbirding ship Carl, and to save himself turned Queen's evidence at the trial of his officers for murder. Eighty natives were collected by the simple expedient of throwing pig iron into their canoes and then knocking them insensible as they swam in the water. When these men created a disturbance in the hold of the ship, and armed themselves by breaking up the bunks, the crew were forced to fire on them all night. In the morning only five were unwounded and sixty blackbirds were dead. The men were acquitted, as was usually the case in these trials, for natives, not understanding the nature of an oath, were not allowed to give testimony.

However, in 1884, two men, officers of the ship Hopeful, were actually convicted of particularly brutal and wanton murders and were sentenced to be hanged. But six years later they were given free pardons, a petition for their release with 28,000 signatures having been presented to the Queensland government. Of course, all the killings were not on one side. The period provides a dark and bloody chapter of outrage and murder, worse than anything the Spanish perpetrated in these same islands in 1606, two and three quarter centuries earlier. There were killings of missionaries, massacres of boat crews on the one hand, and on the other shellings of innocent villages by warships, and countless individual murders. This was part of the price of being discovered.

In one respect Hawaii was fortunate. Its discovery took place before the white colonization of other Pacific lands and the consequent exploitation of native manpower. The timing of that discovery was also opportune in that it antedated the development of the Russian fur trade in the northwest—otherwise, it might have been Russian ships that sailed south in search of a winter haven and came upon these islands. Later, the Russians displayed considerable interest in both Oahu and Kauai where they built forts. These efforts were probably in the nature of trial balloons, but by this time both America and England had established prior claims to the Sandwich Islands as being within their respective spheres of influence. In any case, the Russians were thrown out.

Quite probably, all the currents of Hawaiian history were changed because of Cook's death. Had he returned to England, enthusiastic about his discovery, missionary and trading interest in Hawaii would have been vastly quickened. As it was, the natives took thirty years to live down their evil reputation in Europe as treacherous and bloody-minded savages who had killed a great Englishman. American visitors received an entirely different impression of the nature of the Hawaiians.

CHAPTER II

Home Is the Sailor

PROBABLY the most important fact that you can state about an Hawaiian is a very obvious one. He is an islander. This environmental circumstance has determined his history. It has also colored his whole psychology and character. As is well known, the Hawaiians are a branch of the Polynesian race, and only a sea-faring people could reach these islands. Such folk have their own characteristic slants on life. They are a peculiar people.

The significance of their migrations can only be realized when we study the relationship of Hawaii to other Pacific lands. Over two thousand miles of unbroken ocean separate us from mainland America, a stretch next to impossible to bridge by canoes. Northward, an even greater waste of waters reaches to the Aleutians. In a northwesterly direction from the main Hawaiian Islands there is a chain of small islands and smaller reefs extending past Niihau, through Necker, Laysan, and Hermes reef to Midway, about a thousand miles distant. But between Midway and the next large island group, the Marianas, roll another two thousand miles of Pacific Ocean. To the south a direct course would pass through the Line Islands, which includes Palmyra and Christmas Island, and if curved slightly to the west would bring you to Samoa, 2,200 miles from Honolulu. If you swing a little easterly, you may reach Tahiti and the Tuamotu group, which is 2,300 miles distant. Still farther south is New Zealand, populated by Maoris, another great division of Polynesians. Easter Island forms the other angle at the base of what is called the Polynesian triangle, and it is 4,000 miles away from the apex in Hawaii. You could thus set a compass, with its legs separated to represent 2,000 miles, and draw a circle around Hawaii, which would include only tiny Howland and Baker Islands in one spot, Canton in another, with no other land inside the ring except little Palmyra and Midway, all of these about 1,000 miles distant.

We are losing all notion of the meaning of distance through the astonishing increase in our own surface velocity. Only when you have traveled by more primitive means do you begin to translate miles into effort. On long journeys a horse team can manage twenty miles a day, a camel train eighteen to twenty miles, a donkey team twelve to fourteen, and an ox wagon eight to ten miles—all requiring occasional days to rest and graze.

If you are interested in these facts, you might pay some attention to the country you see through your Pullman window on your next transcontinental journey, especially passing through Kansas, Utah, or Arizona. You will begin to realize what the words Oregon Trail really meant to those who, early in American history, made the great trek. What impression would eight or ten miles travel make on these vast distances? In a day's march, where would the traveler find water; where is there a practicable route for wagons across the rivers or between these buttes or mountains? Where could you find a safe campsite while the oxen were spelled? Would it be wise to have that butte at the back of your ring of wagons, or would it give raiding Apaches a road for surprise and descent upon the camp? What a vast amount of trail experience, knowledge of country, cattle, and Indians was needed by those who guided their wagon trains through the prairies and beyond.

So the next time you are at sea on a great Matson liner crossing the Pacific, try and imagine your progress under conditions faced by those early Polynesian navigators. How would those long sweeping rollers look from a little platform built between the hulls of two dugout canoes? Think about the unceasing labor of baling to prevent being swamped in a choppy sea. Then there is the matter of finding your way without benefit of compass or sextant. And if you have any capacity at all for putting yourself in the other fellow's place—what the psychologists call empathy—try to savor, however faintly, the mariner's fears and distresses. Far worse perhaps than storm would be the dead calm, when the sun stands still above the mast and the ocean is like burnished glass. But the ancient mariner's ship, though it stood as idle as a painted ship upon a painted ocean, was still a ship and not a canoe.

Captain Beechy, who sailed these seas in 1824, tells of meeting a canoe party blown 600 miles out of their course on a 250 mile voyage between islands in the Tuamotus. First came a violent storm, then the canoes were left becalmed. Another storm drove them hundreds of miles in the wrong direction, and this was followed by a long calm, during which food and water were exhausted and seventeen of the party died. A rain storm and the capture of three sharks gave the survivors strength to reach an uninhabited island, where they spent almost a year in refitting. On the voyage home, they damaged their canoe and spent eight months on another island gathering stores of dried fish and pandanus flour to carry them home. Thus an ordinary two weeks' journey lasted nearly two years.

As you idle on the beach at Waikiki, you might notice that the northeast trade wind blows almost unceasingly—about 300 days out of the year. Hence, to journey south through the Line Islands down to Tahiti would have been easy except that these are mere dots in a great expanse of water and could be very easily missed. But the northerly course to Hawaii could only be compassed under the most fortunate circumstances of wind and sea.

These old Polynesians must have known the face of the waters upon which they moved as you know the faces of your friends. The canoes were first of all carefully lined up with points on shore that gave them the exact direction of their destination. Then they fixed their course by the first bright star directly ahead. When it sank, they chose a star following this one. This meant that the navigator must be able to recognize all stars that rose in the same *rua* or pit, i.e., the same spot on the eastern horizon, thus following in their path across the sky the same degree of latitude, to their setting in the west. When clouds obscured the western horizon, the navigator stood at the stern and watched the stars as they rose, steering by the canoe's wake. The wind in the sails made of pandanus matting drove them on, but the course had to be kept by means of the heavy paddles. The voyagers must know the currents prevailing at the time of year and be alert to every minor shift of wind. As they neared a landfall, they must study the movements of the fish in the ocean and the flight of the seafowl in the air lest they overshoot their mark. Trained vision was required to recognize the loom of the land—the greenish tinge in the sky that was the reflection of the lagoon below. It has been stated that some canoes carried live pigs whose behavior was carefully watched as they were supposed to be able to smell the land many miles away.

Nautical experience was not gained in several voyages, but was gathered in a thousand years of acquaintance with the sea. Wrote Stevenson for his epitaph:

> "Home is the hunter, home from the hill,
> And the sailor, home from the sea."

But the sailor's way home was much, much longer than the hunter's, and beset with a thousand more perils. So all the lore of the sea was preserved and imparted—perhaps as men sat outside the reef when the fish were not biting, or on beaches of little islands, or beside the fires of driftwood on seaweed gathering expeditions, or more indirectly in the chants and legends recited at sacred places or *maraes*.

Careful planning was also essential, for on these long voyages there was no more than a razor's edge of safety. If the craft were too well found with a great heap of green coconuts, baskets of dried fish, live pigs and chickens, and dogs for sustenance, with bamboo and gourd water containers, spare sails, paddles and balers, the canoes would ride low in the water and be so hard to handle in storms that everything might be swept overboard.

For long exploratory voyages, the matter of a good crew was essential, the choice being restricted to tried men, strong swimmers, and expert fishers, but above all to men of good heart who would hang on while even a thread of hope remained, and to whose spirit all that was adventure appealed. It would be a great wonder if the voyager's temperament, with all its faults and virtues, were not transmitted to his descendants. Down the years only the strongest and most determined survived.

In addition to the lure of great adventure, there were other reasons that drove the Polynesians on, to pierce unknown horizons. The total land area of all the islands of the Pacific is very tiny in relation to the vast expanse of water that surrounds them. The island of Hawaii, with its quite insignificant 4,000 square miles, is one of the largest land masses. The North and South Islands of New Zealand are of much larger size but they are very far down in the extreme south—"The Land of the High Mists," or "The Long White Cloud"—these native names signifying more winter than the sun-loving Polynesians appreciated. Nevertheless, expeditions from the ancient homeland took place regularly to New Zealand, voyages of settlement and discovery that continued until the Maori people were well established. These journeys ended probably five centuries ago.

The central dispersal point, the cultural hub of Polynesia, is identified as Hawaiki, which you will note is Hawaii with a *k*. Dr. Peter Buck in his fascinating book *Vikings of the Sunrise* insists on spelling the name of the Hawaiian Islands Hawai'i, the inverted comma representing a glottal stop that took the place of the *k*. The name of this island was a nostalgic reminder to the Hawaiians of their original home in Raiatea and Tahiti, the true Hawaiki. It was from there that Kupe sailed in about the tenth century to discover New Zealand.

When these ancient navigators reached Easter Island, their eastward journey ended, for there they met the great swells that rolled unchecked from the South American coast. Undoubtedly, these keen observers had noted the annual flight of the *kolea* or golden plover from its summer home in Alaska. Land, they reasoned, must therefore lie to the north and thither the stream of exploration turned.

Overpopulation has always been the great promoter both of war and pioneering. The whole of the Society Islands, where Hawaiki lay, cannot total in area much more than 500 square miles, not as large as the island of Oahu. The Polynesians, both ancient and modern, are a virile people, their men vigorous and capable, their women broad bosomed, warm hearted, and greatly fertile. Seafaring folk have never been behindhand as regards reproductive processes, and population undoubtedly grew apace. Pandanus, coconut, and breadfruit trees provided food, but never in lavish quantities. Coconuts especially are slow maturing, and the trees are scarce enough in some places to make the felling of one a very serious offense. Good land available for the cultivation of taro, sweet potatoes, or yams was never plentiful.

Then, too, Polynesian hospitality called for abundance. There were feasts on every possible occasion, when the building of a house or canoe was begun and when it was completed. Then to keep the workmen in good heart, additional feasts were offered in between-times. Marriage, the birth of a child, its weaning, all called for celebration, and even death was marked by a feast. From October to February war was tabu, work practically ceased, and after the people had paid their taxes, they gave themselves over to feasting in honor of the good god Lono, who made things grow. It would be a great disgrace to the family and a terrible loss in prestige if food supplies were niggardly on such occasions.

Another fact to be borne in mind is that this settling of the Pacific was no peaceful penetration. Tradition speaks of a still older people called *menehunes* or *manehunes* who inhabited the islands. Probably they represented the first waves of migration, the descendants of groups driven ashore by storms on various uninhabited islands. In any case, these people were either annihilated or absorbed. Land utilization thus depended on conquest and its maintenance by force. These Polynesians were a restless people. Every cliff had its watchman, and there was no morning during the favorable sailing season but what the lookout might not detect those black specks on the horizon that signified an oncoming fleet of canoes. The combats that ensued were real battles. Though the bow and arrow were used for sport, they were disdained for warfare. The only manly way to fight was to get to grips with your enemy in hand to hand struggle. Many a coral strand was dyed red and sharks inside the reef fed well.

In every community that lives by fighting, the great warrior is the people's head and front, and he maintains his power by building around himself a military caste. Wherever these conditions occur, you will find highly developed ideas of rank, succession, and hereditary privilege. Strength, bravery, fighting skill, sagacity in leadership are at a premium, and the man who combines these in his person can demand and receives personal devotion. The men he depends on are trained for war and away from industry. Those who exhibited more brain than brawn became the counselors, the priests or *kahunas,* whose main business was not only divining and magic working, but also preserving the lore of the race, often concealed in chants which only the initiated would understand. Thus an island aristocracy grew up which exploited its privileges to the utmost. They enjoyed better food, leisure for manly sport, athletic and warlike training. Hence, there appeared to be two types of people, sometimes so distinct that they suggested a different racial origin— a common folk called *makaainana,* who did all the work, and a herrenfolk, the *alii,* who did none of the work and only some of the fighting. Among the latter, rituals of honor and chivalry prevailed, as in our own history in the days when knighthood was in flower. Rank was highly respected, but if the hands that held the scepter became old or impotent, there were always others ready to stretch out and snatch it away.

The islands were divided among the high chiefs under an *alii nui,* or paramount chief. If he ruled over the whole island, he would be accorded the title of *moi,* or king. Any interruption in the royal line meant a redistribution of land and usually bloody civil war.[1] So often did this occur, that the king's chief adviser was called the "island carver." Even when times were comparatively settled, there was the problem of the younger brother, popular enough to get a following, but unable or unwilling to challenge the power of the

---

An accusation commonly leveled against the whites is that they acquired land that belonged to the Hawaiians. The question is—which Hawaiians?

ruling chief. This was the setting for many an expedition—the young chief gathering the canoes and setting forth with his followers, their wives and children, and, no doubt, the blessing of the older brother.

Life, then, on the atolls and high volcanic islands of the Pacific was never static. The tides of conquest and settlement flowed swiftly thither and yon. In time the old blood ties were forgotten, intergroup visits were discontinued, and each division of Polynesians developed its own traditions and genealogies which fused with those of other Pacific peoples only in the mythical past. Changes in dialect also took place. Maoris of New Zealand retained the *r* which was displaced in Hawaii by *l*, giving the language a more mellifluous, less virile ring, compensated for, however, by the substitution of the harsher *k* for *t*. The Samoans, another great division of Polynesians, used *f* instead of *h*, so that *hale* (house) became *fale* in Samoa. These changes in speech fashions signify the breakdown in communication, the disuse of the ocean pathways.

But life remained full of incident, even for the common man. Fishing, as an industry, had affinities with hunting. Success was not only a matter of skill, but of luck as well. The harvest of the sea must be gathered often and not merely once a year. There were, therefore, more chances involved in success. Luck was so important that nothing was done to spoil it. No one asked the outgoing fisherman where he was going nor even wished him success. In the old days the fishing party rose before dawn and no one spoke till the fishing grounds were reached. Their wives were forbidden to gossip, go visiting, or receive company during their husbands' absence at sea. Quite possibly this tabu was helpful in keeping the fisherman's mind on his job. He would not be worrying as to what might be happening at home while he was away. If there was bad luck at the fishing grounds, it behooved the wife to have ready proofs of her fidelity to her household tasks against her husband's return.

It is a strange fact that men who live dangerously are less inclined to trust in their unaided strength or ability. If you look for lost islands or depend on surprise to make a landing on a hostile shore, or if you are to escape the path of the hurricane, or avoid a rotting calm, you need the gods on your side. You are easily persuaded that something watches over you, either for good or ill. Signs and portents are not important to the stay-at-homes, but if you are one of those who continually survive by narrow margins, it seems foolish not to make all possible effort, either to cajole or divert the spirits by charms or gifts.

Next to life on the sea as a breeder of superstitions comes life in the desert, and for the same reason. Something must be relied upon to balance or counteract the vicissitudes of existence. Hence, in the Kalahari Desert in Africa, no one goes forth on a journey without casting the bones. One bone represents authority and the chief, the second women and children, the third property, and the fourth the game. From their position when blown upon and thrown, the diviner foretells the success or otherwise of the journey. But even if these signs are right, there are other necessary precautions. A necklace of lion's teeth, the whiskers or claws of a leopard, a splinter of a tree struck by lightning—all these confer protection.

In the same way the Polynesian neglected no chances either to propitiate whatever gods there be or to avert their anger. He practiced much of what is called sympathetic magic. So before the stone adze could be put to the tree that was to be felled and hollowed for a canoe, the tools were soaked in sea water, the element in which the vessel must float. The canoe *kahuna*, the priest known as *kalaiwaa*, watched the tree for days. If the *elepaio*, a bird with some of the habits of the woodpecker, went slowly along the trunk looking for grubs, the tree was rejected as unsound. Red fish were eaten in a feast given to the workmen and red feathers offered when the ship was finished, for red was the royal color and sacred to Ku, the god of war. At its launching, the craft must be slightly dipped to drink sea water so that it would not then be thirsty on its voyages and ship the waves. In considering these superstitions, we must not forget that the canoe was the high point of Hawaiian industry. A Polynesian without his canoe was not lost but partially immobilized, and to be anchored in one spot did not suit his temperament.

The accusation of indolence is frequently leveled against the islander, the popular picture of the ancient Hawaiian being that of a sun-bronzed individual who sat in the shade, waiting for his dinner to fall from a coconut tree or reaching out occasionally for a bunch of ripe bananas. He might vary these ardors of existence by reclining on a rock waiting for the fish to bite. But this picture does not accord with that of an old-time canoe, 70 to 100 feet long, hewn by stone tools out of a solid tree trunk. The koa, out of which it was made, has a very hard wood, and trees of a sufficient height grew only in the mountains. Furthermore, the craft had to be made more seaworthy by lashing stout planks to its sides to give additional freeboard. There was no way of making each of these planks except by whittling down whole trees. Then holes must be bored, both in plank and hull, and the former lashed in place with sennit[2] braid. Consider further that all this hewing and planing had to be done with a stone adze, which itself had been patiently fashioned out of close-grained basalt, first split into blocks, then shaped by striking with a stone hammer, and finally ground down to a cutting edge. The basalt stone quarries were usually near the summits of the highest mountains, and the grinding was done by the use of sand and water, aided by what is called "elbow grease," otherwise hard work. It would be interesting to know how many foot pounds and hand pounds were spent in shaping one of these carefully made tools. The stone adze, the double canoe, the thousand-mile voyage— here is a sequence in industry and adventure, the story of which if woven together with a little imagination would rival any of the old world sagas. The myth of Polynesian indolence fades away in the face of these things.

It is among such considerations that we must look for the key to Hawaiian character. There is no such thing known to science as an hereditary love for the sea, any more than there could be an heredi-

---

[2] Sennit was braided or twisted coconut fiber obtained from the husks which enclosed the nuts.

tary love for taxi-driving. Sailors are not born, but made. But inherent in human personality are certain traits of temperament which fit a man for a career of adventure. Bodily strength, physical and mental restlessness, a competitive spirit, willingness to take a chance, the drive for new experiences, an inquiring intelligence— all these in varying combinations and degree are the stuff out of which men of action are made. One combination gives you the pioneer, the explorer, or the sailor; another, the scientist, creative genius, the researcher. These qualities may be either blunted or sharpened by use and experience, but they must be present in order to undergo development. Environmental influences are like the grinding and polishing of the stone adze, but first of all the basalt must be of the right kind to make a good working tool.

In a rather depressing sense the Hawaiian is home from the sea. True, he no longer combs the damp forest for the koa hulls, nor shivers in the quarries of Mauna Kea or Haleakala. He has forgotten the contours of the ocean bed around his islands, the position, boundaries, and depth of the fishing *koas*—the holes where the deep sea fishes feed. Steamers, not outrigger canoes, ply between the island ports, and luxurious Matson liners, with little concern for storm or current and none at all for sailing omens, now link the once far-flung Polynesian lands. The Hawaiian no longer needs to keep a watch along the shore for invaders; he can leave that to his white protectors, who on at least one memorable occasion kept the watch badly. He has forgotten the old chants and meles, and the reciting of thousand-year genealogies of his family no longer interests him. He is fortunate if he knows who his grandparents are. The people whose ancestors ate some of their bravest enemies, in order to take into their veins their qualities of greatness, have suffered many infusions of lesser blood. In a short hundred years the features of their ancient life have become well-nigh unrecognizable. Their arts, their crafts, their traditions, their history are preserved—in a museum.

But in the days of the first three Kamehamehas, the spirit of adventure was by no means dead. The descendants of the old

Polynesian navigators, once they got over their amazement at the huge bulk of the white man's vessels, were eager to get on board and go to sea. These were no peasants with the peasants' attachment to the soil, to a sedentary existence, and to the institutions that thrive with stability of population, and around which the groundling's life revolves. Far wider horizons than their forefathers' double canoes ever penetrated were insistently beckoning. The very magnitude of Hawaii, a circumstance which had tended to dampen enthusiasm for overseas wandering, seemed now shrunken to such small proportions that once again an island environment became limited and oppressive to a man of spirit. Nor were opportunities to enlarge their experience lacking to the Hawaiians.

It seems odd to record that, with a climate at sea level that ordinarily uses only thirty degrees of the thermometer—from 56° to 86°—Hawaii, in its development, was in any degree dependent upon the fur trade. Yet such was the case. The earliest shipments of sandalwood to China met with a very poor market. This stuff, of small size, was only fit to burn in joss houses, and the Chinese, shrewd traders that they were, depressed the market still more by calling the timber spurious. But the ships' masters noted how eagerly furs, mainly of the sea otter, were snapped up by buyers, who no doubt traded them inland in exchange for concubines, a trade relationship that has not yet wholly disappeared in countries other than China. At once a brisk trade sprang up between the west and northwest coasts of America, where sea otters were being caught in large numbers. By 1801, this traffic was almost entirely in American hands, and ships were finding it most convenient to call at the islands for fresh provisions, water, and other supplies. Hawaii had also other advantages. Honolulu provided excellent anchorage while ships were undergoing repairs, native ropes were much in demand, while most important of all was the fact that, under Kamehameha's firm rule, sailors found there was no safer place in the world in which to spend their time ashore. Moreover, it provided entertainment near to a sailor's comfort.

After the fur supplies were depleted and trade languished,

whaling took first place in commercial importance. From 1820 onwards, almost all the whaling ships made port in Hawaii, on their way to and from the three great whale-hunting areas in the Pacific. One was south of Hawaii near the equator, another near Japan, and the third between Alaska and Kamchatka. The various allurements of island life caused wholesale desertions, but the skippers did not care greatly. Many of the sailors from other ships, the joys of land liberty having palled somewhat, were ready to ship again, and if not, there were crowds of eager Hawaiians who were soon found to be docile as well as excellent sailors. Some of them took readily to harpooning, a most dangerous and responsible job.

So insistent was the lure of the sea that the Wilkes U. S. Exploring Expedition was able to recruit fifty Hawaiian sailors in 1840-41, and soon men of this seafaring people were to be found in every ocean. Bradley, the historian,[2] quotes Sir George Simpson, an official of the Hudson's Bay Company, as asserting that nearly one thousand men in the prime of life left the islands annually. In 1844, from three to four hundred were resident in Oregon, most of them finding employment with the Company in trapping and other pursuits congenial to their variety-loving temperaments.

From that time to this, monotonous toil in the cane field has never appealed to the native islander, but the establishment of large cattle ranches on Hawaii and Maui has provided him with opportunities for varied activities, Hawaiian cowboys having competed on favorable terms with the best riders of the Southwest. But now some of the romance of ranch life has disappeared. The mechanization of plantation industry offers some chance of expression to the Hawaiian's love of speed and power, while college sports, such as football, are sufficiently bruising and competitive to appeal to the old-time spirit.

He wants no part of the routine of business, and in any case money is something to be spent, not hoarded. Hardly an Hawaiian name appears among commercial concerns. Even fishing, now that it has become an industry requiring power boats, refrigeration, and

[2]Bradley, H. W. *The American Frontier in Hawaii.* Stanford University Press, 1942.

miles of lines and nets, had, before the war, been captured from him by the Japanese. Koa bowls or kapa that you purchase are probably now all factory-made, and the only articles of native industry left are lauhala mats and flower leis.

There is, however, one occupation that did not call for sustained effort, which provided the stimulus of contest, with sometimes valuable prizes attached. This was the business of politics into which the old time Hawaiian entered with the zest of a game. It also offered great opportunities for declamation, at which the Polynesian excels, and which occasionally reaches a certain pitch of oratory. For the most part this depends for effect on repetition and exaggerated statements. For example, a common welcoming speech in the old days dwelt on the weariness of spirit and the darkness of the night until the visitor appeared.

> "But now it is dawn, it is dawn,
> It is light."

This declamation lent itself not only to hyperbole, but to stylistic patterns of use. In New Zealand, the Maoris heightened the dramatic effect of speech by movement. The speaker began each sentence from a point to the right of the platform, then as he moved to the left the statement gained emphasis, the trick being to end each period with both feet on the ground. Additional force was lent by the appropriate use of a green-stone club held in the proper ceremonial manner in the right hand. Then while the rhetorical point sank into the minds of the audience, the speaker turned and either walked or trotted back to the starting point in readiness for the next burst of eloquence.

The formal use of the exaggerated phrase provides on occasion a fine outlet for the Polynesian sense of humor, which is never lacking. To deliver a set speech, full of classical allusions, drawn from the poetry and traditions of the people, and packed with the devices of studied eloquence, the whole devoted to some insignificant subject, touches off that sense of parody that makes a Polynesian audience writhe with suppressed delight.

One of the most delightful stories the writer has heard is

Dr. Peter Buck's description of a ceremonial visit by a Maori party which he was induced to accompany. The purpose was to demand satisfaction from another village for a public injury, involving, I believe, a slight case of seduction.

The offending villagers entered into the spirit of the occasion by acknowledging responsibility for their erring kinsman, and brought forth their gifts of restitution which were piled in the meeting place, where each man extolled the value of his gift and his great personal sacrifice. The climax was reached when one man proclaimed the matchless pedigree of the horse he was about to devote to this debt of honor, its dazzling speed, its thoroughbred beauty, its triumphs of the turf, the stamina of its progeny—and then gravely led forth this Man-of-War—a wall-eyed, spavined, goose-rumped, broken-winded, harness-galled old gelding. It was just as gravely accepted—but tides of concealed mirth swept the minds of the assemblage, shown only by the glint in the eyes of each man as he secretly savored the flavor of this joke of jokes, so exquisite that even a smile would detract from its quality.

This deep suspicion that, after all, politics is a game, and government by the people instead of by the high chiefs is something of a joke, has not wholly departed from the mind of the modern Hawaiian. He takes his politics seriously, as he takes any game, but with no bitterness of feeling, so that the local Legislature is one of the best humored in the world. The days of impassioned speech are by no means over, but it is passion with a smile. One of the fieriest speeches in local legislative history, yet one which was filled with covert humor, was directed against a bill for the sterilization of defectives. It was mainly on the theme "what God hath joined let no man put asunder," the orator being somewhat confused as to the type of operation suggested.

Some years ago, a legislator let himself go in a speech on a bill to provide a home for defectives. His fellow members sat mystified as he launched into a moving description of the perils of a policeman's life, his long hours, and the weariness that comes from pounding the pavements—until they realized that the speaker, who was none too literate, had misread the title of the bill as "a home for detectives," and wanted to insure that foot patrolmen received equal consideration.

The sympathies of the Hawaiian are easily stirred, and an appeal for the underdog is always effective. In early political days, one man was elected to public office on the plea that he had eleven children and needed the money. Another had himself appointed to a committee investigating the prison on grounds that he had inside information, having served a penal term.

The shutting away from society of the leprous or the feeble-minded has never been wholly accepted as a humane public policy. These people have done no wrong! At a legislative investigation of Waimano Home, the institution for defectives, one lawmaker asserted that people were confined there without cause. He had interviewed three girl inmates and all had denied that they were feeble-minded. There is also the story of the girl who met a friend on the island of Kauai. "You go Waimano, no?" she asked. "No more," was the reply. "I go Honolulu, take examination for *eediot*. I no pass."

It is worth while emphasizing that the acquisitive spirit was never characteristic of the Hawaiian. In some other Pacific lands the accumulation of wealth or its symbols is a passion, the main business of life. In the New Hebrides, for example, there was a highly developed "pig culture," in which almost all of life revolved around the acquisition of boars whose lower tusks had been allowed to grow in circles. This was done by removing the top incisors which normally kept the lower tusks ground down. After the operation, the growing tusks bend backwards and continue growing, sometimes entering the lower jaw and penetrating it to emerge again and complete another full circle.

The prototype of the Melanesian millionaire was the man who owned a two-circle tusker, while the multimillionaire was represented by the man who possessed a three-circle pig. This animal was so rare that other men would give a pig in payment just to look at it. Such animal treasures must of course be tethered, lest they broke a tusk in fighting, or by rooting in hard ground. They received constant care by women and were fed only the softest and richest food. The great danger was that the animal might die a natural death, as then the owner would lose the tremendous prestige attendant upon the tusker's final ceremonial slaughter. Outside of the social status that pig ownership conferred, the animals had little use or value.

The Hawaiians had no such concepts or symbols of wealth. It must be remembered that they were the farthest-flung division of the Pacific peoples. They were the latest adventurers and had found neither the time nor the place for accumulating wealth. Even the feather cloaks, most prized of the chief's possessions, were symbols of authority rather than riches. Hence we find the young chief Kamehameha visiting one of Cook's vessels and trading his cape for some iron daggers.

With unusual sagacity, this king, after the whites came, began to accumulate property, particularly ships and money. On the occasion of an exchange of a ship for a cargo of sandalwood, Kamehameha prevented the firing of the usual royal salute from her guns, because the fireworks would be at his expense. The much more usual reaction would have been—let's have the big noise, and never mind the expense.

The acquisitive habit was so new that it became quite promiscuous in its objects. Lloyd Osbourne, stepson of R. L. S., in his preface to *The Wrecker* tells of the contents of the storehouse of the king of Apemama, which this "Napoleon of the Gilbert Islands" put at Stevenson's disposal. It contained a large rocking horse, French clocks, perambulators, toy steam engines, sewing machines, surgical instrument cases, etc.—anything from a schooner's trade room that took the king's eye. An early writer describes Kamehameha's storehouses as similarly overflowing with articles useless in Hawaii.

Sailors, having the nomadic temperament, rarely acquire property in large amounts, and generally the Hawaiians were not exempt from this negative tendency. They did not believe in giving hostages to fortune. This idea extended to land, which was for use, not absolute possession. They lived under a most complete feudal system in which land was granted by the king to the *alii,* from them to the *makaainana,* while the landless serfs were the *kauwa.* A change of kings by conquest meant a complete redistribution of land holdings. This feudal idea was probably the basis of the "cession" of the kingdom to the British in Vancouver's day. It was merely an acknowledgment of overlordship, a purely symbolic transfer of ownership, in order to gain the king of England's protection.

A feudal relationship was probably the understanding of the Hawaiian kings when they granted land to the missionaries in return for their services. Proof of this was given when the royal family ordered Mrs. Bingham to make five shirts for the king and a number of dresses for the queen. Such a service was entirely in line with a feudal retainer's obligations.

It is interesting to note that some recent writers have credited the missionaries and their descendants with establishing—and perpetuating—a feudal system in Hawaii.[4] Not until 1848 was the conflict between the two opposing systems of land tenure settled in the white man's way. The Great Mahele, or land division, divided the land in three parts, one for the king, one for the chiefs, and one for the common people, and established the fee simple idea. But the decree did not bring understanding. It did not make sense in the eyes of the Hawaiians. Many of them gave up their landed rights for a mere token payment and expected in return lifelong support and protection from the new owners. The trouble was that the Hawaiian was neither peasant nor dirt farmer. He was ready to till the land for sustenance but not for profit. He was sedentary by accident, not by design. His home was on the sea.

Those of us who have the greatest *aloha* for Hawaiians cannot blind ourselves to their faults. Not being acquisitive themselves, they did not respect this trait in others. They could not understand this identification of the white man with his possessions. Having

---

[4] Bingham, the missionary writer, condemned the feudal system as "a low and revolting state of society."

prostrated themselves before the new chief and thus acknowledged his overlordship, it was, according to their notion and habit, entirely excusable to help themselves from his superabundance of wealth. Their own chiefs' possessions were open to them, provided, of course, the property had not been placed under tabu. Much of the so-called thieving from the early navigators was done by petty chiefs. Shooting a man for a small theft seemed to them an extremely harsh and unnecessary punishment, when all the white man had to do was to declare a tabu, either through chief or king or priest, and by the setting up of the tabu signals, usually white flags. No one would then think of trespass or theft.

Respect for property is a matter of rigid training, and to an open-handed, generous people that training came hard. It was no wonder then that carelessness rather than dishonesty in money matters was recognized for many years as a common Hawaiian trait of character. Things held in trust for another could be converted to use if need arose, and no blame attached. Stevenson, a warm friend of our island people, remarked that honest and upright Hawaiians have stumbled on the narrow path of trusteeship. If, too, what you have today may be lost to you tomorrow, why not enjoy it while you can? This philosophy of living naturally led to intemperance in various directions, a vice which the canny, provident, foresighted New England missionary roundly condemned. What the preacher described as unchristian, may have been merely unwhite.

Another trait of behavior which the white man had difficulty in understanding in the Polynesian was the looseness of natural family ties. As Stevenson declared, "their family affection is strong but unerect." Their ideas of trusteeship in the matter of children were similar to those regarding property. Children were given for enjoyment, not responsibility. Hawaiians loved their children dearly, but cared for them little, allowing them all the freedom of action which they as adults demanded for themselves. Biological ties were weak, ties of association strong. That is how Stevenson's statement may be interpreted.

For these reasons exchange of children, even outright gifts of children, were common. Such attitudes, stemming as they do from the temperament of the people, persist to a remarkable extent. Social workers in Hawaii will tell you that it was always easy to find an adoptive home for an Hawaiian or part-Hawaiian child. If there had been enough Hawaiian families, there would have been no difficulty in the home placement of any or every child. They will also tell you that this adoption will cover food and clothing and all bodily needs within the resources of the foster parent. It will not always guarantee conventional training, prudent control, and a wise upbringing.

But the greatest conflict of all between two opposing moralities, that of the respectable home-body and that of the adventurer, is in the field of sex relationships. The Hawaiian attitude in such matters was influenced by the two attitudes just discussed, namely, that property was held for use but not in absolute possession, and laxity in home control of the young and adolescent was normal. Sexual freedom was horrifying to the New Englander. What to one people was warmhearted responsiveness and a commendable absence of possessive jealousy, was to the other the most degraded licentiousness. The nonmissionary whites exploited the easy generosity of the Hawaiian women to the full. There were other things besides a safe winter haven that attracted four hundred whaling vessels in a season to Lahaina. Women, themselves of sea-going ancestry, understood the needs of men from the sea.

On the other hand, jealousy, another phase of white possessiveness, was not understood by the Hawaiian. Kaahumanu, favorite queen of Kamehameha, in her late fifties became a paragon of virtue and the brightest jewel in the missionaries' crown; but a few years earlier she had had her fling. She slept with a chief, Kanihonui, and when the scandal was discovered, it was he who suffered death at the king's hands, not on account of jealousy, but because he had broken the royal tabu. The matter caused a temporary estrangement between the king and queen, but, with Vancouver as go-between, the breach was soon healed. Stevenson, by the way, placed Kaahumanu above

Mary Queen of Scots; in his opinion, she was "the nobler woman, with the nobler story."

Among the Hawaiians themselves, this freedom of intercourse meant little, but under conditions of free contact with whites it meant national disaster. Hawaiians themselves recognized and lamented this sexual laxity. Kepelino, in his *Traditions of Hawaii,* made this sad confession about his people: *Ma na aina e o na Kanaka 100 makahiki;* he says, "one might live to be hundreds of years in other lands, and not know so much mischief as a small child of five or six years in Hawaii." Then he continues: "The Hawaiian race is a kindly and affectionate one, hospitable and helpful to one another; a race grateful to those who have been good to them. Such were the ways of the Hawaiians of the old days. Now they are changed." The sailor was home from the sea.

The attitude of the Hawaiians towards sexual morality, as we understand the term, is best illustrated by two of their once popular games, described by David Malo, their own historian.

The first was called *ume* and was played by the common people. Husbands and wives gathered together in a house called the *ume-hale,* the ancient site of which is now occupied by a less romantic institution, the Bank of Bishop. When everybody was present, the leader called out *"Puheoheo,"* to which all the people replied *"Puheo-heoheo,"* a word with a derivation appropriate to the game.[5] He then proceeded to touch the shoulders of men and women, in pairs, with a wand. The couples thus designated retired for the night with no questions asked, and no jealous after-complaints. If you didn't want to play, you stayed at home. Virgins and unmarried women, says Emerson in his notes on Malo's work, did not usually attend the *ume-hale.*

It should be noted that only the lower classes of people played this game, which was considered very crude and licentious. The *alii,* or upper class, patronized a much more dignified sport called *kilu.* This was really a game of skill like bowls. The players, male and

[5] *Pu* is a gathering together, for play; *heoheo* is the end of the penis. As Malo remarks, "it was an adulterous sport."

female, sat opposite each other with wooden pins (pobs, Alexander calls them) standing in front of them. Each contestant took turns to bowl a disc cut out of a coconut shell at the other person's pin. If the pin was knocked over, the tallykeeper recited a verse which Emerson translates very discreetly, but which is full of double meanings of an erotic nature. Only after the pins had been knocked over ten times was it proper for the couple to retire for the night. If a person really preferred some other partner, it was possible to buy off with a forfeit of land or other possessions. Only people of high rank played *ḳilu;* no self-respecting chief would indulge in the rude game of *ume.*

Once contact with civilization was established, such easy-going, extra-marital relationships were not compatible either with the new morality nor with the order of co-prosperity which the missionaries worked so diligently to establish in the Hawaiian Islands. Perhaps the Hawaiians were too modern for the missionaries. In any case, for the welfare of the new community, the latter had to stand between the people and some of their natural impulses. Only in one place have their efforts met with lasting success. The people of the island of Niihau represent a strictly controlled engrafting of mission morality upon Hawaiian character. The results cannot as yet be properly reported. The social psychologist has been forbidden the island by its white owners; he might carry with him the seeds of social corruption. It is by no means impossible. In Niihau, the sailor is home from the sea. He is safely at anchor—in the seaman's home.

Niihau lies off the coast of Kauai and is owned by the Robinson family, long-time residents of the latter island. Much of its coast-line consists of steep cliffs, with a low range of mountains, 1,200 feet high, running up the northwest side. At the southern end is still another elevation, while in between is a plain covered with tall grass, an occasional kiawe tree, and scattered volcanic boulders. The whole island is 20 miles long and from four to five miles wide. Cattle, turkeys, and honey are its main products, with wild pigs and peacocks roaming at large in the mountains.

The island is noted for its isolation. There are about 180 people living there, almost all of them Niihau natives for very many generations, speaking Hawaiian fluently, with very little knowledge of English. There is one quarter-Japanese family, the descendants of a Japanese man who was shipwrecked on the island sixty years ago and who married a native girl. Two other Japanese men came from Kauai to look after the bees.

The natives are very clannish, and while perfectly polite to strangers, regard them with considerable distrust. One man seemed to a visitor to be treated somewhat as an outsider. The explanation was that he was a stranger who had come from Hilo thirty years before and had married into a Niihau family. He is still the stranger. Tobacco and liquor and strange haoles are tabu, consequently there is no vice, and only one or two *hapa-haoles* (half-whites) live on the island.

If the inhabitants wish to invite friends or relatives from the other islands to visit them, they must first obtain permission from the owners who provide transportation on the sampan that brings supplies weekly from Kauai. Should anyone wish to leave Niihau he may do so, but unless the trip is approved, he may not return.

In spite of all these restrictions, the natives seem to be extremely happy. Four of the men act as overseers, and working conditions are apparently most harmonious. The owner does not obtrude his authority, being careful merely to suggest rather than to issue orders.

Missionary influence by tradition is extremely strong. The natives of their own accord keep Sunday very strictly. They will not ride, swim, fish, hunt, nor even pick up shells on the Sabbath day, but all attend church. In every home, each day is begun with prayer. Even when the father has to leave the house for his daily work at 4 a.m., the whole family rises to sing and pray with him before he departs. When Mr. Robinson, one of the owners, is on the island, he drives an old-fashioned carriage to church, drawn by a pair of thoroughbred horses. Until the army landed a detachment of soldiers after the blitz, no motor vehicle had ever been seen on the island.

From this almost idyllic seclusion, Niihau emerged most dramatically on December 7, 1941. The story of the Japanese invasion has been told several times, but no one has apparently pointed out how closely the occurrences fit in with the plot of an extremely bad Hollywood scenario.

The opening scene shows the Hawaiian community at church on this little Pacific island, bathed in peaceful sunshine. Then comes the unaccustomed roar of two planes that circle the spot, one of them spluttering and smoking. They disappear out to sea and presently one comes back to make a forced landing, crashing against a hidden boulder. The brave cowboy dashes up to the plane, seizes the aviator's pistol and a mysterious bundle of papers which the enemy is seeking to destroy.

Now enters the villain of the piece, a Japanese named Harada, who had come from Kauai about a year previously to act as assistant beekeeper. Under pretense of helping take care of the prisoner, he leads him to a house where he had previously hidden firearms. The cowboy guard is overcome, and the enemy pair rush off to the plane, get out the machine gun and set off to overawe the villagers and retrieve the mysterious papers.

In true Hollywood tradition, the cowboy frees himself, and jumping down twenty feet from a window, takes a short cut to the village to warn the inhabitants. They run and hide with the exception of one old woman who sits calmly reading her Hawaiian bible in spite of all threats of death or torture unless she reveals the papers' hiding place. The Japanese search feverishly and in their rage machine gun the village.

At night the natives gather at the church and decide to fire the headland beacon which in former days brought help from Kauai. But in case the meaning of the old signal has been forgotten, someone must go for assistance. The cowboys crawl into the stable to get the thoroughbreds just as the enemy also arrive there. The former vault on the horses' backs and ride off under a hail of bullets, the Japanese being apparently unable to hit the side of a barn. Then follows a wild ride across the island, the sound effect man doing a fine job with the drumming of the horses' hooves. In the glare of the beacon, the natives man the whale boat and do a most effective fadeout into the darkness of a wild sea.

Then appears the real hero of the story—old Kanahele, still the strong man of the island, who kills wild boars with his bare hands and nonchalantly carries 260-pound boxes filled with honey down the cliffs to the beach when the stuff is being shipped away. He sneaks up to the plane at night and removes all the spare machine gun ammunition, but next morning he and his wife are ambushed and captured. The Jap aviator threatens Kanahele with his pistol and orders him to lead him to the hidden papers.

"Put that little gun down," says Kanahele, "or I will take it from you." He grapples with the man while Harada struggles with Kanahele's wife, who prevents him from shooting her husband. The aviator wrenches his pistol arm free and shoots Kanahele, first in the stomach, then in the groin, and last of all in the leg. But Kanahele's fighting blood—all that is left of it—is up, and, seizing the enemy by the leg, dashes his head against a rock. Harada, realizing the game is up, shoots himself, and Kanahele's wife picks up a stone to finish the aviator.

"Let be, woman," says the old cowboy, "the man is *pau*. Let us go home and wait for Mr. Robinson and explain to him what we have done." Then off he walks, stomach, groin, and leg wounds notwithstanding. The final scene, of course, is his decoration by the general, Stars and Stripes waving, the bands playing, and Kanahele wondering why all the fuss.

This is nothing but the rankest kind of melodrama, produced under the most amateurish direction, a commonplace Western thriller, naïvely transplanted to an Hawaiian location. The strangest thing about the whole performance is that it is literally all true.

In Niihau, the sailor is home from the sea. His life may be over-regulated and weighted down with missionary tradition, but he still retains all of his old-time spirit. When he comes to the defense of his island home, his mixture of piety and fearlessness makes of the one-time seafarer a man to be reckoned with.

CHAPTER III

Polynesian Potentates

MOST PEOPLE, perhaps because they have a secret urge to be submissive before princely pomp and circumstance, show a decided interest in royalty. Nowhere is this interest keener than in democratic countries. In all America there is only one place where kings and queens reigned for nearly a hundred years, and that is Hawaii. At the Capitol Building, once the royal palace, the visitor can stand in an authentic throne room where once monarchs sat in state, surrounded by all the gold braid and consular dignity of the representatives of the Great Powers. He can sit in the very chair where, fifty years ago, a queen sat, attended by her anxious court, waiting for the die to be cast that was ultimately to make this territory American.

But even if he should not visit the Capitol, the visitor will find other reminders of kingship in the islands. He could hardly miss seeing, in front of the Judiciary Building, the statue of Kamehameha I, showing a man of solidly athletic build arrayed in a helmet and a *mamo* cape, a *malo* or girdle, and considerable dignity. From the descriptions that have come down to us, the form of the statue is really lifelike. Kamehameha was just such a man.

Incidentally, it may be remarked that the king's attire is perhaps as rare in material and workmanship as any of the royal robes of the kings of Europe. The Hawaiian symbol for kingship, here represented, was this golden cape, six feet long, and eight or nine feet wide, which was made of the feathers of 80,000 birds and took the labor of nine generations of skilled cloakmakers to complete fully. The bird was the *mamo,* extinct since 1870, from which was plucked a tiny tuft of yellow feathers from above and below the tail. These birds were snared by a special guild of bird-catchers, the *poe*

Photo by Hawaiian Airlines
Black lava sands form beaches at Kalapana, Hawaii

Photo by R. J. Baker
Bubbles and caves in old lava become "The Boiling Pots,"
near Hilo

Sugar mills and plantations line the Hamakua coast, Hawaii

Steep gulches score the lower flanks of Mauna Kea

ʞahai, who studied their habits and trapped them with a kind of native birdline. The cloak was made by first knotting together a net of fine olona fibers, made from the inner bark of a species of Hawaiian nettle. Then with infinite care the quill of each feather was bent and tied firmly in place so that each overlapped smoothly with its fellows, presenting an unbroken golden surface. It was a garment fit for a king.

The helmet, or *mahiole,* had a wickerwork base covered by a network of rootlets of a tough plant *(ieie—*a tough name), to which were attached the feathers of the *mamo,* or of the scarlet *iiwi,* the latter still one of the commoner birds of the Hawaiian forest. The shape of the helmet, with its forward-looking crest, is one of the indirect proofs relied upon to bolster the rather shaky hypothesis that Juan Gaetano, the Spaniard, discovered these islands in or about 1555. The rest of the evidence consists of vague native tradition of shipwrecks on their shores and an old Spanish chart showing three islands in the right latitude, but with the longitude woefully wrong. If the Spaniards stayed long enough for the Hawaiians to copy their helmets, the latter should have learned much more about civilization. In any case, the form of the helmet is Roman or Grecian, not Spanish. Then, too, if the Spaniards knew of Hawaii, they did nothing with their knowledge. It has even been suggested that they deliberately kept the existence of the islands a secret, another Spanish buried treasure, so to speak.

If the Hawaiians borrowed the helmet, at least the feather cape was a Polynesian idea, for red feather capes formed part of the trappings with which chiefs of the Society Islands were invested. There they were called *ahuula,* a general name for capes in Hawaii. But here, yellow displaced red as the royal color.

If the most substantial basis of kingship is power, then Kamehameha was truly regal. No monarch ever exercised more autocratic rights over his subjects than did this Hawaiian king. No common man dared enter his presence nor dive into his swimming hole nor stand on a special stone which he used when drying himself. Neither chief nor commoner could use any of the king's property nor expectorate in the king's cuspidor which was ringed around with his ancestors' teeth, thus ensuring a befitting continuity of contact.[1] If any person's shadow fell on the king, or if he by chance occupied a more elevated position within the king's sight, if he came into the royal presence with his head wet, or if he failed to prostrate himself, not only when his majesty passed by, but also when food or water was being carried into the king's household, the penalty was death. When two princesses offended by bathing in the king's private swimming hole, their tutor, who should have taught them better, was immediately executed. It was an unfortunate Hawaiian who set foot on a ship's deck not knowing that the king was below, thus setting himself above his ruler. Such an unwitting presumption was also a capital offense.

A sample of these rigid restrictions with regard to rank was observed by Hawaii's white discoverer. Royal honors were accorded to Captain Cook when he landed at Kealakekua Bay in 1779. As the Captain walked along, crowds of people prostrated themselves until he had passed, and were then promptly trampled on by the multitude behind who were rushing up to view the spectacle, much in the manner of crowds at a golf championship match. This was a little hard on the feelings of the downtrodden herd, who finally compromised by running alongside on all fours so as to keep up with Cook's progress and still pay him proper respect. It must have been a joyous sight — a great concourse of Hawaiian men and women, most of them notably broad in the beam, scuttling along on hands and knees, determined to miss no part of the sight of the century.

Some writers on Hawaii have been guilty of making some extremely inept comparisons. Iao Valley, on Maui, for example, has been likened to Yosemite, and Kamehameha has been called the Napoleon of the Pacific. As a matter of sober fact, these two personages resembled each other about as much as Iao resembles Yosemite. The comparison does justice to neither man. Kameha-

[1] A special officer was given the job of looking after the royal cuspidor. It is a common belief among untutored peoples that if an ill-disposed person can get hold of anything intimately connected with a person they can work all kinds of black magic against him.

meha had only a fraction of Napoleon's military genius, and in international stature they were not even comparable. It is idle to speculate what the Hawaiian king could have accomplished with Napoleon's opportunities. On the other hand, the sagacity and shrewdness of foresight that the former displayed would, I believe, have saved him from Napoleon's overweening ambition and lust for power, at any cost. Kamehameha attained his ambition by conquering all in sight and became superior in his field of action just as Napoleon did. But there the comparison should end.

Warfare in his day, like our own medieval contests, was a highly stylized affair. It was not considered quite the thing to take your enemy by surprise nor to use any dirty tricks like lying in wait for him. In the case of one invasion, the attacking forces were not only unopposed on landing, but were given suitable time to rest and recover from their fatigue before the defenders fell upon them. There were interesting preliminaries to battle, such as mortal challenges to individual combat. A special name, *lehua,* was given to the first man killed, and time out was taken to drag him to the priest to be offered to his war god. The foreigners in Kamehameha's service—he had fifty of them at the time of his projected invasion of Kauai—introduced some innovations into the rules of warfare. An opposing champion while reciting his genealogy to prove his fitness as a challenger was liable to get shot before he had climbed very far up his family tree.

White assistants, however, came later in Kamehameha's career. First of all, he had to defeat his cousin, the young king Kiwalao, and very nearly lost the battle and his life-long chief supporter, Keeaumoku. Someone tripped up the latter with a long spear, and two chiefs, crying "Strike the yellow-backed crab,"[2] fell upon him and stabbed him twice. Kiwalao, however, who was anxious to get Keeaumoku's whale-tooth ornament from round his neck before it was stained by blood, intervened, and was felled by a slingstone. Keeaumoku had strength enough to crawl over and cut Kiwalao's throat with a shark's-tooth dagger, upon which the young king's

[2] This probably referred to the yellow cape he would be wearing to denote his high rank.

party fled. Soon after, Kamehameha invaded Hilo, and at Waiakea he was soundly drubbed for his pains by the late king's uncle, assisted by some warriors from Maui. In another raid on Puna, some doughty fisherman batted Kamehameha over the head with a paddle when he had his foot caught in a rock, and nearly killed him. Shortly after, the king, through capture, obtained the services of Isaac Davis and John Young, which proved the turning point in his fortunes. The circumstances were as follows:

In 1789 the islands had been visited by the notorious Captain Metcalf, an American fur trader, in the snow[3] Eleanor, accompanied by a small schooner called the Fair American in command of his son, whose mate was Isaac Davis. While anchored off Maui, the Eleanor's boat was cut adrift at night and the sailor guarding it killed, the boat being broken up for the nails which it contained. The Hawaiians didn't think much of the boat but valued the nails highly for making fishhooks. Soon afterwards Metcalf, while trading off Olowalu on Maui, insisted on all the natives' canoes being collected on the starboard side of his vessel. He then opened his ports and fired a broadside into them. The slaughter was indescribable. The canoes were smashed, and over a hundred Hawaiians killed, while others floated ashore with, as the native account said, "their brains running out of their heads."

The Fair American, this occurrence being still unknown to its crew, anchored off Kawaihae and was suddenly attacked. All on board were killed but Davis, who, when he was thrown overboard, called out the only Hawaiian word he knew, "aloha," and was spared. John Young, boatswain of the Eleanor, who had been left ashore on Hawaii, was detained by Kamehameha until the Eleanor sailed. Both white men then entered the king's service. The cannon from the Fair American were removed, and Davis and Young mounted them on land carriages. They also trained some men in the use of muskets. The king was now ready to invade Maui, and in a battle near Wailuku, the cannon fire scared the wits out of Maui

---

[3] A snow was a square-rigged vessel differing slightly from a brig.

warriors. So many of them were killed in Iao stream that the battle was called Kapaniwai, the damming of the waters.

At this time Keoua, the chief of Hilo, declared war, and two indecisive battles were fought with him at Hamakua, Hawaii, about forty miles from Hilo. But in November of 1790 disaster overtook his army in the explosive eruption of Kilauea, described in a later chapter. Keoua was marching on Kau when an earthquake occurred which was so terrific that no man could stand upright. Then followed the blast of gas and hot ashes which overwhelmed Keoua's main body. It was quite evident to everybody that Pele, the goddess of volcanic fires, was on Kamehameha's side, and except for one rebellion, his reign on Hawaii remained from that time undisturbed.

Young and Davis were also most helpful in winning a naval engagement for Kamehameha against a fleet of canoes representing the combined forces of Oahu and Kauai. They manned the Fair American with cannon and scattered the canoes of the opposing warriors who possessed only spears and muskets. About this time, Keoua, the king's old rival, was persuaded to visit Kohala where he was stabbed to death by Keeaumoku, the old king-killer, this being his second victim of royal blood. Vancouver, in his three visits to Hawaii, also gave Kamehameha valuable military advice and his officers even helped to drill the king's bodyguard. By this time Young and Davis were comfortably settled in Hawaii. Both became high chiefs and married women of great rank. Young's granddaughter afterwards became Queen Emma.

Of course, with these changes, the old methods of warfare went by the board. No longer were the manner and place of battle prearranged. Previously, if there was a nice open space available, the two armies met and arranged themselves in a crescent, the kings and their bodyguards in the center, the slingshot men and other skirmishers on the flanks. The tactics were to envelop the opposing wings and fold them back on the center where the stones and javelins could create confusion and pave the way for a charge by the spearmen. If both sides were evenly matched, the contest might go on for days. If there were notable losses in both armies, the leaders

might declare themselves *luku lua,* "both sides beaten," and go home
to fight again another day.

If the battle took place in a narrow valley, the younger untried
warriors, who had a reputation to make, formed the spearpoint or
welau. They were strictly expendable. The chief and his picked men
drove in behind the point and thus were called the *pohiwi,* or
shoulder. When the ground was broken, the army advanced with
a screen of slingshot men backed by another body of javelin throwers,
while the main army was formed into clumps of warriors called
waa kaua, the war canoes, each under its special chief. The horrid
appearance of the Hawaiian idols can be attributed to the fact that
they were intended to throw a scare into the enemy when carried
into battle by the priests, who let out the most bloodthirsty yells to
prove that the spirits of the gods were really present.

I suspect that Davis and Young, being shrewd men, chose positions for their cannon so as to bring the "war canoes" under direct
fire. These white men were good fighters but very poor sports. Even
the priests ran for the places of refuge when they saw their gods
smashed to pieces by grapeshot. One of the largest of these sanc-
tuaries was the one still to be seen at Honaunau on Hawaii. Ellis
gives its dimensions as 715 feet long, 404 feet wide, with walls
12 feet high and 15 feet thick. Any criminal or fugitive from king,
chief, or other enemy could be pursued to the walls but no farther.
The enclosure was very jealously guarded. There were *puuhonuas* or
places of 'refuge on every island.

In 1794, just one hundred and fifty years ago, Kamehameha
gathered a large force and overran Maui, Lanai, and Molokai. The
next year the battle of Oahu took place. At the outset of the campaign, Kamehameha was deserted by Kaiana, his second in command, who went over with his following to Kalanikupule, the king
of Oahu, who had gathered his forces behind a stone wall three miles
up Nuuanu Valley. A lucky shot from a field piece manned by
Young killed Kaiana and sent part of the wall toppling onto its
defenders. This was such a blow to morale that the army broke,
pursued by Kamehameha's men. The last stand was made at the

Pali, where three hundred of the Oahu men were killed and the rest driven over the precipice.

In 1804, the conqueror raised a large army, said to number 16,000 men, with which to invade Kauai. The penalty against conscientious or other objectors to conscription was to have their ears cropped and then to be dragged by a rope around their waists to the army. Kamehameha's martial preparations, however, were needless, for the king of Kauai was induced to acknowledge his overlordship, thus bringing the whole territory under the one king.

From these accounts it seems doubtful whether Kamehameha should be regarded as a military genius, for without the help of the white men he could hardly have made himself supreme. His claims to respect as a ruler and a great personage rest on a more substantial basis. He proved himself to be a man of extraordinary sagacity, stable temperament, undoubted courage, and foresight.

As regards his personal strength and fighting prowess, these are likely to grow rather than be diminished in the telling. Vancouver describes a sham fight in which six spears hurled at the king were either caught or diverted. The spearmen, no doubt, took good care not to come too close to his sacred person, having in mind what would happen to the unlucky man who scored a hit. One marksman who made a mistake and hit a mere chief's son had his eyes "scooped out," to use the expressive term of the contemporary account.

But even discounting somewhat these legendary feats of Kamehameha, we are still left with the figure of a man—one who by reason of native qualities could take his place with the kings of his time. It should be remembered that these included George III of England (five times insane), Catharine of Russia, the dissolute, Alexander II, the vain, and many other rulers, who, by any reasonable standards of morals, intelligence, or judgment, were hardly admirable, and with whom, considering his limited education and experience, Kamehameha could well be compared.

One of the proofs of Kamehameha's sagacity was the restraint he exercised over his chiefs. They were a turbulent and avaricious lot, hailing the appearance of a ship off the coast as a signal for deep-laid plans for its capture and looting. Sometimes these schemes were at least temporarily successful. The captains of two English vessels lying off Waikiki were killed and their vessels captured. The king of Oahu then set off to Hawaii intending to induce Kamehameha to come on board when they would take the opportunity to kill him. However, the Hawaiians, unused to the motion of a ship, became violently seasick and were overpowered by the white crews. Chiefs on Hawaii were also full of similar nefarious schemes, which were frustrated by Kamehameha, who insisted on fair and honest dealings with visiting ships. Perhaps it was to check the cupidity of the chiefs that, as Douglass records, "he kicked them all by turns, without mercy, and without resistance," with what might be called stern justice. No doubt they deserved it.

Some other instances of foresight, unusual in Polynesian chiefs, were noted by missionary recorders. Kamehameha put a ten years' tabu on the cattle landed by Vancouver; he forbade the cutting down of young sandalwood trees "so that our children may live"; he directed the release of birds after the few feathers had been plucked for cape making; he kept the potential troublemakers in the kingdom at court, under his eye.

The common people enjoyed this restraint of the chiefs. As Jarves said, "Kamehameha allowed no crimes but his own to exist with impunity"; to which Bingham adds his rather unwilling testimony: "To check the violence which existed in a disturbed country, he interdicted murder, theft and robbery, and so far, at length, restored the peace of the realm that, as people say in his praise, 'the aged could journey and sleep by the way'." This was in contrast to the state of affairs described by David Malo, the Hawaiian historian, who said that it was wrong for a chief to stay the night at a commoner's house because his men usually robbed the place thoroughly and seduced or ravished all the women of the household.

Bingham naturally disapproved of the king's connubial state, with his 21 wives and 24 children. The missionary extended his sympathy to Queen Kaahumanu (a later convert) on account of the loss of domestic happiness that must ensue from the small share of attention that was hers under such circumstances. But a high spirited young woman like Kaahumanu did not suffer the situation too meekly. There was a lot of gossip about her relations with Kaiana, a fine upstanding chief of some 6 feet 5 inches, who afterwards deserted Kamehameha in the battle of Oahu. Then, too, there was a near relative who was strangled because of suspected familiarities with the queen. She herself suffered several severe beatings at the royal hands, once because she referred to a young man as "handsome." Evidently Kaahumanu had the same idea as Bingham. However, age had a mellowing effect on the queen's temperament. When she was over 50 years of age she saw the error of her ways, put away her younger co-husband, who was her own stepson, and became the mission's prize convert.

Kamehameha was an apt learner. When he sent a shipload of sandalwood to the Orient, all his profits were taken away from him by harbor dues, etc. So he decided that others could play the same game, and clapped on similar levies with regard to ships in Hawaii, but not severe enough to kill the goose that laid the golden egg. Incidentally, the diving boys' performance, which you may have seen in Honolulu harbor, dates back to Kamehameha's time. The king wanted an anvil from a ship; the request was granted but the heavy anvil was tipped over into sixty feet of water. It was too heavy for the Hawaiians to bring up, so they went down in relays and rolled it along the bottom of the sea right on to the land.

Jarves devotes almost a whole chapter to a recital of Kamehameha's virtues as a man and ruler. Typical of his comments is the following: "He had the faculty of inspiring those about him with his lofty and generous sentiments, and creating in them a resolution and energy of purpose, second only to his own." The country was organized, the taxes regulated, and excellent governors appointed over the various islands. In his relations with foreigners, Kamehameha was hospitable to scientists, shrewd yet honorable in his dealings with traders. He built forts, armed them with batteries of heavy guns, set up military discipline, encouraged learning, acquired wealth and a considerable fleet. It was Jarves who first compared Kamehameha with Napoleon and thought that, considering his lack of advantages, he had equal military skill, as vigorous an intellect and as keen judgment. Jarves considered Kamehameha's rejection of Christianity as his chief weakness. To one who wished to convert him Kamehameha said, "By faith in your God, you say anything can be accomplished, and the Christian will be preserved from all harm. If so, cast yourself down from yonder precipice, and if you are preserved, I will believe." Jarves seems to think that the apostle was a little clumsy in his approach, and had he been cleverer might have had more luck with the king. But this is very doubtful.

Twenty-four years after Kamehameha's death, this historian could write: "To this day his memory warms the heart and illumines the national feelings of every Hawaiian." That was high tribute. A most extraordinary fact is that now, a century and a quarter after this heathen king's death, those words are just as true today. There are few kings of whom this might be said.

The character of Kamehameha is highlighted by contrast with that of his son Liholiho, who succeeded him as king. Kamehameha may not have been a Napoleon, but Liholiho was certainly the play-boy of the Pacific. His was really a notable capacity for enjoyment, heightened by a royal capacity for rum. On his accession in 1819, Liholiho abolished some of the annoying restrictions of the tabu system, especially those which forbade men to eat with women or to partake of anything that women had cooked. Since the men of Hawaii had to be the cooks, the tabu put a considerable strain on a good husband's domesticity. When Liholiho feasted with the females of his household, no fire from heaven came down to punish their impiety, and the people cried, "The tabus are broken—the gods are a lie!" The jibes directed by foreigners at their superstitious worship were remembered, and the high priest himself led the way in an idol-burning campaign. The old heiaus were allowed to fall apart and much was destroyed that the museums of today would readily have sacrificed a missionary or two to possess.

Liholiho proceeded to have a gay time. Foreigners "stimulated his thirst for ardent spirits and gambling. Under the patronage of this weak and pleasure-loving king," says Jarves, "the whole court became corrupted, and aggravated misery the lot of the common orders. Days were spent in bestial drunkenness, debauchery, dancing and gambling, and all their attendant crimes." In his sober moments the king was affable and studious, and soon learned to read and write. Missionaries' expostulations on the subjects of rum, revelry, and riotous living produced at least one delightful discussion.

Catching the king awake one midnight, when the missionary himself could not sleep, Bingham thought it a good time to urge him to repentance. The king, however, could not see a complete and sudden reformation. "I am a very wicked man," he said, "probably the wickedest in the whole kingdom. My sins are as thick as ohelo berries—yet you expect me to drop them all at once. Why don't you get after So-and-so, who is already a fairly good man? He hasn't much to give up. *He nui loa kuu hewa* (My wickedness is too great). In five years I will turn and forsake sin." But Bingham couldn't approve salvation on the instalment plan: "You can't be sure of five years," he told the king, "or even five days or five hours. Now is the time to repent if you want to save your soul."

"Brother Bingham," replied his majesty politely, "I've often heard the missionaries say 'one thing at a time.' Well, that is how I want to drop my sins, one at a time. In five years I should be a good man."

As a matter of record, Liholiho began his reformation right then, and stayed sober for some time till, as Bingham sadly records, he was "enticed into intoxication by a gentleman of standing from the United States, who prevailed by the artful offer of cherry brandy, accompanied by the assurance that it would not harm him." The gentleman must indeed have been of considerable standing if he could drink the king down. Thus Liholiho's five year plan failed, and shortly after he and his queen died of measles when on a visit to London. As Bingham with some self-satisfaction points out, only half of the allotted reformation period was up.

People have spoken slightingly about our island royalty and have gone so far as to suggest that Hawaii was somewhat of a comic opera kingdom. It is undoubtedly true that the characters of some of its rulers were not distinguished by strength or wisdom of purpose. Liholiho (Kamehameha II) seemed to value his position more for the pleasures it afforded than for its high responsibilities. After his death, Kauikeaouli, his young brother, succeeded to the kingship with the title of Kamehameha III. The missionary party was greatly disappointed in him as "it was evident he found more pleasure in billiards, horses and rum than in prayers and sermons." His easy manners and refusal to take his position seriously brought criticism from others. As Bradley records, "he often might have been found playing billiards or bowling with some of the foreign residents or visiting seamen. On such occasions all pretense of ceremony was cast aside, and one visitor to Honolulu observed, in 1836, that the young king was on the most friendly terms with the 'commonest skippers that visit the port, who did not hesitate to address him by name or put their arms about his neck'."

Such unceremonious behavior did not accord with visitors' ideas of how a king should behave, but neither does it partake of the nature of *opera bouffe,* as one writer has described the Hawaiian court. On the contrary, pretensions to pomp and dignity might well have been comic in the king of the Sandwich Islands. It seems that his actions, taken in conjunction with the generally expressed opinion that he was "frank, kind and generous" indicated a sensible and realistic view of his position.

Between Kamehameha's death and the final deposition of Queen Liliuokalani in January 1893, and the setting up of President Dole's provisional government, six kings and a queen reigned in Hawaii.[4] During this period there is considerable justification for the statement that this was a comic opera kingdom, but the comedy was supplied not by the Hawaiians, but by the representatives of the Great Powers. There was a never-ending succession of international inci-

These rulers and the dates of their accessions were: Kamehameha II (Liholiho), 1819; Kamehameha III (Kauikeouli), 1824; Kamehameha IV (Alexander Liholiho), 1854; Kamehameha V (Lot), 1863; Lunalilo, 1873; Kalakaua, 1874; and Queen Liliuokalani, 1891.

dents, in which a warship lined itself up with all its great guns trained on Honolulu, threatening to flatten a number of grass shacks unless some imposing array of demands were instantly met.

In another chapter reference is made to the threats of Percival that he would bombard the place unless women were allowed on board the U.S. Dolphin to quench the amorous fires that were raging on his ship. Then there was the ultimatum delivered by Laplace of the French frigate Artemise, which included demands that his ship be given a salute of twenty-one guns, plus $20,000 indemnity for the alleged ill-treatment of French citizens, of whom there were four in the islands. None of these had suffered any invidious treatment whatsoever. Another demand was that French brandy should be admitted free of duty. This was all done under cover of the pretext of establishing Roman Catholic missionaries in the islands, two of whom had been previously excluded. Some of the Catholic converts had been ill-treated by the chiefs, but they were not French citizens.

If a treaty acceding to these demands were not signed immediately, war would at once commence, with all its devastating and calamitous consequences. Moreover, Laplace promised that it would be a war of extermination against the native rulers and their missionary counselors, in which neither man, woman, nor child would be spared. In the face of such terrific threats, the chiefs gave way and borrowed the money for the indemnity "at a high rate of interest" from the foreign merchants. Laplace landed two hundred seamen with fixed bayonets, and mass was celebrated "in a straw palace of the king's." Some years later the indemnity was returned to Hawaii in the original boxes with the seals intact. The only ones who gained were the foreign traders who got their high rate of interest. But which people, the French or Hawaiians, provided the comedy?

But in 1849 there was no question as to who occupied the farcical position. Admiral de Tromelin, in a French warship, arrived with ten demands. He also required a salute of twenty-one guns, and among other things the punishment of some impious school boys who had made rude noises in church. He landed an armed force with field pieces, scaling ladders, etc., and took possession of the empty fort, the Customs House, the king's yacht, and other property. Barrels of French brandy were seized in the Customs House, the guns of the fort were spiked, and so too were most of the French invaders. Then the warship withdrew. Whether the school boys were punished for their rude noises, it is impossible to find out; history is silent on this important point.

And among all this comic relief, some at least was provided by the British. In 1843, Lord George Paulet, in command of the British frigate Carysfort, made a series of demands, two of which were the same as those of the French. Paulet wanted Great Britain's might acknowledged by the benighted Hawaiians with a salute of twenty-one guns; but whereas Laplace wanted the whole jury handpicked by the French consul when a Frenchman was on trial, Paulet was content if the British consul, under similar circumstances affecting one of his countrymen, packed only half the jury. He made up for this concession, however, by raising the British claims for damages to $80,000. The king then decided that Paulet might as well take everything, and he then ceded the country to Great Britain. Though other commission governments have been proposed for Hawaii, Paulet's was the first actually in operation. It consisted of a civilian and two naval officers with full power over every department of government. When the commission took over, all the Hawaiian flags were destroyed, the vessels in the harbor were put under the Union Jack, and a small standing army, "The Queen's Regiment," was enlisted.

Then Admiral Thomas arrived in his flagship and everything was off again. The cession of the country to the British was repudiated and the Hawaiian flag restored in formal ceremonies on an open space that has since been gratefully named Thomas Square. What must have pleased the Hawaiians most was to see the men from the Carysfort in the parade and to hear her saluting with twenty-one guns the power and dignity of Hawaii. This was a most honorable reversal of policy—but the joke, if any, was certainly on the British.

In 1893, after King Kalakaua had died and Queen Liliuokalani had succeeded him, came the famous revolution which also had its humorous aspects. This same revolution was not only bloodless but it was gutless as well. As far as can be judged by reading the accounts written at the time, it was a case of one side being frightened and the other not being game. But the revolutionists played a better brand of poker. They bluffed a little more convincingly and the Hawaiians conceded the jackpot. Neither side had anything but a very weak hand.

President Cleveland, after the revolution, sent Colonel Blount to report on the situation. He gave initial offense to the whites by declining "the customary social courtesies usually extended to people in his position coming to the islands." Blount reported that the constitution of 1887, which had been forced on Kalakaua, put a property restriction on voters which gave the whites three-fourths of the power in electing nobles to the Hawaiian legislature, through whom they were able to control legislation; also, that Portuguese laborers on the plantations who were not naturalized but had taken an oath to support this constitution were taken to the polls to join with other unnaturalized foreigners "to balance the native vote."

Admittedly, the reign of Kalakaua contained abuses entirely subversive to good business. For example, the legislature of 1890, which the whites alleged had been elected on the strength of gin supplied by the king, passed a law authorizing the use and sale of opium. Kalakaua promptly sold the concession to one Aki for $75,000, and immediately turned around and sold the same concession to a Chinese syndicate for $80,000. But Blount alleges that Kalakaua was the American party's own choice of a ruler when an election took place, in opposition to Queen Emma, who favored the British. Now Queen Liliuokalani wanted to bring in a new constitution returning power into the hands of the Hawaiians, and the battle was joined.

A committee of public safety was formed and a mass meeting held, at which a prominent spokesman for the American party declared that it was not the queen's fault "the streets have not run red with blood." (One man was wounded in the whole affair.) It is doubtful if the committee intended that any of their blood should run, although they talked a great deal about it. The speaker went on to ask: "Has the tropic sun thinned our blood, or have we flowing in our veins the warm rich blood which makes men love liberty and die for it?" This was, of course, a rhetorical question, but the answer perhaps might be found in an appeal which the committee forthwith addressed to the American consul. "We are unable to protect ourselves without aid, and therefore pray for the protection of the United States forces."

Troops from the U.S. warship Boston were accordingly landed in response to this appeal, and since the simple Hawaiians naturally thought that they would support the whites, the royalists lost all hope. After a scout discovered that there were only eight clerks and no guards in the government building (now the Judiciary Building), the committee of public safety with an armed force of one volunteer rifleman took possession of the center of government. The name of this hero is unfortunately not recorded. From the front steps of the building a proclamation setting up the provisional government was read to the crowd. More volunteer riflemen arrived and the city was placed under martial law. But President Cleveland accepted Blount's report and ordered the removal of the troops and requested President Dole to restore Queen Liliuokalani, which he refused to do. Congress overrode Cleveland and supported the new republic.

It is altogether too late to debate the rights and wrongs of the revolution or whether the white merchants were ready to die for liberty or good business, or to die at all. There is absolutely no shadow of doubt, however, regarding the expediency of the queen's dethronement, and expediency seems to be the dominant factor in most changes of government. The revolution decided the fate of the islands and determined that Pearl Harbor became an American naval base rather than a Japanese conquest. But it should be emphasized that this was no glorious historical chapter, no blood and thunder affair. Its essential motivation can be judged from an impassioned speech of another member of the public safety committee: "There can be no business prosperity here at home, and our credit abroad must be of the flimsiest and most uncertain nature. And you business men who are toiling honestly for your bread and butter will have to put up with thin bread and much thinner butter if this farcical work is continued."

So ended the business men's revolution. By 1893 it was apparent there was more butter than poi in the calabash.

CHAPTER IV

Myths and Missionaries

THE VISITOR to Hawaii, before the war, often became quite interested in strange looking glass balls, weathered in many colors, that occasionally could be picked up on our beaches. He could see them also in curio stores and in the beach houses of his friends. He soon learned that these were the glass floats used instead of cork for keeping deep-sea fishing nets in place, and that they had drifted here from shores as distant as the Philippines and Japan. Evidently great currents, imperceptible to view, swept around these islands, casting up from afar things of strange appearance and use. The islanders have always watched the beaches; in the early days, for wreckage from which could be pried loose much-prized nails and other scraps of precious metal, or for pine logs that could be much more easily hewn into canoes than the native koa. Strange things are still to be found, and after severe storms the glass floats come ashore in the greatest numbers.

Nor will the visitor live long in Hawaii before he learns that there are some very controversial currents constantly running around these islands, currents that originated a long way off, and which cast up quantities of flotsam and jetsam that have been in the water a long time. Ancient scandals, almost forgotten dissensions, century-old criticisms have a habit of bobbing up again like glass floats on our shores. Now and then some journalistic journeyman in his beach-combing makes quite a collection and then writes a book about his discoveries. If he has picked up a particularly large and finely discolored ball or two, they may excite some local comment and interest. There may be some foolish attempts to suppress his story. Someone is either persuaded or hired to write a booklet in the attempt to prove that these are not glass floats at all, that they came from nowhere, and are really figments of the beachcomber's imagination. The rest of us when we happen on one of these curious artifacts usually pick it up, look at it with passing interest, and then either throw it away or give it to a mainland visitor to take home with him.

To change the simile somewhat, there is a fairly general belief that Honolulu's best houses are full of locked cupboards, in which some terrible family skeletons reside. Any that I have seen opened contain no more than an old mouldering bone or two and a few dusty, indecipherable records. I doubt if there is a whole skeleton of scandal among the lot. The trouble is that there is too much mystery, and more people sensitive about their grandfathers' reputations here than anywhere else. It is true that we have no Cabots or Lodges hereabouts, but a surprising number of people who claim that their ancestors talked with God.

One of the most highly colored and largest glass floats you will come across in Hawaii might be labeled, "The Great Missionary Myth." For at least forty years after their coming, the missionaries wrote nearly all the history of the islands; in fact, they and their doings *were* the history of the Sandwich Islands at that time. In the opinion of many people, especially if they can claim descent from the 128 missionaries (61 male and 67 female) who labored here in the quarter of a century between 1820 and 1845, these mission folk were a band of devoted individuals striving mightily to uplift and ennoble the Hawaiian character, sunk, alas, in utter depravity. The missionaries hoped to bring about this result by transplanting to these shores that dour, condemnatory conscience of the variety called New England, but no more indigenous there than doughnuts. In the mild air and salubrious climate of Hawaii, the spiny cactus throve and burst forth into rare and exotic blooms of righteousness. But these blossomings were very evanescent, and when picked to adorn the House of the Lord, they often drooped and shriveled in the saddest fashion.

But along with this night-blooming righteousness, the missionaries brought for transplantation a goodly stock of the hardy perennials of education, temperance, social decency, sanitation, health—

benefits less showy than religious conversion, but more lasting in their effects. About these things there is no dispute, but there are some people who have the idea that the missionaries were the first white people to live in these islands and that every gift and abuse of civilization which we see around us was their responsibility. They were also supposed to have done their work under conditions of extreme personal danger, persecution, hardships, loneliness, and privation. In short, they were saints of the Lord, animated solely by selfless zeal.

That is one view. The other, to which credence was given at the time and for long afterwards, was that the missionaries turned into a rapacious band of robbers. By insidious stratagems, they established a hold over the kings, their queens, and chiefs, and taking advantage of this position of dominance, they got into the hands of the mission society and later into their own, the most valuable and productive lands and all the great natural wealth of this country. Thus they laid the foundation of immense fortunes, all of course at the expense of the poor Hawaiians. This view is expressed by a well-known writer, who complained that the missionaries who "came to give the bread of life remained to gobble up the whole heathen feast." In plain terms, the missionaries were really shrewd New England hoss-traders who, under the cloak of religion, robbed the Hawaiian people of their birthright or, at best, bought it for a mess of evangelical pottage. In other words, they got their fingers into the poi bowl first and never gave the rest of us a chance. The proof of the pudding, say these critics, is in the eating, and the pudding is completely eaten. The first families have divided even the crumbs of the pudding. The bitterest and perhaps the cleverest wisecrack of the lot is that the missionaries came to Hawaii to do good and did well.

These views, it might be said at the outset, are just as ridiculous as the supposition that all the Hawaiian missionaries and their helpers were earthly saints. But in the very violence of these cross-currents of opinion and denunciation, the visitor is sure to become confused. Some unbiased attempt should be made to steer him clear of the rapids and to give him a background of facts against which the general history of these islands might be viewed. In this attempt, the writer proposes to use the missionaries' own published records, applying in places his own interpretations, leaving the reader to do the same. Such an effort will, of course, please no one; an impartial view is never acceptable to partisans.

There should be no complaint of this use of missionary records for, as will be seen, the cause of the missions was most unfortunate in its choice of a champion and chief historian, Hiram Bingham, who published in 1849 *A Residence of Twenty-one Years in the Sandwich Islands, or the Civil, Religious, and Political History of Those Islands, Comprising a Particular View of the Missionary Operations Connected With the Introduction and Progress of Civilization Among the Hawaiian People.* There it is, as you may say, in a nutshell—of 616 pages.

On October 23, 1819, the brig Thaddeus left Boston bearing the seven members of the pioneer band of missionaries and their wives. They were accompanied by three Hawaiians who had made their way as sailors to the East coast and there had been converted and sent to school. Asa Thurston and Hiram Bingham were the two ministers in the party, though later Mr. Whitney was ordained. Chamberlain, Ruggles, Loomis, and Dr. Holman were the other male members of the pilgrim party. The travelers went on board to the strains of a farewell hymn, which considering the big island's rainfall, rather maligns Hawaii.

> "Though in distant lands we sigh
> Parched beneath a hostile sky."

There was, of course, no Tourist Bureau to correct such unfair statements.

The ship rounded Cape Horn with, for those days, a minimum of difficulty. The only excitement other than shark fishing seemed to be when Brother Whitney, who was painting the stern of the ship for exercise, fell overboard when they were only three days' sail from Hawaii. Someone threw him a bench on which he knelt and prayed until the ship could put about and rescue him.

On March 31, 1820, after a five months' voyage, the Thaddeus reached Kohala, on the island of Hawaii. In view of the fact that the activities and influence of the missions were afterward so severely criticized, it is perhaps no wonder that Bingham in his history took pains to point the contrast in the natives before and after taking pious instruction. But his description of their sad original state seems a little overdone. "The appearance," he says, "of destitution, degradation, and barbarism, among the chattering, and almost naked savages, whose heads and feet, and much of their sunburned swarthy skins, were bare, was appalling. Some of our number, with gushing tears, turned away from the spectacle. Others with firmer nerve continued their gaze, but were ready to exclaim, 'Can these be human beings! How dark and comfortless their state of mind and heart! How imminent the danger to the immortal soul, shrouded in this deep pagan gloom! Can such beings be civilized? Can they be Christianized? Can we throw ourselves upon these rude shores, and take up our abode, for life, among such a people, for the purpose of training them for Heaven?' "

In considering this fervent outburst, it must be remembered that the missionaries need not have been so shocked at the appearance of Hawaiians since they had had three natives on board with them for five months. Moreover, no one before or since has ever seen a Polynesian in a canoe "shrouded in deep gloom," pagan or otherwise. As to bare skins and sunburn, it is a pity that the Reverend Hiram cannot revisit Hawaii. He might consider the shores of modern Waikiki much ruder than those of Kohala at the time of his arrival there. He might easily see a larger gross area of sunburn than sand.

The story has often been told of the remarkable events which made the arrival of the missionaries in 1820 so opportune. King Kamehameha had been dead only a year, and his successor, Liholiho, though personally a disappointment to the newcomers, was, fortunately for them, a somewhat weak ruler. The old king took what he wanted from civilization, but resisted with all his strength the inroads of ideas that seemed to threaten the Hawaiian way of life.

In pursuance of this desire for survival, he deemed it wise to preserve intact the forms of native custom and religious belief. Through contact with the white traders and sailors, the people were beginning to question the validity of the old notions, especially when confronted with the skepticism of these white strangers whose material culture was so superior to their own. Even the priests themselves, who were undoubtedly among the most intelligent of the Hawaiians, were beginning to look askance at their idols and to doubt their power. The people were ripe for religious revolution.

Thus it was not long after the old king's death that Liholiho, his resolution sapped by drink and the persuasions of those most interested, relaxed one of the most important tabus, that against men and women eating together. This restriction had been supported by the severest sanctions, and when no fire from heaven descended to punish the offenders, the waves of revolt spread until they overthrew the walls of the heiaus and the idols were destroyed. The knell of paganism had sounded, and to the missionaries it was no less miraculous than the blast of the prophet's trumpet before which the walls of Jericho fell. But it is well to remember that while the outward forms of native religion were overthrown, many Hawaiian superstitions merely went underground. It was always a matter of sorrow and perplexity to some of the most earnest missionaries that the Hawaiian, though religiously converted, was not changed. The disposition and temperament that belonged with the old Adam remained.

But in the meantime, the substitution of missionary for *kahuna*, or priest, must have lifted a heavy burden of fear from the minds of the people. To Bingham, Hawaiian idolatry was "besotted" and its priests "more like fiends than anything else that walks the earth." As a matter of fact, blood-letting does not come amiss to the mind of the savage. He has almost as little respect for human life as his civilized brothers. Individuals who had broken tabus or had offended the chiefs or priests were offered as human sacrifices on various special occasions. The victims were marked down beforehand and were quietly knocked on the head as they went about their avocations, by men specially deputed for the purpose. The executioners took care to mutilate the bodies as little as possible. Eleven men were required for the dedication services at the heiau of Kaili, Kamehameha's war god. The building is still standing at Kawaihae on Hawaii. A revolting practice was to put the victims in a row face downwards before the altar, and then lay the bodies of hogs upon them at right angles, the whole being left to decay together. On the death of Kamehameha, the sacrifices, according to priestly injunction, must go up on a sliding scale, one man if before the corpse was moved, four victims if it had left the house, ten if the sacrifice were offered at the grave, but if delayed until next day, the quota of victims would have to go up to forty. Three hundred dogs, then quite a delicacy in Hawaiian diet, were sacrificed on this occasion. Naturally enough, the missionaries did not hold the religion of the Hawaiians in much respect. Says Bingham: "Polygamy, fornication, adultery, incest, infant murder, desertion of husbands and wives, parents and children, sorcery, covetousness and oppression extensively prevailed and seem hardly to have been forbidden or rebuked by their religion."

Idolatry was, however, considered the worst sin. As we have seen, even the slaying of Captain Cook was held by the missionaries to be a judgment upon him because he allowed himself to be worshipped as the god Lono; it served him right. Notwithstanding the enmity of the preachers, the heathen *kahunas* showed a commendable absence of professional jealousy, hailing the missionaries as "brother priests." Hewahewa, the high priest, was most helpful in persuading the king to give the missionaries permission to remain in Hawaii—a really valuable assistance which Bingham grudgingly acknowledges, but with no show of gratitude.

That the natives knew no better than to practice idolatry was little excuse. Reason, conscience, and nature should, in Bingham's view, have forbidden them "to prefer as deities the workmanship of their own vile hands, or the vilest objects in creation, or the viler creatures of their polluted imagination." Then to this triumph of vilification, with its odd comparison of vile, vilest, viler, he adds, "pollution, violence, fraud, sensuality, pestiferous action of the mass of corruption all around, degradation, licentiousness and odious character," as prevailing on what he calls "the dreary and dark shores of Hawaii."

The tabu system also came in for its share of condemnation. "It grew up into a bloody system of violence and pollution, suited to the lust, pride and malice of the priests." Nevertheless, the missionaries, on occasions, found tabu a very useful means of enforcing morality by checking licentious conduct. The chiefs and governors of Lahaina and Honolulu were induced to place a tabu on the ships in harbor so that loose women could not go aboard. At once there was a frightful rumpus. The seamen on whaling vessels and men-of-war usually were at sea for very long periods and made for Hawaii with the liveliest anticipations of the special kind of entertainment which had always been offered them in the past. Their rage when they found that no woman dared come on board knew no bounds, and their officers protested against what they considered a most highhanded and unjust imposition, enforcing unwelcome restraint on women who were not only willing, but eager to be accommodating. Lieutenant Percival of the U.S. schooner Dolphin complained to the Queen Regent that because of this enforced morality "his ship was just like fire." Riots, assaults on missionaries, and threats of bombardment finally forced the lifting of the tabu for the ten weeks that the Dolphin was in port, much to the delight of the sailors and many of the foreign residents who loudly cheered the first boatloads of women to go on board. This setback to the cause of morality was hailed with satisfaction by a section of the white population which was beginning to show cordial hate for the missionaries.

Prostitution was a very sore subject, and the favorite target of Bingham's denunciations was carnal lust. You may make of this what you will, but the fact is that he never neglected to call attention to the loose sexual habits of the people, and words like pollution and licentiousness were constantly on his lips. The morals of Massachusetts were not easily transplanted among a Polynesian people who had never placed any special emphasis on chastity and sexual restraint. There were many and frequent falls from grace. One of the very best roads in all the islands was part of the highway to Hana on Maui, which was built, according to the Reverend Cheever, "by the convicts of adultery some years ago, when the laws relating to that and other crimes were first enacted." The reverend gentleman found the road most convenient, and almost, as he says, blessed it unawares, hailing it as a marvelous work "which Sin has wrought on Maui." In another place he calls it "altogether the noblest and best Hawaiian work of internal improvement I have anywhere seen." Either the law was changed, or the supply of philanderers ran out on Maui, for the road was finished for only fifteen or twenty miles. If the law could have been revived for a season, it might be possible to have a good road all the way to Hana. Cheever regarded it "as great a work for Hawaiians, as digging the Erie Canal to Americans." These Maui adulterers must have been a strong-backed, hard-working crew.

A most powerful factor in the success of the missionaries was that the chiefs remained their very staunch friends. There was one motive for this newfound zeal for an alien morality that has not, apparently, been noted by the historians. It has been pointed out elsewhere that the islanders were a fighting breed, warriors as well as maritime adventurers, truly Vikings of the Pacific, as Buck has called them. But after the conquests of Kamehameha and the arrival of the missionaries, there came to the land a kind of *pax ecclesiastica*— a missionary peace. The warrior laid down the sword, but was unwilling, or did not know how to turn it into a ploughshare. The militant missionary spirit appealed greatly to the minds of the rulers of Hawaii, who were themselves men and women of courage and high spirit. When Bingham's life was in danger from the attacks of sailors of the Dolphin, who were infuriated by the ban against prostitution, the chiefs stood calmly by. "Do you not help me?" cried Bingham. "We help," was the laconic reply, and with that they promptly felled his attackers, some of whom would undoubtedly have been killed except for his intercession.

In the long disputes be⁺ween the "foreigners," or traders, and the missionaries, the chiefs ranged themselves firmly on the side of the latter party. Some of the missions' devoted adherents were Kaumualii, king of Kauai, Kalanimoku, the old king's advisor, and two of his queens, Keopuolani and Kaahumanu. Governor Hoapili on Maui, and Governor Kuakini on Oahu were two staunch supporters whose zeal carried them to such lengths that it was a cause of embarrassment to the more moderate-minded missionaries. It was the governor of Maui who issued a decree linking learning and wedlock by forbidding the marriage of those who could not read. "This was intended," explains Bingham, "not as an obstacle to marriage, but as a spur to education, so far, at least, to enable the people to read God's word." He commends the people for their submission to a decree that even he considered a little harsh. Hoapili evidently thought it was better for people to live in sin than intellectual darkness, but as the laws against fornication were equally severe, it is probable that there were many earnest students of God's word on Maui in those days.

Kuakini, who had been a supporter of the missions in Kona, and later became governor of Oahu, was not an outstanding example of piety, since he occasionally took a glass of "ardent spirits" and thought, as Bingham put it, "a *careful* attention to the increase of wealth was quite allowable." But on the other hand, he was most diligent in applying the "blue laws." It seemed to give him extreme satisfaction to enforce them against the traders and other non-missionary whites, much to their infuriation. He did not hesitate to order his police to impound the horses of people caught riding on Sunday, nor to enter a house and compel the host to remove liquor from his table. The white residents blamed all of these small tyrannies on Bingham, Dibble, Chamberlain, etc., and denounced them for setting up an alliance between church and state. The probability is that Kuakini, or Governor Adams as he liked to be called, was actuated in large part by hatred for these white traders and sailors, who thought themselves superior to the natives, and above their laws.

In spite of this ardent support by the rulers, the missionaries were at times discouraged by backslidings in the church, and particularly by the idea prevalent among native Christians that a mere confession of sin in lieu of true repentance was all that should be sufficient to restore a man to good church standing. A letter from one of Mr. Bond's pupils in his school at Kohala said: "There is trouble in the church. Some of the brethren have been drinking sour potato and smoking tobacco." On the credit side, however, is to be recorded the contribution from a native group of a bed quilt to help cover the destitute of New York City. Truly the missionaries labored mightily to make Hawaii "a reprint of Puritanism."

Another storm that threatened the peace of mind of the missionaries was the constant effort of Roman Catholic priests to gain admission to the islands. The missionaries, for all the terrible moral turpitude which they ascribed to the Hawaiians, wanted a monopoly on salvation, and to keep for themselves exclusive evangelical rights in this territory. They looked on the uprooting of sin as their special privilege. All other uplifters, *kapu*. So they diligently spread the idea that Roman Catholicism was just another form of that idolatry which the Hawaiians had renounced. The name for this religion was *pule palani*, *pule* meaning a form of worship, while *palani* was the word for the French who were trying to compel the government to admit the priests and incidentally French brandy freely. *Palani,* however, is also the name of a surgeon fish which emits a very rank odor. Hence, *palani* also meant "to stink," so that Roman Catholicism could be obliquely referred to as the religion that smells.

In 1826, a Catholic party was excluded by order of Kaahumanu, the queen regent. The commander of a French warship with threats of bombardment insisted on the priests' debarkation, but they had to promise to withdraw as soon as possible. Two years later some of the *pule palani,* or stinkers, were arrested and punished for image worship,[1] the Reverend Hiram being careful to make the point that the punishment was not for being papists but

---

[1] Some of the other missionaries, such as Bishop, made most earnest and vigorous protests against any religious persecution.

for practicing idolatry. Then in July 1839, the commander of a French frigate insisted on the admission not only of the Catholic priests, but of the French brandy and spirits, plus the payment of an indemnity of $20,000. These were indeed harsh terms and Bingham might be allowed some reasonable indignation. He praises on the one hand the Hawaiians for their forbearance, and comments on their "manly energy, refusing to receive the last and stereotyped edition of Romanism, and foreign spirits"; and, on the other, "the sleepless cunning of Jesuitism, the proud assumption of the Potentate of the Seven Hills, and the naval power of the citizen king (of France), all attempting to force the admission of the teachers of an eschewed error upon these carefully guarded, but still defenceless shores, and open the floodgates of inundation and ruin." Though such intolerance can hardly be defended, strict justice impels the opinion that, had the position been reversed with the Catholic priests in command, the missionaries might have had a similarly harsh reception. Bigotry was a common characteristic of most religious sects in those days. When Church and State went hand in hand you could be sure that each had an eye to advantage. Jarves, the historian, shares the distrust common to the time when he cites the experience of the Tahitian and Marquesan islanders, and says, "The native governments have occasion to be suspicious of Roman priestcraft."

As will be gathered from these pages, the work of the missions was not happy in its chief exponent. As Hiram Bingham portrayed himself, he was narrow-minded and proud of it. Like Calvin Coolidge's favorite preacher, he was "agin sin" in any shape or manner, and at the appearance of any sinner, he at once girded himself with what another preacher called the short sword and the dagger of tract-giving and Christian admonition. With these he smote alike the heathen, the Roman priests, English and American traders, or "foreigners" as he called them, the licentious sailors, their careless captains, and the British consul, hip and thigh. But there was no question of his sincerity or courage.

He records that on one occasion he was sitting in the mild evening air on a mat with Liholiho, instructing the king on various matters, when a native approached with a square bottle of spirits. "I gently took the uncorked bottle," says Hiram, "and offering it rather to the earth than to his Majesty, turned it bottom up on the mat." The king was very offended, and "muttered indignation in terms which I did not fully comprehend." The chiefs advised the missionary to leave the king's presence, which he did. Liholiho, however, bore him no malice. Much more serious consequences would happen nowadays to a man in the Islands who offered such an outrage to a bottle of spirits of any shape. The king's restraint was really marvelous.

Even Jarves, who, after an initial prejudice against the missionaries, became friendly to their cause, offers some guarded yet none the less severe criticism of Bingham. While praising his sincerity and firmness, he says: "But it must be acknowledged he possessed a tenacity of opinion, and a sectarian zeal which at times separated him in some degree from his friends and marred his usefulness." It is easy, of course, to be critical, but it is well to remember that religious people of one hundred years ago were not noted for their tolerance. They firmly believed that the natural inclinations of man were bestial, his heart desperately wicked. Mere morality, unless combined with faith in the accepted creed, was of no avail. Missionaries of Bingham's sincerity and forthrightness literally plucked sinners like brands from the burning and were none too gentle in the process. The realities of hellfire were so vivid that many a hesitant soul was hustled into the Kingdom. Indeed, the quick conversion of the Hawaiians was furthered because the missionaries had at hand the fires of Pele to serve as illustrations of the tortures of damnation. To be eternally imprisoned in such a hell was a prospect that no suggestible Hawaiian could look at without terror. You had to be tough to die a sinner in those days.

The early reception of the missionaries by the whites, some of whom had resided in Hawaii for thirty years, was quite friendly. At their first landing in Honolulu, three native houses were set aside for their use by Messrs. Winship, Lewis, and Navarro, while Captain Pigot of New York, seeing them fatigued with the toils of disembarkation, "considerately and kindly gave us, at evening, a hospitable cup of tea, truly acceptable to poor pilgrims in our circumstances, so far from the sympathies of home."

Thus the trials and dangers of early days in Hawaii were just a cup of tea as compared with the experiences of the pioneers who crossed the plains of the West in their covered wagons. Though relatively uncivilized, the Hawaiians were gentlemen compared with the Apache, Comanche, and Sioux. Hawaii was no dark and bloody ground, and though there had been killings following that of Captain Cook, notably of a British lieutenant and seaman from the ship Daedalus in 1792, the islanders had lived down their evil reputation. As a matter of fact, the natives offered friendship rather than enmity to the visitors so that one fear, that of leaving "delicate females accustomed to polished and refined society" alone to the tender mercies of savages, proved groundless. The missionaries had to take long journeys from home, but there was only one case in twenty-five years in which a missionary's wife suffered a minor molestation, and the drunken offender would have been instantly slain by the chief except for the missionary's interposition. Not a bad record for a people who were called brutified, violent, and licentious!

During these early years, the only danger and threats which the missionaries suffered were from people of their own color, especially certain "lewd men of the baser sort" who had settled in the islands. Sympathy from traders and others was extended to the missions as evinced by an early contribution of $600 for the purpose of establishing a school for orphan children. Nor were other kindnesses wanting.

But the storm clouds soon gathered. The preachments of the missionaries could not help but be resented by many who had come to the islands as an escape from law and order and decent living. What kind of men these were, we can readily guess. Here was a country ruled by natives who were so untutored as to look up to the white man as a superior being. The Hawaiians were as lambs ready for the shearing, and were promptly shorn. Their women were kindly and accommodating and even sought association with whites no matter how low-class. Offspring from these unions, if any, imposed no ties nor obligations. There was no supervision of conduct, and provided the foreigner did not incur the hostility of king or chief, he could be a law to himself. Now these New England busybodies, with their tabus on dancing, drinking, fornication, recreation, and even travel on the Sabbath, dared to come between these men and their easy pleasures, and to undermine their prestige with the natives. These Boston hell-hunters even went so far as to persuade the Queen Regent to root up a crop of sugar cane to prevent it from going to the distillery to be made into spirits. As regards whites of better social standing, the traders who bought sandalwood, or supplied visiting whalers with provisions, native rope, and ships' supplies at high prices, found it paid to stand in well with the native rulers. They soon discovered that King Liholiho, drunk or half drunk, could be easily talked into making all kinds of valuable material concessions. Then, too, it was easy to take advantage of the king's passion for gambling. As regards the lowest class of adventurers, such as one party of escaped convicts from Botany Bay, their ill-gotten gains were transient, for their motto of "easy come, easy go," kept income and outgo well balanced. But the traders were shrewd and soon began to resent bitterly the missionaries' interference with their selfish schemes and to complain of their influence over the rulers of the kingdom.

Soon reports of missionary high-handedness spread to America, so that Jarves, who came to Hawaii in 1837, quite prepared to condemn the influence of the missions, at first was very dubious as to their value. His statement is that "he had formed the opinion that the Hawaiians, though bettered in morals, were a priest-ridden people; that sectarianism and worldly aggrandizement were the cogent motives of their spiritual teachers; and that they had succeeded in establishing a system of government, which for influence and secrecy of design might justly be compared to the dominion of the Jesuits in South America." After observing at first hand the work of the missionaries, and the scheming of their enemies, he changed his attitude and condemned the opposition of evil-loving individuals for whom

Moku Manana or Rabbit Island, framed by a Kamani Tree

Hawaii's second largest industry. Pineapples on Oahu

Pineapple plants and cities of plantation people; both follow straight-line patterns

Landing stages, roads and pineapple fields have transformed a barren island into a great productive area

"no artifice was too low for them to commit, or falsehood too gross to be circulated. Originating in a few worthless vagabonds, the contamination gradually spread to persons, if not of better principles, of more knowledge; and the falsities so diligently uttered by the former, found their way into journals and reviews." It is no wonder that the criticisms occasionally re-echo to this day. Though we cheerfully recognize that there were plaster saints among the elect, it would take an ocean of whitewash to make the characters of their opponents presentable.

The only charge that has "stuck" has been that of worldly aggrandizement. It would be idle to pretend that the missionaries neglected to use every bit of influence possible in behalf of their pet schemes for the improvement of the Hawaiian people, and equally foolish to assume that there were no self-seekers among them. In regard to the charge of commercialism, the missions were again unfortunate in their defenders. The Reverend Henry Cheever visited these islands and wrote in 1851 a book which he called *Life in the Sandwich Islands or The Heart of the Pacific.* The best thing about the volume is its subtitle, though its pages are plentifully besprinkled with lines of poor poetry and tags of Latin. Along with his account of the islands, he is quite concerned to prove that piety pays. He tells the story of a young wheelwright in Massachusetts who was induced to contribute a dollar to the mission in the Sandwich Islands. "He paid it," says Cheever, "but with the feeling that the dollar was thrown away. Within the present year this same wheelwright has received an order from these islands of twenty pairs of cartwheels and bodies, at $90 a pair. To this he adds that if men want a dividend of 1800 per cent, they had better "put it into the treasury of missions."

But if selfish advantage were really the missionaries' aim, they were singularly slow in attaining it. So far as can be judged, there were no great windfalls of fortune for anyone in Hawaii. Outside the sandalwood trade, there was nothing that looked like easy money in these islands. King Kamehameha got together a fair sized fleet on the basis of an exchange of a hull full of sandalwood for the ship itself, but he tended to keep this lucrative business in his own hands. The missionaries, at least, seem to have had no share in it. A hundred years ago, Mr. Locke's school at Waialua grew seven acres of sugar cane, but between fortunes in sandalwood and money in sugar, there was at least a gap of sixty years.

Tropical and subtropical islands will support life with a minimum of effort for a minimum number of people. Coconuts, breadfruit, bananas, yams will grow without cultivation. This means that a vegetarian can live without much exertion, but if you wish to climb a notch higher in the scale of sustenance, you must work for it and under conditions where hard labor is not exactly pleasant.

Sugar, the great commercial mainstay of these islands, must be raised, not simply caught by tapping a maple tree and watching the juice drip into a keg. Clearing land, plowing, seeding, weeding, burning, cutting, loading, trucking, crushing, refining, retrucking, shipping, unshipping, again refining, marketing—these are the stages in the sugar industry and none of them has ever been described as easy. What little mixture of molasses and missions there was took place in the pioneering days of the industry, long before there was any hint of fortunes in sugar. Since that time, tolerably large chunks have stuck to the fingers of agents, executives, and even shareholders, but only temporarily. You have probably heard of the Federal income tax.

The first quarter of a century of missions certainly did not result in any great accession of wealth to any individual, for up to this time all property was vested in the American Board of Missions in Boston. In 1843 a general missionary meeting in Hawaii resolved that, however proper it was for other men to engage in speculation and accumulate property, "we cannot consistently with our calling engage in business for the purpose of private gain." This action was superseded five years later by another resolution stating that missionaries' salaries could be used according to their own discretion, "accountable only to God, our own conscience, and an enlightened public sentiment." In 1853 the American Board cut the missions adrift to achieve their own support. Not till 1876, twenty-three years later, or fifty-six years after the arrival of the missionaries, was a reciprocal trade treaty with America approved, which allowed Hawaiian unrefined sugar free entry into the United States. Up to this time the annual export of sugar amounted to about 1,000 tons, and certainly no one got rich on the proceeds. The reciprocal treaty, however, according to Joseph Barber in his book, *Hawaii—Restless Rampart,* was the turning point in Hawaiian commercial affairs. "With a sure sugar market, it was easier to attract the necessary capital. More acres were planted in cane; irrigation systems were built to bring water to the thirsty fields; . . . . and up went production figures, climbing steadily year by year." But again the facts are worth emphasizing that all this prosperity took one hundred years of unstinted effort, and that for at least three quarters of a century there were no huge fortunes established, and certainly, for the first fifty years, no one in the islands achieved more than a modest competence.

The chief reason why wealth is at present centered mainly in the missionary families is because they, of all the one-time residents of Hawaii, looked on this as their permanent home. Traders and other business men, who made money in the islands, went back to where they belonged in Germany, America, and England.

In any fair appraisal of the value or otherwise of the missions to the Hawaiian people, certain considerations must be borne in mind. It is worth while to reiterate that civilized contacts did not first of all come about through the missionaries, but through voyagers such as Cook and Vancouver, traders such as Portlock and Dixon, whalers, fur traders, and a minor host of adventurers, not by any means the salt of the earth. Along with "ardent spirits" and similar cultural blessings, these foreigners brought with them the common cold, influenza, measles, tuberculosis, plague, cholera, small-pox, and probably leprosy. Possibly less fatal to the individual but inimical in the greatest degree to the race were the twin diseases, gonorrhea and syphilis. Pulmonary troubles were not helped by the natives going clothed, often hotly clad in the warmest season and quite exposed in the cold weather if, as was likely, their clothes had worn out in the meantime. The sandalwood trade, which according to

Jarves brought in $400,000 a year, demanded the labors of many Hawaiians in high altitudes, to which they were unaccustomed. Prior to the arrival of the missionaries, depopulation due to wars and pestilence had proceeded at an alarming rate. Cook, in 1778, estimated the number of natives at 400,000, but he did not take into account the fact that curious crowds followed his ships along the coast from place to place. The best informed opinion is that the population was about 300,000. In 1823, it had fallen to 130,000.

What would have been the early fate of the Hawaiians if this religious invasion had not taken place? The newcomers, bigoted and intolerant as many of them were, established salutary rules and tabus against drunkenness, gambling, adultery, prostitution, and infanticide, all of which immoral practices were greatly harmful to social welfare and human survival. Medical men were included in missionary companies; care was given to the sick, sanitation was improved, a variety of foods was introduced, orphans were rescued and educated, and zealous attempts made to regulate conduct, all in healthful ways. Missionary influence checked, though it could not arrest, decline in population. Without these efforts the native Hawaiian would soon have disappeared from the scene.

In the second place, the benefits of education, such as they are, were conveyed to the people, a large proportion of whom became literate. Printing presses were set up, the language was stabilized by reducing its sounds to an alphabet of 12 letters, the Bible was translated into Hawaiian, thousands of school books were printed and distributed. Along with the common people, the kings and chiefs underwent instruction, being thus better equipped to deal with the representatives of civilized nations. Written treaties were entered into and recorded.

Thirdly, through the parent society in Boston, the ties with America were strengthened, laying a sure foundation for the claim that the American people had a predominant interest in, and influence over the country. Though the United States was slow to take advantage of this fact, her claims of dominance were such that no other country could dispute them.

Any unbiased view of the history of these islands will inevitably lead to the conclusion that in their development the most important factor was the work of the missionaries. Perhaps we may get the fairest understanding of their zeal, character, and puritanical outlook when we remember that their expedition to Hawaii was in the nature of a religious counter-offensive. New England in their day was experiencing the inroads of Unitarianism in religion and Republicanism in politics, both of which developments were distressing to the fundamentalists, religious or political. Here in the Pacific lay a whole new territory to be developed and a hundred thousand souls to be saved. The missionaries' instructions included covering this new land with fruitful fields and pleasant dwellings. Christianity and civilization were to go hand in hand. The natives were to be lifted out of moral, social, and pagan degradation. The primary purpose, of course, was religious salvation, the visible fruits of which were chastity or continence, total abstinence from liquor and tobacco, rigid Sunday observance, and subjection to the discipline of the church.

For a time all the missionaries' purposes prospered. Aided by the regent Kaahumanu, the new religious influence spread like wildfire. By 1832, just before her death, Sunday congregations in Honolulu numbered as many as three thousand, while fifty thousand pupils were enrolled in island schools. So general was this thirst for the new knowledge that visitors, such as Kotzebue, condemned the schools for the inattention to agriculture. The taro patches were wilted and full of weeds—the farmer was away at school. Natives came from all over the islands to attend the four-day public examinations, even though many of them had to go without adequate food or shelter during this period.

Bradley, in his book, makes an excellent appraisal of the factors in this remarkable achievement. First of all is the fact that the Hawaiians were naturally a religious people, and the sudden destruction of their own traditional beliefs made a gap which the new religion filled. Next was the prestige of the new teachers, particularly in the field of education. The support and example of the chiefs was of great importance, but most potent of all was the force of character and the determination of the missionaries themselves. Whether they succeeded in their efforts "to transfer the religious and social ideals of New England to the Hawaiian Islands" is another question. One wonders what their reactions would be if they could return now to the scene of their labors.

Finally, the action of the American Board in cutting off their support and making the missions financially self-supporting had far-reaching effects. The missionary families were hardworking as well as religious. They turned their hands to every craft and experimented with every kind of crop. They also trained every type of artisan. Their influence with the kings was so salutary that Jarves could write in 1843: "Among no other community on the globe, can the traveller sojourn at the present day, with greater security of person and property." Testimony to the great value of the missions is also given by John Young after a residence of over thirty years in Hawaii, although from the language of his statement there is considerable suspicion that while he signed the document, it was dictated, or written by a missionary hand.

Though it may seem absurd to have to make such an obvious statement, the missionaries did not take any vows of poverty on behalf of their descendants. Piety *does* pay if mixed with good business sense. It is no wonder that Cheever's prediction came true in the islands when he said, "As prosperous or as happy as the child of a missionary may yet become a proverb." Ministers' sons are notorious for falling out of the religious cradles in which they were nurtured, but it is astonishing how many of them fall on their feet. There are more of them in "Who's Who" than children of any other group of professional men.

Even if we admit that the missionaries came to Hawaii to do good and their grandsons did well—what of it? Business enterprise, shrewd investments, rugged individualism are not anywhere looked down upon in America, and to have some religion mixed up with them does not seem to do any harm.

There was a man of a very peculiar religious sect in Australia who always had remarkable luck in keeping the flocks of predatory parrots away from his peach crop. When a friend inquired how he did it, he answered, "By prayer." "Oh, come," said the friend, "that's not being neighborly. How *do* you keep the parrots away?" "By prayer," the man insisted, "and an occasional shot." It is really marvelous what can be accomplished by prayer and an occasional shot. The missionary's child developed a good eye and a very steady trigger finger.

Looking back on missionary days and efforts in Hawaii, a competent observer, in the writer's opinion, could not fail to come to certain definite conclusions. During the first seventy years, many of the missionary band died, but none of them died rich. One of those who by common repute enriched himself greatly at the expense of the poor Hawaiians died in 1872,[2] after fifty years' residence in the islands. He left $15,000, one third of which estate came from land inherited by his wife in Rochester, New York. The rest was accumulated by making and selling dairy products after the American Board had withdrawn their support from the missionaries. Saving the sum of $10,000 in fifty years can hardly be described as amassing wealth, nor was it accomplished at the expense of the Hawaiians.

From the beginning the missionaries envisaged a broad program of improvement for the natives, so that printers, teachers, farmers, and doctors were included in their companies, about one third being ordained ministers. Some of these were undoubtedly intolerant, in an age of bigotry and intolerance. But quite apart from their evangelical zeal, this band of men and their devoted wives stood between the Hawaiians and the unscrupulous whites who sought to exploit them. Acting thus as buffers, they absorbed many a shock of hatred and calumny but never wavered. No matter what their individual faults of temperament happened to be, courage, devotion, foresight, sincerity, and a single-minded purpose must be placed to their credit. What higher encomiums could a group of men and women earn?

[2] Reverend Artemas Bishop.

CHAPTER V

Of Sugar and Shekels

THERE CAN BE no doubt that if thousands of human beings were to devote themselves to a single purpose for a period of one hundred years the results would be magnificent. Even though slave labor built the pyramids of Egypt, they still are a tremendous accomplishment. So, too, is the Great Wall of China. But if with all your coolie laborers you mix a great company of skilled artisans, traders, inventors, scientists, yes, even money changers and investors and men who go down to the sea in ships, their achievement cannot fail to be of epic proportions, its story, if it could be told, a great saga.

In 1835, over a hundred years ago, the first commercial venture in the growing and processing of sugar was set up at Koloa on Kauai. The enterprising firm was Ladd and Company, and it is a great pity that their name was afterward associated with a secret and shady deal that fortunately failed of fruition. But to them must be accredited the vision and purpose to establish an industry which has since grown to mammoth proportions.

From the standpoint of any standard of progress, whether it be merely the multiplication of products, like the making of two stalks of wheat to grow where only one grew before, the development of this industry is remarkable. In 1838, after a dam had been built at Koloa and considerable land put into cultivation, one acre produced 12 tons of cane, from which was recovered 2½ tons of salable sugar—by no means a mean accomplishment. Now the same acre has produced up to 80 tons of cane, with a notable sugar yield, a thirty-two-fold increase. In 1865 the total yield for Hawaii after many years of experiment and effort was less than a thousand tons. Since then it has topped the million ton mark. If the comparison were on the basis of money value, it would be equally astounding. Making two million stalks of cane grow where only two stalks grew before might still be an understatement.

It is difficult for the reader to take much interest in, or appreciate such staggering figures. He can have no adequate conception of what a million tons of sugar would look like, how big a heap it would make if tipped out on one spot. It would be also difficult to say how long it would take to drive through 250,000 acres of cane, if all the sugar plantations of the Territory were joined end to end. We do know that the green cane runs for miles and miles, and that this sugar production, though perhaps a minor item in national business, is of vital consideration to us. In short, if the American people should suddenly practice austerity to the extent of going without sugar in their tea or coffee, it would be a minor deprivation to them, but a major tragedy for Hawaii. For many years we have put most of our financial eggs in the one sugar bag.

But if we have little care about figures, we might have about men and men's effort. No one can write the saga of sugar; too many forgotten men's lives have gone into it. There have been too many broken backs, too much anxiety and heartache, too much blood, sweat, and tears, for it to be one long song of triumph. There have been lying and cheating and injustice also in the building of Hawaii's great pyramid. That is inevitable in a hundred years' effort to raise two tons of sugar to a million. But compared with business ethics prevalent elsewhere during that period, Hawaii's record is astonishingly good.

There are still preserved for us some intriguing pictures. One contrast is particularly interesting to consider. On the one hand is a stone mill consisting of two revolving cylindrical rollers of granite, with a laborer sitting on his hunkers feeding into it a couple of stalks of cane each three times between the rollers, watching the juice run into a groove cut in a granite slab at the base of the cylinders, and being collected in a tub sunk in the ground alongside. On the other hand, there is the steel grab at a modern mill, gaping wide as it descends from a steam hoist to lift half a truck load of cane at a time, to be fed into the whirling, clattering machinery. At heart, the man that fed the stone mill and the modern mill superintendent are not so different. The same glint of pride came to the eye of the one as he announced that he had collected three hundred pounds of juice in a day's crushing as may be seen in the look of the other as he says, "Another hundred-ton day today."[1]

It probably took just as much human ingenuity to figure out the mechanical principles involved in the primitive mill, with its granite rollers mortised at the top to receive the wooden cogs of a block to which was attached the bent branch of a tree so that a mule walking in a circle would make the mill grind, as it did to devise the machinery of a modern mill. The setting up of the latter was a great task, but so, too, was the chiseling into shape of the granite rollers. And no doubt the man who fed the cane into the stone mill was just as tired at the end of the day as the modern sugar boiler, who was so pleased with his hundred-ton day. Cane cutters' aches and pains, alas, are just the same whether suffered in 1835 or 1935.

A graphic description of the difficulties besetting the way of the sugar planters of early days is to be found in Vandercook's *King Cane*. He records the scarcity of beasts of burden, especially draught animals, and how in desperation the manager of Koloa Plantation hitched forty Hawaiians to a plow to turn up his field. It must be admitted it was also a little difficult for the Hawaiians.

This manager was a man named Hooper who made mill rollers out of hardwood, built a dam to supply his farm with power and water, printed paper money redeemable in goods by his workers, and imported pans and earthenware pots from China, as well as experts to carry out the boiling and refining of the sugar. The stone sugar mill was also run by Chinese and turned out three hundred pounds of brown sugar a day, when cane could be had for the grinding.

[1] This was at one of the smaller mills. Some of the large ones can turn out 300 tons of sugar daily.

The debt of the Hawaiian sugar industry to the Chinese has never been adequately acknowledged. The Egyptians made sugar and purified it by adding a mixture of white lime and albumen and washing the molasses out with water. The Chinese worked out their own methods. A writing of the fourth century A.D. records that the sap of the sweet bamboo, if dried in the sun, was sweet and melted in the mouth. It was the Chinese who came to the rescue of the planters when the "temperamental incapacity," as Vandercook calls it, of the Hawaiians to till the ground, cut cane, and carry it to the mills became more and more apparent. Perhaps it would be better to call it plain unwillingness. Hawaiians everywhere were popular as sailors but nowhere did they take to such an eventless occupation as farming, especially if it included pulling a plow with forty of their fellows.

With the good earth between his toes and a yoke on his shoulders, the Chinese peasant, on the other hand, felt perfectly at home. He would be rich before he could afford to be temperamental. Wages of three to six dollars a month were low, but much higher than he was used to at home, and offered ultimate independence of plantation labor. With this end in view, the plodding determination of the peasant could even suffer the overseer's black snake whip across his shoulders.[2] Perhaps Sing Loo and Fung Tai had visions of their grandchildren as wealthy merchants, doctors, lawyers, and legislators in this new land of their adoption.

By any standards other than his own, the Chinese laborer's bargain was a hard one, with wages four dollars a month for ten hours in the fields or twelve in the mills, about two cents an hour. It cost $59 to transport him from China, and $41 of this amount was deducted from his wages, enabling him to earn $119 by three years' work. Food, mainly rice, was provided, and housing for single men, six to forty in a building.

A labor report of the time states that the men worked in gangs "supervised by an overseer who directs the work, corrects mistakes,

[2] These were the conditions of seventy years ago, when the lot of labor elsewhere was hard. Later, the treatment of laborers in Hawaii compared to that of white miners, mill workers, or sailors was most favorable.

instructs the ignorant, and stimulates the lazy." Perhaps too much stimulation was the reason why the new immigrants showed "a considerable disposition to hang themselves." The report rather unnecessarily declares that "the plantations are not carried on primarily for the purpose of elevating the laborer to the standard of Western civilization and morals any more than other corporations." In time, conditions improved, and over 46,000 Chinese came to Hawaii.

Nor should the debt of the Hawaiian sugar industry to other nationalities be forgotten, particularly that to the Portuguese, who like the Chinese bore the early heat and burden of the day. In all, 20,000 of them came from the Azores and Madeira, bringing their wives and families with them, intending to make their homes in Hawaii. They drove the mule teams, looked after the huge stables and plantation dairies, tended the machinery, took over most of the semi-skilled and skilled jobs in the mills and elsewhere on the plantation. Soon they were putting up neat houses and planting gardens on the lower mountain slopes just above the sugar belt, had settled themselves in, and were rearing thriving families. As soon as possible they planted familiar fruits and flowers around their homesteads to make them look as much like home as they could. Thus they showed a disposition to "stay put," and formed for many years a steady reservoir of labor for plantation use. They, too, laid courses in the pyramid of sugar.

Most numerous of all, 180,000 Japanese entered Hawaii during the third of a century ending in 1908, and labored mightily. How many acres of cleared land, how many miles of tunnels driven into the mountains to tap the water trapped between volcanic dikes, how many thousands of miles of irrigation ditches, how many million man-days they have given to sugar, who can tell? It is true that they found much better conditions than the first comers to Hawaii, for wages had gone up to $12.50 a month for men and $8.00 a month for women, while food, housing and, later, medical attention, fuel and water were provided on a much improved scale. But labor in the fields was still hard. Hoeing the cane, burning the cane, cutting the cane—the work went on, with Papa-san and Mama-san showing a steadiness and stability through the years that any group might envy.

The latest of all the racial groups to fill the gaps in the ranks of the labor army have been the Filipinos, over 60,000 of them, small men but handling themselves well; good little men as the saying goes, dark-eyed, brown-skinned, voluble but soft-voiced, with a thirst for gay apparel and a keen eye for a likely bird for cock fighting. During nearly a quarter of a century they have proved themselves docile, thrifty, industrious people.

In the saga of sugar the common laborer, be he Chinese, Portuguese, Japanese, or Filipino, has contributed his share. He has bent his back and applied his strength to its full capacity. If credit is due for the building of an immense industry, then a great amount of it should go to the men with the hoe and the cane knife. That is in fact why it is called *industry*. Of course, the laborer was hired for the job and paid for it; but who wasn't? There have been no dollar-a-year men in sugar.

On the other hand, because their efforts paid, and paid well, is no reason why praise should be withheld from those who did the initial engineering and laid the foundations of the pyramid so broadly that its final elevation was possible. We can admit freely that the prime motive of each man, whether he be the *hapai ko* (carry cane) laborer, the plantation manager, or the bold investor of capital, was selfish—the desire to get along, to obtain that little or much above a survival minimum that spells mental ease, a sense of freedom and security. But the selfish motive, though primary, is not the only one. There is that other determination, entirely laudable, to do a good job, to leave no weeds in the row, to see that the water spreads evenly through the cane, to plot the cultivation contours correctly, to tap every available irrigation source, to give that last ounce of effort, and that last minute of thought, that spells success in any endeavor. To this end, the man with the hoe, the manager of the plantation, the agricultural scientist, the marketing agent do their work as efficiently as they know how. A man can be hired to drive nails, but the inner force that makes him drive them straight cannot be purchased.

The name of the first pioneer of the sugar industry in Hawaii has been lost, but it would be worth a good wager at long odds that it was a Chinese. In 1811 Stephen Reynolds was a seaman on board the brig New Hazard lying off Oahu, and his diary entry of March 5th of that year says, "Went ashore in cutter with Captain; saw the king's cane mill and boiler." Since Kamehameha had traded extensively with China prior to that time, it is very probable that his ships brought back some of the "dried sap of the sweet bamboo," and as sugar cane was cultivated in Cook's time in Hawaii, the king probably imported men from China to build the mill and operate it. In 1825 an Englishman named John Wilkinson planted a hundred acres of cane in Manoa Valley. At his death two years later, Boki, the governor of Oahu, proposed to sell the cane to a distillery for making rum. This made Queen Kaahumanu so angry that she ordered the cane plowed under and sweet potatoes planted in its stead.

The Ladd and Company venture at Koloa has been previously mentioned, and the tremendous efforts of the manager of this plantation to put it on a paying basis. Every pyramid must have its shady side, and a deal in which Ladd and Company and Brinsmade, the American consul, were the prime movers, is a part of the shadows. It was a scheme by which Ladd and Company, having won the confidence of King Kamehameha III, obtained his signature to a contract secretly drawn up by Brinsmade and Richards, a former missionary, but at that time the Court's economic adviser. This contract allowed Ladd and Company the privilege of "leasing any now unoccupied and unimproved localities" at a low rental for a term of one hundred years. Fifteen acres in each locality was granted for a millsite, and two hundred acres of adjoining land for cultivation. Private property rights were to be carefully respected, but as these rights as well as occupancy and improvement were ill-defined in those days, the contract could be stretched to take in most of the arable land in the islands.

This contract was conditional upon the recognition of the independence of the kingdom of Hawaii by both England and France
as well as by the United States, a highly desirable event. Sir George
Simpson, an official of the Hudson's Bay Company, agreed to assist
with regard to England, and he and Richards and Haalilio, the
king's secretary, were appointed plenipotentiaries, Richards holding
the king's full power of attorney. Brinsmade, who seems to have
been the villain of the piece, arranged to turn the contract over to
the "Belgian Company of Colonization," of which King Leopold
was a large stockholder. Four hundred thousand dollars were to
be invested in the Hawaiian branch of the Belgian Company and
4% interest was guaranteed on the capital, secured by a mortgage
on the revenues of the kingdom of Hawaii for six years. Emigrants,
presumably Belgian, were to be given fifty acres of land in fee
simple. The value of the contract may be judged from the fact
that Ladd and Company were to be paid $200,000 for its privileges.
Kamehameha III was to be a partner in the company and Richards
a director. Whether because of the king's repudiation of the contract or the indignation aroused in the islands by this ill-advised
plan, the scheme fell through. Its far-reaching and adverse effects
should have been obvious. Richards no doubt was honest, but his
lack of foresight in this instance was lamentable. Ladd and Company went into bankruptcy.

The next forty years of the industry reveal spectacular ups and
downs. Gold in California brought the ships of the world to the
Pacific Coast. Prices of commodities soared, and sugar reached the
unheard of price of 18 to 20 cents a pound. Soon inferior Manila
and China sugars flooded the California market, and with the
uncertainties of supply and demand, what might be worth a small
fortune today salable only at a loss tomorrow. Around 1850,
failures were frequent; so, too, were advertisements offering "sugar
mill machinery, almost new, for sale." That year only 335 tons of
sugar were produced in Hawaii, though it was estimated there were
224,000 acres of sugar land, capable of an average yield of 1 ton
of sugar per acre, in the islands.

It is strange how incidental events seem to set the pattern for future developments. Stephen Reynolds, who went ashore in 1811 to see the king's mill, returned to the islands some years later as a merchant and finally got into the sugar business by the purchase of a half-interest in a plantation on Maui, which later through the foreclosure of a mortgage passed entirely into his hands. Reynolds' original investment may well have been a development of his interest which began thirty-nine years before. In 1856 the land was purchased by C. Brewer II and Captain Makee, and later became the Brewer Plantation.

For many years the surplus sugar had to be disposed of in uncertain markets in Chile, California, and Australia. These places were thousands of miles away across the ocean, and the safety of the cargoes and the ships themselves were dependent upon the skill and courage of the men who sailed them. In the early days traders were desperate, and old vessels with foul and leaky bottoms went to sea, keeping afloat by the grace of God and good seamanship. The people of the islands knew these perils well. Hunnewell, founder of the firm that preceded Brewer and Company, reached Hawaii from Boston by sailing the Missionary Packet, no bigger than a fair-sized sampan, loaded within a foot of the water with merchandise for sale in the islands. Hunnewell took nine months, weathered many storms, took refuge thirty times in twenty different ports, and finally rounded the Horn. Perhaps in memory of these dangers, he later instructed his young partner, Peirce, "to avoid the purchase of a vessel or goods of a perishable nature." Sugar and ships between them make up the greater part of the early history of Hawaii, as we shall see later. It was the fur trading and whaling ships that first created the demand for sugar, and after the whaling industry declined, marketing abroad became essential, necessitating all kinds of monetary exchange that ultimately led to the formation of the sugar agencies or factors.

Along with fluctuations in price, financial panics and shipping losses, the industry had several remarkable fillips. One was the situation created by the Civil War, which took mainland sugar areas out of production; the other was the Reciprocity Treaty of 1876, which gave the island industry a chance to export sugar into America free of duty. The next important development was the movement towards co-operation within the industry through the formation of the Royal Hawaiian Agricultural Society in 1850. This was succeeded in 1882 by "The Planters Labor and Supply Company," with the announced aim of resolving jealousies and promoting the welfare of the whole industry. This was in turn succeeded by the Hawaiian Sugar Planters Association in 1895, which devoted its efforts mainly to increased productivity. Without this co-operative effort the industry could not have continued, yet the pooling of its resources has many times been condemned as forming an iniquitous monopoly.

From the early days a serious problem was the small acreage in the islands suitable for farming. Water and sunshine were the great essentials, water to grow the cane, sunshine to improve its sugar content. Where the rainfall was adequate, there was not enough sun. Where there was sun enough, the land was too dry. Obviously, the answer was irrigation, and to provide this seemed an impossible undertaking. A leeward valley like Manoa had a rainfall of 133 inches at its head and 20 inches where it opened on to the plain. The other islands were similarly divided between drought and saturation.

In the waist of the island of Maui, for example, there is a large, open, but very arid area. Flanking it on one side and shielding it from the rains stands the huge tumulus of Haleakala, a great burnt out crater 10,000 feet high. Up the windward slopes sweep the tradewind-driven clouds. But half way around the mountain the rain belt ceases. To windward, forty miles from the open plain, the combination of cumulus and tumulus brings about precipitation measured better by feet than inches. How could this water be impounded and carried round the mountain to make some of the most fertile land in the islands productive?

Smooth though the tumulus of Haleakala looks from a distance, the torrents that tear down its windward side have furrowed the old slag, cinder, and lava heap into a hundred deep gorges. If the planter wanted this water, he must turn his back on planting. He must forget his crops, his grinding mill and all profits from them for the time being. He must persuade the merchants in Honolulu that there were really shekels in sugar so that they would join in the gamble and back his seemingly impossible scheme with money. Fortunately, there were optimists willing to take the risk, their business being already full of such chances. As one of them said, "A man with sugar on the brain is a queer animal. Even if on the verge of bankruptcy, they all think themselves millionaires."

The main ditch obviously must run high enough on the side of the mountain to head the smaller gorges, and where the larger streams had gouged out steep precipices the water must go into pipes to be siphoned down and up the farther side. Then, too, tributary ditches must fan out to the head waters of all the main catchment areas to keep the big ditch full; and where the residual ridges were too high to be circumvented by open cuts, tunnels must be dug.

Since the army of men, the rank and file who built this colossus of sugar, cannot be counted, it seems reasonable to keep names out of the record, even of those who planned this great achievement. But in speaking of the Hamakua ditch on Maui, it is difficult to avoid mention of S. T. Alexander and H. P. Baldwin, missionaries' children who conceived and carried through this project. Money later built a larger ditch on Maui, one which delivered fifty million gallons of water daily, but it was not Maui men who planned and paid for it. Money alone did not build the Hamakua ditch. Baldwin, with a rope twisted round his one arm—the other had been too enthusiastically fed between sugar mill rollers—let himself down the precipices to supervise the laying of the siphon pipes down and over the Maliko Gulch. It took stamina as well as money to do this work. Money may command impressive undertakings, but in this Maui accomplishment the partners lived in the mountain camps, slipped and climbed through the gulches, were daily soaked in torrential rains, and came out of the game caked with mud and triumph. It was an all-Hawaiian venture, and its co-operative financing in Honolulu also required plenty of courage and faith.

Then there was the manager of a plantation on another island where irrigation would help production substantially. Engineering experts from Honolulu said it would cost $120,000, would require high flumes, expensive to maintain, and two years' work. The manager had a Japanese boy in his office who knew something of surveying, and the two of them disappeared for a few days into the mountains. Their report was that by driving a two-mile tunnel, fluming would be avoided, the job would cost $30,000 and could be finished in six months. The agents for the plantation gave a very dubious assent, the penalty for failure being, of course, the manager's head. The two halves of the tunnel, begun from both ends simultaneously, met within a foot of alignment, the cost was below the estimate, and the work was done on time. The name of the Japanese boy has been forgotten, so for the purpose of this record, the manager shall be nameless also.

Not all the notable achievements have to do with irrigation. There is, on Hawaii, a plantation which straddles the government road around the island. If a lateral road near sea level could be built, the cane would not require to be hauled up an 800-foot elevation to the highway and down again to the mill site. But there was the old problem of crossing the gulches torn out of the mountain by the rains and getting steeper and larger as they descended. But under the manager's eye, with the work being carried out by David, the Hawaiian boss of the plantation's road building operations, hillsides were blasted down, cuttings were gouged out, bridges built, and a road put in that wormed its way across the mouths of the gulches and thence on easy grades to the mill. It looked in places like pictures of the Burma road, but it served. The work cost only one life. For years an Hawaiian had longed to set off a big blast, and while the road gang was at lunch he sneaked down and tamped in a big dynamite charge. He attained his lifelong ambition, and on that high note of accomplishment his existence fittingly ended. He blew himself and the side of the gulch to Hawaiian heaven.

But if the planters had to turn their backs on the fields and go into the mountains to get water, this was nothing to the journeyings to and fro upon the earth undertaken by scientists to find allies in the planters' battle against the insect enemies of sugar. This is surely one of the most interesting chapters in the story of *Saccharum officinarum* in these islands. The first of these mortal assaults by insect foes was carried on by hordes of the saccharicidal leafhopper— *Perkinsiella saccharicida*—an insect undoubtedly introduced along with some plant from Queensland. One plantation had its yield reduced, by reason of these leafhoppers, to one tenth of its former production. The only way by which the entomologist could defeat the attacker was literally by boring from within. From Northern Australia the bug-hunters imported a tiny insect which laid its eggs within the body of the leafhopper and the larvae did the rest. The principle was established that when a pest makes himself particularly obnoxious in Hawaii, he is probably only an escapist from his enemies in his own home territory. Bring some of his lifetime foes to his new abode and he will soon be put in his place. It is a dirty entomological trick, but effective.

Then in 1906 the tables were almost turned on the entomologists. They had brought in a borer to settle the leafhopper menace but now they were almost beaten by another borer which drilled into the stems of the sugar cane. The jungles of Malaysia and Java were diligently scoured by scientists and their native helpers, but no parasite appeared. By canoe up tropical rivers, through leech-ridden swamps, under humid forests, on savannahs alternately drenched with sun and rain, the search went on. At last Frederick Muir, chief scout for the H.S.P.A., found the same borer in the sago palms of Amboina in the Dutch East Indies. There it was being effectively held in check by its particular enemy, a parasitical New Guinea fly.

But this fly, called *Tachinid*, though its business was boring, found the journey from New Guinea excessively so, and died on the way. It was only after four years, when breeding stations had been set up in Australia and Fiji, where the *Tachinids* could settle down, complete their life cycle, and hand on their mission of hate to their descendants, that the allied invasion of Hawaii could take place. But in six months' time the cane borers were reduced to the proportions of a normal pest.

Knowing scientists as I do, and the knack of making oneself comfortable in the wilds, I have a shrewd suspicion that they should divide credit with their native assistants, who probably did most of the dirty work. It is astonishing how much the native appreciates the white man's vices. For two sticks of nigger-twist tobacco, two Australian aborigines cheerfully swam and paddled twelve miles across a current-swept, shark-infested strait in northern Australia to carry a message for me to a neighboring island. In Africa, also, powdered tobacco mixed into a cone with cowdung will bring the non-perspiring naturalist all the biological specimens in the neighborhood, while in central Australia aborigines will chase and capture rare marsupials for the fun of it. Once the bug-hunter can convince the natives that he is not really crazy, they will catch bugs for him until he goes home. The native in his home territory is the best naturalist in the world, and as a collector can lick any entomologist hands and knees down. No doubt many of them performed sterling service on behalf of the Hawaiian sugar industry.

So much for the bright side of the story of the building of the great pyramid of sugar. There are some people, however, who believe that the shadow of that pyramid extends over every home, business, and institution in this Territory and that this constitutes an unhealthy condition for growth and development. They are usually ready to admit that shade can be beneficial as well as harmful, and that many things which now flourish in Hawaii would have perished from heat and aridity except for the fact that they have grown up in the shadow of sugar cane. For example, no one would deny that the far-reaching agricultural experiments of the Hawaiian Sugar Planters Association are of the utmost importance to very many other people besides the growers of cane. What the critics dislike most is apparently the size of the industry and its co-ordinated control by five agencies. To their minds there seems to be some malevolent magic in the number five. If there were twelve or fifteen large enterprises flourishing in Hawaii, there would apparently be little cause for complaint or suspicion. They apparently reason that a dozen pyramids would cast less of a shadow on Hawaii.

This is the view set forth by one author in a book[3] which turns a distrustful eye on the economic and military situation existing in these islands. He devotes a good deal of space to a critical review of the powerful influence exerted over Hawaiian affairs by the quintet of sugar factors, popularly, or more unpopularly, known as "The Big Five," and describes the developments whereby these firms obtained their power. Speaking of the time subsequent to 1890, he says, "With their representatives more or less arbiters of local affairs, they were also becoming assured of a practical monopoly not only of the many sources of income arising from the handling of the sugar business, but of island merchandising and insurance. . . ."

But in respect to present day conditions, the picture seems to have changed. If the system of concentrated control of business in Hawaii is deserving of condemnation, then the indictment should be broadened to include other large "interests." There is, for example, the Matson Company, with headquarters in San Francisco, which through its steamship lines and hotel holdings has invested so heavily in Hawaii's past, present, and future. Then, too, there are the Dillingham interests which control the Oahu Railway Company,[4] with its large land holdings, and also maritime piers and a great construction business. The Bishop Estate, an eleemosynary corporation established by an Hawaiian princess for the educational benefit of Hawaiians, owns 350,000 acres including many residential areas and is now immensely wealthy. On the island of Hawaii is the huge Parker Ranch, claiming the largest herd of purebred Hereford cattle in the world. On Kauai and Maui are situated the Rice and Wilcox holdings. These two families are of missionary descent but are distinct from the Big Five. Finally, two trading firms—Kress, and Sears, Roebuck—whose business tentacles cover the United States, are also established here.

[3] Barber, Joseph. *Hawaii: Restless Rampart*. Bobbs Merrill Co., New York, 1941.
[4] This company paid more than a million dollars in taxes in 1944.

All this can be summarized in a simple statement—big business controls big business in Hawaii. It is not in the hands of a single concern, nor of five companies, but is divided between, possibly, twenty-five large firms. This is far from a monopoly, or economic fascism, or whatever the writers like to call it. If the same names appear several times on different boards of directors, that is not to be wondered at in a community of small size. There is both competition and co-operation in island affairs. If there is more of the latter than is usual in mainland communities, that, too, may be ascribed to our historical background and insular conditions.

Another author[5] is very severely critical of the supposed dominance of island business and affairs by the Big Five, but he makes a most significant admission. He states, in effect, that what has come about in Hawaii is no isolated occurrence, and is not even a rare hothouse variety of the rule-by-the-few system. He affirms, without fear of contradiction, that the Hawaiian plant is a *species Americanus,* thriving particularly luxuriantly on American soil. Thus the matter is plain. It is no indigenous devil that must be cast out of the islands, but the familiar evil spirit of American capitalism. If there were any way of building a fleet of steamers, or a huge irrigation project without capital, we should undoubtedly adopt it.

If, too, as this author points out, the names of certain business directors appear frequently on the boards of education, social welfare, community chests, etc., two interpretations may be ascribed to that fact. By the over-suspicious it may be interpreted as a malevolent lust for power, a desire to manipulate all the strings that might move this community. It might also mean a long-continued and deep-seated interest on the part of business men in the welfare of a community that has been home to these directors or their families for very many years. The motivation behind any public service is always subject to suspicion. The only way to judge of its character is to consider its record. With all due allowance for the weak-

[5]MacDonald, Alexander. *Revolt in Paradise.*

nesses of human nature, involving individual desires for prominence and the exercise of authority, achievement in the fields of education, research, and social service in Hawaii is such that there is no fear of comparison with that of any other community of like size and resources.

Without doubt the sugar agencies are in on the ground floor of Hawaii's commerce, but a brief review of the situation will reveal that they got there when there was only one story to the building. Moreover, if some attention is paid to sugar's forerunners in island trade, the sandalwood, fur, and whaling industries, it becomes apparent that the Big Five moved into the single-storied structure after the previous tenants had found it so shaky that they deemed it wise to move out. For many years, at least forty, their continued occupancy was a matter of doubt. The whole building threatened to fall down about their ears. Gradually, however, its foundations were strengthened and its walls thickened, till finally it became firm enough to support the present imposing structure of island prosperity. Its long-term tenants can hardly be blamed for refusing to leave the preferred positions and to move upstairs.

The background of business in the islands is worth another brief historical summary. At its inception, the sandalwood trade enriched no one in the islands except Kamehameha, who maintained a rather strict monopoly over its sale. The unit of measurement for the wood was the picul, a Malayan word which means a sufficient load for a man's back, and is a little over 133 pounds. Many thousands of piculs were traded by the king, a full cargo of the wood in exchange for the ownership of the ship that carried it.[6] Thus the king planned to do his own shipping to China where the timber was used for chests, coffins, etc. It was only after the war of 1812 that the trade became brisk. The reports of Hawaiian sandalwood written about 1791 had declared it inferior, while Vancouver doubted if the timber were the same as the valuable wood of India which was sold by weight. That Kamehameha found sandalwood a source of wealth is shown by the fact that just before

[6] See also Chapter III.

his death he was able to purchase $8000 worth of guns and ammunition. The king's chief desire, however, was to acquire ships, and Bradley records that he purchased no less than six vessels, and was credited with "immense wealth." After Kamehameha's death, the chiefs continued these exchanges, at one time owning "ten large and elegant brigs," as well as numerous smaller vessels. Other proceeds were wasted in lavish, unnecessary purchases. Some strange bargains were struck. One involved the purchase of Cleopatra's Barge, a most sumptuously appointed vessel built originally at Salem for George Crowninshield at a cost of $50,000. It was bought at auction in America for $15,400 and was then turned over to Liholiho for the equivalent of almost $90,000. Some of the largest business firms in the East, such as Marshall and Wildes, Bryant and Sturges, and John Jacob Astor, were soon eagerly competing for cargoes, but as supplies of sandalwood dwindled, it became increasingly difficult for them to collect their debts.

Nevertheless, the chiefs went on buying. Costly silks, ready-made garments by hundreds, carriages, billiard tables, plate glass, etc., were among their acquisitions. The Eastern firms were afraid to refuse to trade lest they lose both the business and the chance to collect their bills. Soon the traders began prodding the U.S. government to send warships to Hawaii to compel payment. The warships came, but their captains, in fear of international complications, were very cautious. In the meantime, the missionaries, while they preached honesty to the chiefs, were not slow to point out what miserable bargains the latter had made, a procedure which did not endear them to the traders. One of the bitterest complaints was that the missionaries were making the chiefs "too enlightened." When the old chiefs died, the new ones refused to assume the debts. The Eastern firms, in despair, gave up their Hawaiian ventures as too risky or unprofitable, leaving the field open to the small local traders.

In the meantime, the whaling industry was beginning to be important. In 1823, as many as six hundred sailors were in port at the one time, and they spent their wages as only sailors can.

By 1826 the natives were selling thousands of dollars worth of provisions to visiting ships. They spent this money in the local retail stores, buying all kinds of goods, including fine clothes, so that the women of one missionary company were much chagrined to find themselves much less modishly dressed than some of these simple Hawaiian females they had come so far to instruct. The natives' special demands were for things "new and elegant." Razors, pocket pistols, umbrellas, rings, champagne, ink, powder, perfumery, pantaloons, card tables figured in the sales of James Hunnewell, the precursor of the Honolulu firm of C. Brewer and Company.

It should be noted that outside of provisions, Hawaii had no exports that could correct such an unfavorable balance of trade. By 1840 the most important products of the islands were listed as hides, sugar, molasses, salt, goat skins, tobacco, arrowroot, and kukui oil, the total value being below $100,000. The whaling industry itself had extreme fluctuations. Sometimes both whales and money were scarce and there was little or no profit, particularly after the financial panic of 1837. By 1842 there were six commercial firms operating on a moderate scale in Hawaii, two British and four American. Only Peirce and Brewer had a direct continuity with any existing firm. As previously mentioned, one of these six business concerns, Ladd and Company, was the pioneer in sugar production and went bankrupt on account of its venture. For a time silk vied with sugar as a potential commercial product. It was only in the 'fifties that the discovery of gold in California, combined with a more stabilized white population in the islands, and the development of agriculture and Hawaii's combined importance as a transshipment point in Pacific trade improved business prospects and paved the way for the establishment of the quintet of firms now so prominent in the life of the Territory.

The part that sugar has played in island prosperity has been described in interesting detail by Vandercook,[7] while Jared Smith[8] has contributed a brief factual account of the genesis of the Big Five.

[7]Vandercook, John W. *King Cane*. Harper Bros., 1939.
[8]Smith, Jared. "The Big Five." Advertiser Publishing Co., 1943.

From these accounts certain salient facts seem to emerge. Only two of the five sugar agencies, Castle and Cooke, and Alexander and Baldwin, were originally set up by missionaries or their sons. As previously mentioned, C. Brewer and Company was begun by Hunnewell in 1826 and continuity of operation was provided through Peirce, Captain Brewer, and Charles Brewer II, of whom the first two were partners of Hunnewell. American Factors was originally a German firm with headquarters in Bremen, under the name of Hackfeld and Company. Its property was seized and sold during the last war and its enterprises continued and developed by the new firm. A business, begun by an Englishman named Jannion in 1845, came into the hands of Theo. H. Davies in 1868, and has been controlled by his family ever since. Davies had been previously employed as a junior clerk in the business which he later purchased.

The partnership of Alexander and Baldwin, begun in 1874, seems to have been the only firm founded directly to carry on as sugar factors. All the rest began as world traders, making their profits in many markets, carrying on merchandising and insurance and banking, risking their capital in all types of inland ventures, wherever a chance of gain appeared. Only many years after their foundation, when sandalwood, fur, and whale oil had declined or disappeared as profitable commercial products, did these firms become concerned in the growing and marketing of sugar.

Looking backward, then, we find a motley collection of sea captains, missionaries and their descendants, supercargoes, traders, planters, school teachers, bookkeepers, doctors, janitors, and junior clerks, who worked their way to the forefront of Hawaiian industry. They came from London, Liverpool, Boston, San Francisco, Bremen, Hamburg, Sydney, and elsewhere. No common interest brought them together save one, namely, profit making. The fact that such a miscellaneous assemblage of men were able to set up a system of co-operation seems the best proof that they were compelled to do so by force of circumstances. Only by such a plan could they hope, under island conditions, to survive. Profit making is not the kind of activity for which you must prove you have missionary connections before you can participate in it. If missionary families have now a controlling interest in Hawaii's greatest industry, the sugar business, it would seem to be the reward of their own enterprise and vision. Certainly the missionary stock in one respect had no undue advantage over the rest of their business associates. For thirty years, from 1820 to 1850, the field was open to the traders, entirely without missionary competition. This long priority should have been a most important handicap in favor of non-missionary firms.

In any superficial survey of the present island economic structure the tendency is to neglect its historical foundations and to interpret the Big Five's width of operations as being due to a desire to control everything in sight. Undoubtedly, this motive has not been absent from the minds of some individuals, but on the other hand, it should not be forgotten that the condition may be one of the natural consequences of insularity. If these were not islands, there would have been no necessity to import laborers for the plantations and we should not have had such a racially heterogeneous population; our historical precedents and antecedents would have been entirely different; our political, social, and economic structures would not have been nearly so closely knit together; our domestic issues would not come to such instant national focus, and books in such numbers would not be written about us.

Nothing can change the fact that Hawaii is a group of islands over two thousand miles from the nearest mainland community. Because of this isolation, the various activities involving sugar, pineapples, transportation, irrigation, shipping, mechanical equipment, fertilizers, labor, wages, banking, tourists, hotels, etc., had to be developed side by side—*pari passu* as the scientists put it. None of these enterprises could get very far ahead or very far behind the rest without dislocation of business and loss to the Territory. As one example of this necessary co-ordination, we have mentioned banking. Obviously, our geographical isolation, and the early uncertainties of trade in the islands made it imperative that Hawaii should have its own banking institutions, not only to insure the stability of our commercial relationships with the rest of the world, but also to finance local enterprises.

All of these activities, in default of mainland or foreign capital, had to be paid for out of the common purse. There were far too few small investors, and no single firm wealthy enough to undertake more than a limited responsibility. Whether the idea was welcome or not, a pooling of resources was necessary. If any large project, such as the building of the Hamakua Ditch on Maui, had failed from lack of capital, the effect on the rest of the sugar plantations would have been bad. Its success, on the other hand, paved the way for similar projects elsewhere. Thus the leaders of Hawaiian industry became like members of a large family with a joint bank account. They watched each other's expenditures jealously, but continued to pay in to the co-operative account.

We have already mentioned the Hawaiian Sugar Planters Association. None but a common purse could have provided a half million dollars annually to bring together such a body of scientists of high caliber for the solution of sugar's recurrent problems. The work of these chemists, entomologists, agronomists, geneticists, engineers, etc., was vital. In plant breeding alone there were almost countless experiments needed for the development of varieties of cane suitable for different altitudes, temperatures, soils, aspects, sunshine periods, and other conditions. Science in sugar as elsewhere knows no boundaries, certainly no plantation boundaries. What was discovered was for the good of all. Naturally the H.S.P.A. experiment station was controlled by the H.S.P.A.

The sugar business in Hawaii exists in a chronic state of emergency mainly because of the uncertainties of action in Washington. This fact is recognized by Barber, who points out that Congress may amend or repeal Hawaii's constitution, the Organic Act, without consulting the people of the Territory. "Similarly," he says, "it may enact legislation which almost overnight could topple the carefully reared economic and social structure of the islands." A drastic downward revision of Hawaii's sugar quota would, of course, also bring about this result. The prosperity of other communities may likewise hang by a single thread, but if so, they too live in a state of emergency and need co-ordinated leadership to meet any crises effectively.

The best insurance against discriminatory action towards Hawaii is the outstanding success in commercial matters that has been achieved in the islands. The Hawaiian goose may lay a relatively small golden egg, but no one would care to kill it. To discover the basis for this remarkable prosperity we can again rely on a statement by Barber, certainly by no means a friendly witness. After describing the intense waterfront activity in the Territory, the freighters going out loaded with sugar and pineapples and returning with cargoes of all kinds of goods from the mainland, and accepting all this as a gauge of material prosperity, Barber says: *"It could never have come into being but for a unique system of enterprise, which was already functioning when Hawaii was a monarchy"*; in short, when the skyscraper had only one story. This unique system was the Big Five, not malefactors, nor benefactors, merely sugar factors. It is worth while noting also that the bonds of association between them took seventy years to grow and cement.

As there are sixteen thousand shareholders in these concerns and the plantations they control, it would seem that profit participation rests on a fairly wide basis. It is, however, useless to dodge the issue of centralized authority; yet this is what Vandercook does in his description of the growth of the sugar industry. After proving conclusively that these fine mills, these countless miles of contour lines of growing cane, these farflung irrigation systems, this volume of research could not possibly have come about without the closest co-operation within the industry, he weakens his case by suggesting that sugar is produced by individual farmers on ordinary-sized holdings. He continually refers to these huge plantations as "farms."

Competition in business affairs is without doubt a healthy thing, and it is difficult to say just how the right balance between unrestrained competition and co-operation should be struck. One source of complaint is that some plantations have paid as high as eighteen to twenty per cent to their shareholders and that some of these profits should have gone in larger measure to the laborers. Perhaps so; but it is well to remember that other plantations have paid no dividends for many years. If the prosperous plantations paid higher wages, the poorer concerns would either have to raise their wages or go out of business. The former course eventually would mean they would go further "in the red"; the latter would mean a decided detriment to the welfare of many people in the Territory.

If there are excess profits anywhere in the sugar business, the ordinary citizen will be quite content to have them taken care of by taxation. The situation is somewhat like the Biblical story of Joseph and his brethren. When the brothers visited Egypt, the recognition was one-sided, and Joseph hid money in their sacks. But the next time they came, bringing Benjamin, their father's favorite, they again left with the shekels in their sacks, but they did not get very far with the money, for Joseph sent his steward out after them. If there are shekels in sugar, the tax collector knows about it and most of it will be returned to Pharaoh.

CHAPTER VI

Perplexities in Paradise

WHOEVER first called these islands the "Paradise of the Pacific" probably did Hawaii no great service. There is, of course, no paradise on earth, any more than there is a fountain of perpetual youth, which strangely enough, Polynesian tradition once located in Hawaii. Even our much vaunted climate has its bad spots. People who are here for a very short visit, and spend this time in the downtown area, complain of heat and humidity, and are properly skeptical of published temperature records, taken on the top of a high building, well above the sweltering footpaths. These visitors may not know that within a mile or two from the shore they may find a much more pleasant temperature, nor that a thousand feet of elevation—and two thirds of the Territory must surely be above that altitude—gives a climate that is all that can be desired.

To anyone who is fortunate enough to know the islands intimately, their beauty also is most satisfying. Hawaii is one place where man's occupancy has increased its natural charm. The earliest photographs of the present site of Honolulu, for example, show a dry, dusty, almost treeless plain lying at the foot of hills, similarly arid and uninviting. Most of the trees and flowers that make the Territory a garden have been brought here.

But climate and beauty do not complete the inventory of Hawaii's advantages. Among its peoples the visitor may find a tolerant, almost indifferent attitude towards many problems that elsewhere cause bitter strife or controversy. Not that the material for such conflicts does not exist here; it does, in full measure, but somehow these troublesome matters seem to occasion little concern. The observer

Photos by 18th Air Base Photo Laboratory, A.C., Wheeler Field, T.H.

Upper. View of summit of Mauna Loa, showing craters and
old lava flows

Lower. The mountain sides crack open and the lava flows
to the sea

Upper photo by 11th Photo Section, A.C., Luke Field, T.H.
Lower photo by 18th Air Base Photo Laboratory, A.C., Wheeler Field, T.H.

Upper. The empty pit of Halemaumau, Kilauea volcano, Hawaii

Lower. The pit begins to fill with lava
(Note cars lined up in middle foreground)

is sometimes at a loss; he cannot decide whether this calm is due to a broad-minded or an easy-going attitude.

Nevertheless, even all these things added together do not make paradise. As a matter of sober truth, these islands have always had their full share of very perplexing problems, and around them have centered some rather bitter and prolonged controversies.

Nearly a hundred years ago a visitor could write of Hawaii thus: "In such a community as that at Honolulu, to a wayfarer a few years ago, everybody seemed to have everybody else by the ears, and an excessive eagerness for gain, gossiping and news created a state of mind, as in California now, by no means favorable to the general inculcation of truth." Perhaps because our controversies are so well publicized, it may seem to some that strife is endemic here. Books written about us feature revolts and restlessness. The visitor may still hear echoes of "old, unhappy, far-off things, and battles long ago." On the other hand, the fact that this community has successfully weathered so many storms gives ground for future confidence.

As we have already seen, the contest between the early missionaries and traders was one of the longest and sharpest. It is easy to understand how this trouble arose. The one group was so intent on saving the Hawaiian, and incidentally, converting him into a provident, temperate, well-disciplined landsman, while the other group sought to exploit the native's weakness for useless possessions, to the end that they might build up their own fortunes. The trader naturally resented the missionary's attempts to put a halter on the Hawaiian's extravagances, in restraint of trade. Then, even while this feud was still continuing, there occurred a long chain of incidents, in which the chiefs of Hawaii withstood in turn the demands of American commercial agents, British consuls, French admirals, etc. Later, with the decay of the chiefs' influence, the kings were disposed to try and revive their autocratic powers. This brought about that other conflict between business men and royalists, which found the missionary families, once the bolsterers of the kings' power, aligned on the side of the business interests. With these matters settled by annexation, the next troubles that loomed on Hawaii's horizon were those related to labor relations. No sooner did these dissolve, at least temporarily, than another shadow appeared, the specter of economic discrimination against Hawaiian industry and the threat of the loss of territorial self-government through establishment of commission rule.

As if this were not enough, there occurred, about twelve years ago, a most unhappy event. Accusations of a brutal sex assault were brought by a white woman, a "navy wife," against a group of island youths of mixed racial origins. Then followed a punitive murder and the reverberations of this case were heard all over America. The picture of the islands presented by much of the mainland press at that time was hardly that of a paradise but rather of a dark jungle where white women were unsafe. The case presented so many unusual features, and the credibility of the complainant was so much in question that island opinion was acutely divided. On the mainland the ability for self-government by the Territory was seriously doubted, and commission control was proposed.

Now that this storm has died down, another trouble has been laid on Hawaii's doorstep. Thousands of defense workers were suddenly transported to a community which was by no means capable of absorbing this influx without serious dislocation. Housing and transportation and other facilities were restricted and the inconveniences suffered occasioned loud complaints. Nor has this reservoir of potential ill-will and misunderstanding been lowered by the reports of the men of the armed forces who have been stationed here in large numbers. In Honolulu the soldier or sailor finds a city of moderate size and American appearance, but with no large group of white people of the artisan class at all comparable in social grade with those he was accustomed to living among at home. Hawaii is by no means his idea of an earthly paradise. Both the enlisted man, and, to a lesser degree, the officer, often feel that they have been thrown into a social element in which they can neither sink nor swim.

All of these considerations demand the frank admission that

Hawaii is no paradise, and claiming it as such leaves the community open to some deserved jibes. The local Tourist Bureau, which has probably overworked the term "Hawaiian paradise" in its literature, is not, however, to blame for the invention of this somewhat meretricious term. More than ninety years ago, the Rev. Henry Cheever wrote a book called *The Island World of the Pacific,* in which he termed Hawaii "the isles of the blest" and "island paradises." It is probable that Mark Twain, who stayed in these islands for a time and was entranced with their beauty, did most to popularize the phrase.

Cheever, by the way, seemed to think that the isles would be still more blest if people of his own color only, lived here. He had the Hawaiians and the whites all mixed up with the sons of Noah— Japhet and Shem—and on the strength of the prophecy that God would enlarge Japhet so that he would dwell in the tents of Shem, Cheever took this to mean the ultimate dispossession and total disappearance of the natives of these islands. Provided they were first "saved," he was inclined to look on their extinction quite philosophically. In the same spirit, he drew a parallel between this expected event and the "wonderful plague" that "providentially" depopulated New England of its Indian warriors, just prior to the arrival of the Pilgrim Fathers. In Cheever's opinion, Providence was very definitely on the side of the white man.

Nevertheless, this writer had a prophetic eye. Writing in 1851, he foresaw "iron steamers" ferrying crowds of tourists from California and Panama to the volcano at Kilauea, which he predicted would become one of the wonders of the world when some enterprising "Yankee or Yankeefied Hawaiian" would build a house of entertainment on the crater's edge. He was right in every respect, except that a "Yankeefied" Greek built the Volcano House. Cheever likewise envisaged a transpacific line of steamers operating from Hawaii and a "miniature Polynesian University," conferring degrees on native-born Hawaiians. This latter development, however, he associated with Punahou Academy.

This writer also opened up discussion on what has come to be recognized as one of our major perplexities, the question of statehood for Hawaii. After reciting the fact that the islands were "harboring a permanent American population, foremost in energy and influence, now little short of one thousand," he goes on to see "a propriety in their enjoying an American Protectorate, if not an admission under the flag of the American Republic. Linked, as it will speedily become, to our Pacific and Atlantic seaboards by steamer and telegraph, it may suitably be adopted into the sisterhood of the American States. Hawaiian Senators and Representatives may ere long take their seats in the Capitol at Washington, with members from Minnesota, Utah, Deseret, New Mexico, and Santa Fe. The star of Hawaii may yet blaze in the flag of the American Union."

He also noted the fact that in 1849 the islands "consumed nearly a million of dollars' worth of American merchandise." Eighty-eight years later, this amount had increased over a hundred times, and the American population, still energetic and influential, had multiplied seventy fold, but Hawaii is not yet a State.

In 1937 the question had come so much to the fore, that a congressional committee held hearings in Hawaii, thus giving an opportunity for the airing of local doubts as to the wisdom of the move. It was realized that the whole matter constituted a difficult problem, with much to be said on both sides.

In the free-for-all style in which these hearings were conducted, it was inevitable that individuals with personal grievances appeared as witnesses, the complaints ranging all the way from protests against dismissal from a territorial position up to charges of miscarriage of justice in the local courts. There were some suggestions made that witnesses would be intimidated by threats of persecution if they dared oppose statehood. From remarks dropped by committee members, it was evident that, privately, they had met with a considerable "I could, an I would" attitude on the part of residents. Perhaps because of real or fancied apprehensions, or possibly because there existed no actual basis for serious or specific complaint, the hearings were singularly free from recriminations. There was nothing that the Committee could seize upon as evidence of intimidation, and no one had any definite ideas as to how people could be punished for expressing their opinions. When committee members asked questions designed to uncover unhealthy conditions present in the islands, they were often reminded that lobbying for special interests, legislative and voting blocs, business combinations, etc., were to be found quite generally on the mainland. Since they could not deny the facts, the committee was almost driven into the illogical admission that conditions in Hawaii would have to be far superior to those of mainland states before she could be admitted into their political company. One committeeman rather plaintively suggested that perhaps it would be better if some of the states could return to territorial status. It was possible that, judging by Hawaii, they would be happier therein.

When the argument was advanced that Hawaii exceeded so many of the states in federal income tax payments, this drew from Senator Connally the comment that its people were fortunate to have such large taxable incomes. It is, of course, quite easy to be philosophical about the other person's tax burdens.

Apparently one weighty argument against any change of status was that Hawaii had nothing to gain. She was already happy, prosperous, and had full recognition as an integral part of the U.S. The contention was that she should remain as she is, slightly coerced but contented. It was even suggested that with a Committee on Territories of 23 members ready to support the delegate from Hawaii, Hawaii was already much better represented in Congress than if she elected two senators and a representative, a right to which she would be entitled as a state. The committee seemed to think that the Territory should be content with its present dependence and privileges[1] rather than be concerned about rights and independence. Only two main reasons were brought forward for preventing Hawaii from treading the same path that has led other parts of the United States through territorial status to statehood.

[1]Hawaii, as a Territory, must be included, by special provision, in many Federal grants made to States.

The first objection was that in spite of all appearances of happiness, prosperity, and social welfare, the islands were suffering from a most unhealthy state of misgovernment at the hands of that sinister quintet, the Big Five. How this power was being exerted seemed by no means clear. One witness stated that the chief influence of the Big Five in the legislature was directed towards keeping taxes down, yet others gave as a reason for opposing statehood that taxes would go up. Some favored the change in status because it would diminish the Big Five's control, others opposed it because it would give them more power. The committee endeavored to clarify this confusion of opinion by trying to pin witnesses down to specific instances of interference by the sugar interests in governmental affairs.

One witness complained that the plantations directed their employees how to vote to such an extent that independent candidates such as himself "did not at times have the chance of being considered favorably by the voters." However, this same individual was elected to the House of Representatives for several sessions and has since been chosen senator for the island where plantations are most numerous. Incidentally, his vote was the largest of any electoral district on the island. Another witness who thought that with statehood "there would be a little more increase of power" on the part of the Big Five has also been elected to the Senate from another island, supposedly dominated by the sugar planters. Even these apparently mild indictments were not supported by the facts.

How far Hawaii is from unified control is also demonstrated by the history of the 1941 legislature, in which two of the sextet of most powerful corporations disagreed over the location of a new pier on Honolulu's waterfront.[2] The members of the House were so evenly divided on the matter that a legislative deadlock resulted. This affected the passage of the important M-day bill, which received scanty consideration, and in the closing hours of the session lay disregarded on the clerk's table, despite a strenuous last-minute effort

[2] Obviously, whatever the new pier's location, it would have greatly improved Honolulu's congested harbor facilities.

of the chairman of the judiciary committee to have it passed. This neglect necessitated the calling of a special session, during which, with the former bone of contention buried, ten days of discussion and amendment were needed before the M-day measure was finally passed. Thus while the community could unite on a matter of general importance, a move that looked like an attempt to obtain a special advantage on behalf of any of the big corporations brought forth immediate and violent opposition. In the light of these facts, the accusation leveled by the author of the most recent anti-paradisiac, that the population of these islands is politically inert, or supine beneath the heel of a fascist regime, is certainly unjustified. If, as has been suggested, the people of Hawaii are merely puppets and the Big Five the puppeteers, then most of the wires seem to be crossed or broken so that we dance very badly or not at all. Altogether, the basis of complaint as to misgovernment did not seem to be very real, and the committee was compelled to regard this community in the light of individuals who cherish their griefs or are unwilling to give up a long-standing complaint. However, some other difficulties seemed more substantial, particularly the likelihood of a security-weakening conflict between civilian and military interests.

By 1937, at the time of the hearings, the shadows of war were visibly lengthening over the Pacific, and by early 1941 had come very close to the islands. Grim warnings had been issued. Back in 1935 General Drum had declared: "From the beginning of any war we are involved in, every man, woman and child becomes interested to the extent of life itself, in the defense of the islands." The people of Hawaii had not been left in doubt as to their insignificance in the military picture through an earlier statement by Admiral Stirling, then commandant at Pearl Harbor.

"There appears to be a tendency among those who have spent their lives in Hawaii to forget that the major importance of the Hawaiian Islands to the United States lies in their situation as an outpost in the Pacific and not in their agricultural and industrial wealth." Having thus limited the role of Hawaii in the national situation, the admiral went on to prescribe rule by a commission consisting of navy and army officers plus some others whose qualifications seemed to be chiefly negative; they were to be men "not imbued too deeply with the peculiar atmosphere of the islands or with the predominance of interfamily connections"; moreover, they were to be "without preconceived ideas of the value and success of the melting pot." The peculiarity of the Hawaiian atmosphere that the admiral referred to was evidently our ability to live in racially harmonious relations.

It is little wonder that, considering such pronouncements, writers have anticipated a serious conflict between military and civilian interests in the islands. Some of the trouble seems to be in the unthinking acceptance by people of the term "military outpost" as being properly applicable to Hawaii. The word outpost, in military usage, means a small place which is *primarily* of military importance, a station for a detachment of troops, usually placed, for defensive reasons, some distance from the main body's position. Only in this last particular, namely distance from the mainland, does Hawaii fit the description.

To begin with, the Territory, with its 6,453 square miles, can hardly be described as small, nor is the undue emphasis on military importance justifiable. According to data furnished to the Committee on Statehood, the total expenditures of Federal money in the Territory in the 37 years from 1900 to 1936 inclusive amounted to about 715 millions. Of this amount, 453 millions were allotted to the army and 197 millions to the navy. This left 65 millions to be spread over civilian uses. But collections of civilian taxes, customs, etc., amounted in the same period to 241 millions. This means, in effect, that Hawaii contributed 186 millions, or almost a third, of the total cost of peace-time military establishments in the islands. If Hawaii is a defense bastion, then its civilian population has helped hugely to make it so.

But this is by no means all. It is obvious that since the outbreak of war, the armed services have used our streets, highways and bridges, our hospitals, public buildings, and housing, our telephones, electric light and water supply system, all, in fact of the facilities that have made the islands habitable. It may well be asked if this is the civilian contribution that might be naturally expected of a place whose major importance to the United States is "as an outpost in the Pacific"? If this view of the islands' importance had been accepted at annexation, and they had been taken over for purely military purposes, then it would be proper also to suggest that many billions of dollars and years of effort would have been necessary to provide the facilities that the armed forces have so freely used. The civilian stake in the country is too great to be lightly brushed aside as of little national significance.

Hawaii is, of course, too populous and too productive and therefore too important to the nation in other ways, to be considered a mere outpost. The Pacific Coast is, as we all know, mainland America's first line of defense, yet the people of California and Washington would certainly resent any suggestion that their major importance to the United States was military, and that therefore they should be controlled in peace as well as in war by a military commission. To designate Hawaii as a "sugar-coated fortress" is just as much a gross misplacement of emphasis as it would be to call it "a fortified sugar mill."

Fortunately, the anticipated conflict with regard to the status of Hawaii did not occur. According to Barber, the opposing parties were to be, on the one hand, the military authorities who contend that "as a defense outpost, the islands belong to the nation, not to a favored few, whose forebears happened to get there first," and on the other, the missionary families seeking to retain their economic control. The obvious comment is, of course, that the islands for over forty years *have* belonged to the nation, but this situation is by no means inconsistent with the existence of private enterprise.

As events have proved, an excellent working partnership has been established between civilian interests and the military authority. At the first outbreak of war, plantation equipment was at once placed at the disposal of the armed forces, large areas of productive cane land were sacrificed to military necessities, all kinds of restrictions on plantation construction, repairs, supplies, and working activities were more or less cheerfully accepted. For their part, military leaders have recognized that Hawaii as a productive center of utmost importance has claims to consideration, and that the output of sugar, pineapples, island beef, milk, vegetables, etc., should be increased rather than diminished. As a matter of fact, civilian participation in war activities is as marked in Hawaii as it is in any other part of this country. Certainly the war seems much more real than it does to many other places in America.

Incidentally, Barber's book provides proof that civilian foresight as to the probable effects of war on the islands was all too fully justified. Written a year before Pearl Harbor, his words were almost prophetic.

"For obvious reasons of geography, Hawaii's civilians visualize a war with Japan as just about the worst thing that could happen to the islands. Residents would be in the midst of the fray, subject to a multitude of nerve-wracking uncertainties. They might be bombarded by the Japanese fleet, bombed by planes based on Japanese aircraft carriers, starved by enemy blockade cutting off commerce with the mainland." Most of these misfortunes, to greater or less degree, came to Hawaii. Happily, some other dire happenings envisaged, such as paratroop landings and sabotage by disloyal elements, did not occur, though they were not outside the bounds of possibility.

In contrast with this awareness of imminent danger among the residents of the islands, a statement by the chairman of the Committee (Senator King of Utah) may be cited. It is typical of American complacency at that time.

"I have never entertained any undue fear that Japan would attack the United States. It is too absurd. We are impregnable to the attack of Japan and any ally she might have. The whole world could not attack the United States with any degree of success."[3]

During the hearings, the question of the loyalty of American

[3] Statehood for Hawaii. Hearings before the Joint Committee on Hawaii. Congress of the United States. U. S. Government Printing Office, 1938. See p. 145.

Japanese was frequently raised, either through the committee's questions or by direct testimony. It is noteworthy, however, that some who feared the domination of island affairs by the sugar plantations and agents did not believe there was any danger of disloyalty. Among the arguments for statehood, Delegate King's testimony was most positive in regard to the allegiance of the American Japanese group. "Absolutely no one who knows the Japanese, who has worked with them, and who has lived with them, or who has taught them, has the slightest doubt about their fundamental loyalty to America and its ideals, and their desire to fit themselves as American citizens, in which desire they have achieved a great deal of success in a very short time."[5]

Events, as we all know, have fully borne out the delegate's confidence. For a time reports of sabotage and fifth column activities were prevalent on the mainland, some of them so absurd that they seem suited only to a moronic level of credulity. There was, for example, that widely spread story of arrows cut in the sugar cane to direct enemy aviators to Pearl Harbor. To think that men with a shred of intelligence would fly around looking for a compass needle in a canefield when all Pearl Harbor lay stretched out in front of them is ridiculous, yet after a year had elapsed persons newly arrived from the mainland were inquiring as to the truth of the story. Another entirely baseless report was that in the midst of the attack, a Japanese drove a milk wagon on to Hickam Field, dropped the sides of his truck and mowed down our men with a murderous fire from concealed machineguns. Still another allegation was that the Japanese used jalopies to block the roads to Pearl Harbor, thus preventing assistance from reaching the Navy Yard. Every resident of Hawaii knows that all jalopies were at that time seventh day adventists, appearing for their weekly airing every Sunday. No doubt, on the fateful seventh, the roads to Pearl Harbor bore their quota of weekly Japanese excursionists.

----

[4] Some sensitiveness has been displayed by this group with regard to their designation. No stigma is attached to Anglo-Indian or American Indian nor should there be to American Japanese.

[5] Loc. cit., p. 573.

As to the young Americans of Japanese ancestry, their professions of loyalty to America have been amply translated into deeds. The exploits and fighting spirit of these young men have been spread on the records of heroic action in this war. Many of them have evinced an almost passionate determination to fight, and if need be, die for this country. The question of the loyalty of this group is now beyond the pale of discussion.

On the other hand, though the belief that the overwhelming majority of the American Japanese are loyal seems justified, it is too much to expect that a few at least would not be uncertain in their allegiance. There are those who hold that a successful invasion of Hawaii by the Japanese enemy would have brought to light many rifts in the loyalty of the Nisei, or first generation Japanese Americans. They maintain that the disloyal elements did not have the opportunity to show their hand, and point out that on Niihau, the only place where a Japanese aviator made a landing, he found no difficulty in finding an ally who had been born in the islands. This much may be admitted—that if a successful invasion had taken place, many of Hawaii's Japanese-born citizens would have found themselves in a most tragic situation, caught between the upper and the nether millstones. To have gone over to the enemy would have meant being branded as traitors, while if they had remained loyal to America, they would have suffered a far worse fate than the whites.

As regards those aliens who might have been inclined to assist the enemy, they were taken care of effectively by that branch of the service whose duty it was to prepare safeguards against the day when war with Japan would take place. The job of nipping in the bud subversive moves was so well done as to suggest that had our near vision been as good as our long term planning, the disaster at Pearl Harbor would never have occurred.

Sufficient credit has not been given to the military authorities, particularly the G-2 section, for their wise and efficient handling of a difficult situation. After the Pearl Harbor attack there was every opportunity for harsh and repressive measures, and under the circumstances such action would have gone unquestioned. The restraint of the military intelligence group is beyond all praise. They had the power in their hands and used it sparingly. At the same time they must have withstood all kinds of pressure, both from within and without the army, to take stronger action. The surprising thing is that it was the military who stood between the local Japanese and the rest of the community, many of whom demanded repressive measures. Not only for real intelligence operating in a delicate situation, but also for their vindication of Hawaii in respect to accusations of sabotage leveled against the Territory, we owe the officers directing G-2 a great debt. They exhibited a fine blend of tolerance and justice, and at the same time they provided adequately for the community's safety against possible disloyal activities.

If fear of the Hawaiian-born Japanese has been dissipated by the events of the past three years, there still remains a considerable distrust or dislike of the prospects of Japanese political domination of the Territory after the war. This may be called prejudice, but it is nevertheless based on the recognition of racial differences that actually exist. Man is a sociable animal and likes to foregather with individuals of his own kind. Like tends to cleave to like, so that whites are more at home among whites, blacks among blacks, orientals among orientals. This, however, is no innate tendency but one which is the result of circumstances. There is no inborn love of country either, but there is in most individuals a feeling of greater happiness or security among surroundings that we are familiar with, and which we thoroughly understand. The people we grew up with, the kinds of faces we saw, the manner of speech we were accustomed to, plus the familiar physical surroundings, underlie that attachment to home which is extended into love of country, national pride, patriotism. Any intrusion of individuals of an alien culture or physical appearance is often resented by the group. It is a resentment which works both ways. A difference that is easily apparent, such as color, is the most effective stamp of the outsider and therefore constitutes the most serious barrier to acceptance within the group, regardless of political affiliations. This consciousness of differences becomes racial prejudice only when it gives rise to political, social, or educational injustice. These things being so, and regardless of the fact that relations between racial groups in Hawaii are exceptionally good, we shall no doubt continue to live apart and may tend to vote differently.

If human society should become so thoroughly homogeneous that it would no longer consist of aggregations of peoples of different appearances, tastes, habits, religions, and languages, then the world would be free from parochial, national, or racial feelings. But at present the sense of "belonging" is very important to us. Consider the efforts we expend to make ourselves as much like our neighbors as possible, to signify our oneness with the group by the types of shoes we wear, in the way we wear our ties or brush our hair, etc. No matter how strong the individual's urge for variety, it operates strictly within the bounds of variability set by the group.

Possibly, if the time ever comes when a man can say that he is an Englishman, or an American, or even a New Yorker without some sense of separateness, then much of the spice of living will have departed. If travel becomes so easy and habitual that most of us will no longer have a home to go to, then international barriers will completely disappear, and the physical differences that distinguish racial groups will cease to have any significance. But that time is not yet. In the meanwhile, a realistic attitude will induce the recognition of the divisions between peoples, with every effort and even sacrifice devoted to removing the causes of inter-racial irritation and friction. That, at least, is the Hawaiian way.

How will this consciousness of differences affect Hawaii's political situation? It is idle to pretend that racial factors have no influence on bloc voting. The whites certainly exhibit this trend and so do the Hawaiians—and why not the Japanese? But race is rarely the most important factor in obtaining electoral support. Other things being equal, as one witness before the committee on statehood put it, voters will tend to vote for persons of their own race—but things are very seldom equal. The evidence of political observers in Hawaii agreed that the American Japanese were just as likely to be divided politically among themselves as any other group. One American Japanese lawyer asserted that "the time will never come when the voters of Japanese descent will vote alike *en masse*." Another attorney, a part-Hawaiian, stated on behalf of his racial group that "they have no fear of Japanese domination."

With people of Japanese blood making up nearly 40 per cent of the population, the possibility of the election of Japanese Americans to the highest offices under statehood cannot be discounted entirely. Voters who dislike this idea may oppose it by all constitutional means, but it is no valid reason for denying the rights of self-government to the people of the Territory.

As a logical sequence, Hawaii should proceed to full statehood, or should, as an alternative, be governed by a commission. If the argument against statehood is accepted, namely that we are unready or unfit for self-government, those conditions, in the minds of objectors, are not likely to change, and we might as well accept the alternative. But under those circumstances, American citizenship in the islands will have lost its meaning. There surely can be no such thing as a half-American, any more than there can be anyone half-slave, half-free. To treat the people of an integral part of America by any other than democratic principles is to deny those principles.

As regards the rights and responsibilities of American Japanese, the whole question has been brought to a crisis by the war. At one time the restricted citizenship idea found expression in a policy of not asking, nor allowing, this group to take their share even in home defense. They were, on one pretext or another, excluded from the National Guard. This action was at least consistent; but with the enlistment of the A.J.A.'s and their excellent war record, the situation has been completely changed. Opposition to their full citizenship, with all its rights and privileges and duties, is no longer justifiable. It will come with the least grace from the military authorities who accepted their military services and sacrifices. Opinions will differ on the wisdom of enlisting A.J.A.'s and allowing them to fight as a unit, but once that course was taken its implications are indisputable.

As to the alternative plan of government for Hawaii, commission rule, it must be admitted that it has its advantages. It is more effective in certain emergencies, since democratic processes are slow and cumbersome. The turmoil of politics is avoided and community problems can be more directly and decisively attacked. But commission government will not change the character or complexion of our population, and in the greatest crisis of all—an outbreak of war—the military must again assume full control. With all the advantages of commission rule there are decided drawbacks. Without either the correctives or the spur of public opinion, progress loses its impetus. Clumsy and time-consuming as democratic processes undoubtedly are, changes are hammered out on the anvil of public discussion and criticism. But there is surely no need to repeat the arguments for democracy. One inconsistency in the dispute should be noted. It is usually those people who condemn centralized commercial control most heartily who favor the centralization of governmental authority in the hands of a small commission. Democracy claims the right to make its own mistakes, because, no matter who makes the wrong decisions, it is the people who pay for them.

The attitude of the common man towards statehood is excellently exemplified by the evidence of an independent, long-time resident of Hawaii, who was never employed by the big commercial interests, held no public office, nor employed any other means to make his name well known in the Territory. Yet his statement seemed so fair and reasonable that a substantial excerpt from his testimony has been included in an appendix to this chapter. Tolerance and good humor, now characteristic of Hawaii, or what Culman calls "the spirit of Aloha Oe," can be relied upon as the best solvent of future difficulties.

If Hawaii has inherited perplexities due to the mixed nature of our population, we have amassed credits that more than balance the ledger. The sugar planters imported problems as well as laborers from Madeira, China, Japan, and the Philippines. But this mass immigration from lands of less, to one of far greater opportunity has resulted in the release of extraordinary amounts of repressed mental energy. It tapped unlooked-for reservoirs of latent intelligence. Of these contract laborers or their descendants, it can be affirmed that there is no single group which has not contributed greatly to the life of the land. There are Portuguese doctors, dentists, lawyers, judges, legislators, teachers. Chinese and Japanese names appear equally among the lists of professional men. Some of the best students who have passed through the University have been orientals. The Filipinos are also beginning to make their contribution. It is most unlikely that immigrants of similarly low industrial status, drawn from London or Chicago, would have exhibited such a flowering of talent as these descendants of coolie laborers.

The Hawaiians have been the universal blood donors to the melting-pot and exhibit every possible kind of interracial progeny. They have disproved, for all time, the theory that mixed bloods are necessarily inferior. At one time the Chinese-Hawaiian cross enjoyed a deservedly high reputation, but longer experience has shown that the white-Hawaiian mixture is equally superior, while a study of a few years back indicated that the tri-cross, Chinese-white-Hawaiians, are excellently endowed from the standpoint of intelligence. Some of the highest public offices in the Territory have been held with conspicuous success by part-Hawaiians.

But in spite of these facts, the educational road in Hawaii is beset with special difficulties. Mental test results throughout the Territory indicate that the general average of tested intelligence of children in Hawaii would be some points below that of children on the mainland; that is, if the ordinary I.Q. measures are used. An unfortunate feature of life in the islands, and one which affects these I.Q. scores, is the restricted English that is commonly used, and which is somewhat allied to "pidgin."[6] How much this poverty of expression affects the test scores is impossible to measure exactly, but it has undoubted effects.

Teaching, or use of better English, then, remains one of Hawaii's chief perplexities. If the lag in language development could

[6] The Hawaiian form is so superior in content and complexity to that used in other parts of the Pacific or in Africa that it should hardly be called pidgin English. It is, however, restricted enough.

be made up, then the educational sights could be raised all over the Territory, in every department of education from the primary grades to university levels. At present, speech habits are being taught at the University, which would be better inculcated in the kindergarten. Consequently, students are being graduated with college degrees with a knowledge of English that leaves much to be desired. However, this complaint affects mainland colleges as well.[7]

Lest the picture of the mental status of Hawaii's population be considered too discouraging, it should be stated that in the tests of practical intelligence as distinguished from verbal abilities, the children of the Territory are quite up to the mainland average, and this fact accords well with the facts of industrial progress. This, at least, is not one of our perplexities.

Because the peoples of Hawaii have learned to live together, it is not strange that from this amity have sprung several developments of international importance. The Pan-Pacific Union, the result of one man's unrewarded vision,[8] has set the keynote for subsequent developments. Out of this Union came the plan of scientific congresses which were held periodically around the Pacific Basin. Then followed the Institute of Pacific Relations, dedicated to better international understanding and good will. In some respects these developments were fifty years ahead of their times. In the light of events, their attitudes were too idealistic, but their efforts were a thousand times more admirable in every way than do-nothing isolationism. After the specter of militarism has been laid, there may be a healing of wounds, but any hope of permanent peace must be based on a common understanding. The I.P.R. may yet become the Parliament of the Pacific.

What is the reason for Hawaii's tolerant spirit? There are some who believe that we take our racial problems lightly because we take all of our problems in the same careless or happy-go-lucky

[7] If the reader cares to institute a proof of this statement, he might test his college classmates on the pronunciation of such common words as *interesting, premier, inquiry, penalize,* or the spelling and pronunciation of the less familiar *crucial, portentous, erudite.* He will uncover a most remarkable confusion of tongues among supposedly well-educated people.

[8] Alexander Hume Ford.

fashion. They contend that our spirit of Aloha Oe is basically nothing but an easy-going habit, born of an equable climate and pleasant living, which tends to develop a *laissez faire,* live-and-let-live philosophy. If this were so, it would be indeed fortunate, for then the remedy for many national or racial animosities so acute elsewhere, would be wholesale extended vacations in Hawaii. But sometimes this paradise complex works against us. The University once lost the continuation of a Foundation grant through the report of a too-enthusiastic visitor who asked: "How can anyone do serious scientific work in such beautiful surroundings?" The answer to this is to be found in the record of Hawaii's scientific and social achievements.

The reason for Hawaiian tolerance goes beyond the facts of climate. A most important factor is that no one racial group has been numerically strong enough to overshadow and dominate the rest. We have no minority grievances because there is no majority to impose them. With, roughly speaking, 30,000 Portuguese, 30,000 Chinese, 40,000 Filipinos, 50,000 part-Hawaiians, 5,000 Puerto Ricans, 5,000 Koreans, and 70,000 of Northwest European stock, there are so many minorities that there has been no great imbalance. The increase of people of Japanese descent to 160,000 is the development that tends to destroy the symmetry of the picture. They threaten to come nearest to being a dominant group. Hitherto, government has been carried on by means of a coalition between whites and part-Hawaiians. Two factors could restore the balance; one is the increase by birth of the part-Hawaiian group, the other the increase by immigration of the whites. If it were not for their predominant numbers, little would be heard of dislike for people of Japanese blood. An improvement of interracial balance would be to the advantage of all, including the Japanese.

The question then arises—what has Hawaii to offer, what claims does it make on interest and affection so that people will wish to make this their home? Enough has been said to prove that here is no elysium, but nevertheless a better place in which to live than most human beings have a right to expect. We are justly proud of our tolerance; we have really learned to live together on good terms with people of diverse colors, national backgrounds, social customs, and ideas. Perhaps this is because we are all immigrants together; perhaps it is partly the result of a climate that blunts the edge of nervous irritation; or it may be that Polynesian good nature is some-how contagious. For these, or other reasons, the asperities of life become softened, and yet we are not wholly a prey to that unseeing complacency to which continental communities are prone.

Humor, they say, is the saving grace, and good humor may yet be the great solvent of Hawaii's perplexities; if so, it will be con-tributed in large part by Hawaiians. Due mainly to the fact that their introduction to civilization was through men of good will, these people have never become embittered. They have never been made to feel inferior; on the contrary, they have continued to play a large part in the government of their homeland. Hawaiians have retained their good humor and their hospitable habits. They have kept the stage set for good will.

Perhaps they owe some of their evenness of temperament to the fact that their lot has been cast in pleasant places, for, as we shall see, each of the Hawaiian islands has its special interest and charm. The Polynesian has never been insensitive to beauty, and ease of mind and heart can readily be transmuted into laughter; and laugh-ter, as we know, is infectious.

And, finally, we have one great advantage. There is hardly a spot in the islands where a man cannot step aside from his daily work and worries, and refresh himself with some glimpse of satis-fying beauty. Perhaps we have managed to slow down the pace of modern living, because we have, round about us, a land of un-changing loveliness, soft skies and wide horizons upon which the clouds ceaselessly model themselves, a fringing ocean whose depths and shallows are a mixing bowl for almost unbelievable colors. These things by themselves are nothing if they exist side-by-side with human misery and ill-will. But linked with a contented spirit, they spell unusual happiness. This beauty all the islands share. In the remaining chapters some attention must be paid to those things that account for the note of deep interest and affection which you can detect when people say: "These islands are my home."

APPENDIX TO CHAPTER VI

HAWAII STATEHOOD HEARINGS

TESTIMONY OF H. CULMAN

Mr. CULMAN. My name is H. Culman. I came to Hawaii in 1902, and have been here ever since. All my interests are centered in this Territory. I am engaged at the present time in renting cottages. . . .

Senator CONNALLY. Are you for statehood?

The WITNESS. I am for statehood. During my 35 years here I have never known of communism amongst the Japanese. They are the most law-abiding people I have ever seen. I was born on the eastern coast, in Philadelphia. I worked my way across the continent, doing all kinds of labor, in order to earn livelihood, partly from choice and partly from necessity. The conditions I found in Hawaii were such that, after I had served a 2 weeks' probation, after which the employer I came to work for told me he was glad I had come, and I told him if he was not satisfied to let me know —that I would go back and no harm done. Upon that assurance I told him that if I was satisfactory I would send for my wife, and I wrote back to her by that mail out, after I had been here 2 weeks, and I told her there were bigger opportunities in Hawaii than in any place I had been. I knew the United States at that time from the Atlantic coast to the Pacific coast as a working man, and I felt Hawaii offered opportunities from the point of view of the working man. My experience down here has been such that I was justified in my judgment. I am here to say to you that there were then and there are now more opportunities in the Hawaiian Islands for the man who needs to work for a living than any place I know anything about, and under more agreeable conditions than any place else.

Regarding our desire for statehood, I have in the last few days copied the tactics of our friend, the good Senator over here, who told us he had gone out on the street and indiscriminately button-holed the people he saw and asked them how he (they) stood on statehood. He told us he has asked approximately a hundred people whom he met, at random, about how they felt on the question of statehood, and invariably the answer was, without a single exception, that they were not in favor of statehood. I was much interested in his experiment, and I have done the same thing since I heard him. I took my cue from him. Surprisingly I had a similar experience. A few were in favor of statehood, but the vast majority were against statehood. I was surprised.

By the CHAIRMAN:

Q. Did you talk to all classes, American and other Anglo-Saxon, Japanese, and Hawaiians? A. Yes. I might say the last one I asked was a foreman of a street gang on Kalakaua Avenue. I happened to be passing, and I asked him how he stood on the subject and he said he was against statehood and I asked him why and he said, "I am afraid of the Big Five." That has invariably been the answer when I asked the reason, "I am afraid of the Big Five."

Q. How many people did you talk to? A. Probably 25. The second objection they put forth was fear of the Japanese. Those are the two things they are afraid of—the hold which the Big Five exerts, and the problem of the Japanese, which is reinforced by the racial prejudice which at times expresses itself like this: "How would you like to have a Japanese governor? If we have statehood they will outvote us very soon, and then how would you like to have a Japanese governor?" My answer has been, "I have no objection. I am a man who believes in the democratic form of government, that the majority shall rule, and if the majority wants to elect a Japanese to the governorship, I should bow in submission to that choice.

I believe in democracy. I believe the cure for democracy, if there is any cure needed, is more democracy. I believe, under state government, we would have the opportunity to make our own mistakes, and the privilege of suffering for those mistakes, if we make mistakes, and I know we will make mistakes, and we will have in our hands the means of correcting those mistakes. At the present time we don't have that opportunity. We let Washington make our mistakes for us, and we suffer for those mistakes and we have no remedy at our disposal. I am not sure that statehood would be of any advantage at all, except for that reason, that we would administer our own affairs. I am in favor of it, from top to bottom. If I were certain that under statehood we would have to suffer ills we don't have to suffer today, I still would be in favor of it.

I know your very searching investigator, the gentleman from Oklahoma, wants to know what advantages the United States would gain by granting us the status of a State. A bit more loyalty, Mr. Chairman, if possible than you have at the present time; but the question is not what the United States would gain, as I see it, but whether we are or are not ready to be given statehood, not whether we would be better off with it or without it.

As far as the domination of the Big Five is concerned, I came down here as a mechanic, and a blacklisted mechanic at that. The control of the Big Five has not been so prohibitive——

Representative Hope. What do you mean when you say you were a blacklisted mechanic? By whom were you blacklisted?

The Witness. By the Chamber of Commerce of San Francisco, because I was able to talk sensibly to my fellow workmen. I am not the only one in the United States who was blacklisted for the same offense. Fortunately I escaped the jail. Some of my fellow workers did not escape it, and yet they committed no worse crime than I have committed.

As I was saying, the domination of the Big Five was not so very repressive, but what I have prospered in this Territory over and beyond what any man I have ever known in the same number of years, in my position, has prospered. I have not the slightest doubt but that there is a tremendous pressure exerted by what is known as the Big Five, but it is a different caliber than the pressure exerted by big business in other parts of the country. You visitors have probably felt what I would describe under the general terms of Aloha Oe. Even those repressive matters are tinctured with the spirit of Aloha Oe, in the common man on the street as well as by those in control. That there is a great deal of pressure and intimidation is beyond cavil, but that it is more than elsewhere I dispute.

PART TWO

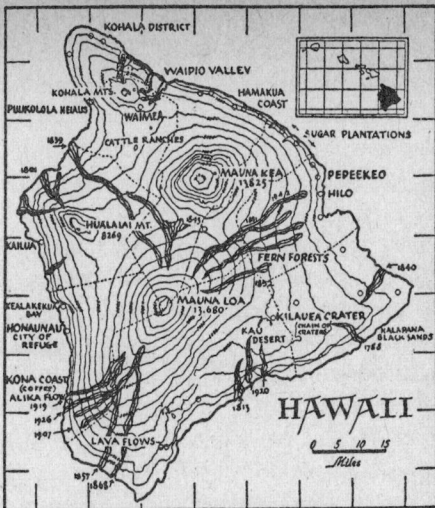

The map shows the island of Hawaii with the following labels:

KOHALA DISTRICT
WAIPIO VALLEY
KOHALA MTS.
PUUKOHOLA HEIAUS
WAIMEA
HAMAKUA COAST
CATTLE RANCHES
SUGAR PLANTATIONS
MAUNA KEA 13,825
PEPEEKEO
HILO
HUALALAI MT. 8269
KAILUA
FERN FORESTS
KEALAKEKUA
MAUNA LOA 13,680
HONAUNAU CITY OF REFUGE
KILAUEA CRATER (CHAIN OF CRATERS)
KAU DESERT
KALAPANA BLACK SANDS
KONA COAST (COFFEE)
ALIKA FLOW 1919
1926
1907
LAVA FLOWS
1887
1868

HAWAII

0 5 10 15
Miles

CHAPTER VII

Terra Infirma

THIS EARTH is not solid, and Mother Nature can forget all her maternal dignity and kindliness and be just as unpredictable and vindictive as any old harridan. These are some of the lessons that the visitor can learn in Hawaii. If he thinks them hardly worth while coming a couple of thousand miles to gain, he can forget his lessons and go ice-skating in the tropics—provided, of course, he brings his equipment with him. Lake Waiau's few acres, at more than thirteen thousand feet elevation atop Mauna Kea, may give him the opportunity. At times there is even skiing to be had, at 20° latitude—probably the nearest approach to a climatic paradox that the visitor's mind can appreciate.

He may even see actually as well as visually an island rising out of the sea, for he is coming to a land half of which is built and the other half building. If fortunate enough, he can watch the process of construction at close hand—the pouring out from cracks on Mauna Loa of billions of tons of molten rock covering thousands of acres. He may realize how infinitely long, in terms of man's experience, the process is, for Mauna Loa also approaches fourteen thousand feet in elevation.

Yet these mountain masses are singularly unimpressive, perhaps because two thirds of their bulk lie beneath the sea. A few miles off the coast is an Hawaiian deep, with soundings nearly four miles in vertical depth. If the waters should recede, these two mountains would appear as peaks higher than Everest.

Naturally, such a steep mass, though buttressed with a mighty weight of water, is none too stable. Part of the island northeast from the volcano of Kilauea is inclined to slip off into the sea. These earth movements are communicated to the ocean in the form of the displacement of untold billions of tons of surface water, which heaps itself up into what we inaptly call tidal waves, moving at an unimaginable rate for waves—three to five hundred miles an hour —and are certainly not tidal.

Your first view of Hawaii's highest mountain begins with the five-hundred-foot cliffs that represent its broken seaward edges. You see three zones: the light green of the sugar cane reaching to about 1,500 feet elevation, the more somber green of the rain forest running to 9,000 feet, and finally the bare, cinder-strewn top of the mountain. Sugar mills are perched just above the edge of the sheer cliffs, in between narrow gulches marked by waterfalls tumbling into the sea. These mills were built in the days of sail, and all their heavy equipment had to be carried ashore—fifteen-ton mill-rollers lashed across pairs of row-boats, and then hauled up the cliff face. It is a reminder that all the amphibious feats do not belong in our day. The machinery for the mills on the Hamakua coast was installed without loss, and the Hilo folk have a ready explanation for this achievement. The engineers were Scotch, and unused to losing anything.

These Hawaiian mountains stay in the background—they seldom dominate the scene. Facts and figures usually detract from appearances, but here the reverse is the case. Elsewhere civic pride would have found some means to emblazon those thirteen thousand eight hundred and twenty-five feet of elevation on Mauna Kea's sides so that he who runs, or rides, or buys real estate might read. Tourist literature refers to the mountain standing alone in majesty —but majesty should never stand alone. It needs the comparison of lesser dignitaries to make it impressive. Perhaps it is the fact that you are looking up an inclined plane to the mountain tops with no lesser heights between, that dwarfs their stature. To appreciate height you must yourself be elevated. So the only realistic views you can get of these Hawaiian altitudes is from the air. When the plane is high enough above the sea to iron out the largest waves to the merest suspicion of wrinkles, you may look away to find Mauna Kea actually towering above you.

All in all, the island of Hawaii succeeds better than any other place on earth in playing down its scenic glories. Even when you leave Hilo for what is proudly advertised as the greatest active crater in the world, there is no build-up for the scene itself.

The strip of concrete road unwinds slowly through a tangle of fern trees, ohias, and purple-flowered Brazilian lasiandras. This is locally called a forest, though in Australia or South Africa it would be merely bush, though of a particularly pretty and verdant kind. Only in one place in thirty miles does the road climb quickly enough to top the forest and give you a view of Mauna Kea in the distance. The experience is rare enough to warrant naming this shoulder of land "Mountain View." Otherwise, the sole indication of altitude is the increasing coolness and some change in the vegetation, not so much in the native flora but in the appearance of wild roses, fuchsias and imported trees of the cedar and cypress family that seldom flourish in the low lands. Still there is no hint of marvels.

Even when, a mile or so past the National Park gates, you roll out on to the edge of the crater, you will find nothing breathtaking. Mauna Loa looms in front of you, a smooth bank giving absolutely no suggestion of height or grandeur. It offers nothing but a rounded brown expanse with irregular dark blotches here and there, as though some artist had done a clumsy job of camouflage. You may mistake these blotches for cloud shadows except that they do not drift as shadows do. Only when you have crossed similar strips on the road to Kona will you recognize them as fields of out-poured lava, miles wide and many miles in length. These be marvels, but marvelously well concealed.

The crater of Kilauea itself cannot be accused of blatant over-display. To begin with, it is not, to anyone's notion, a mountain at all, but a bulge that has imperceptibly lifted itself to an elevation of four thousand feet. The visitor may be told on good authority that a long distance off towards the sea there is a sharp declivity, but nowhere for miles around the crater is there a slope steep enough to bowl a hoop down. This is a mountain top without visible means of support. Only your skin tells you that you are up in the air, for even in July and August fires burn on Kilauea hearths, and by sunset people are crowding close to the blaze. At the old Volcano House the host, George Lycurgus, used to boast that his fire had never been put out for fifty years, until, finally, the fire extinguished its own record by burning the house down.

The crater itself, five hundred feet below the Volcano House, is weird rather than wonderful. Halemaumau, where activity centers, is a pit within the pit, a circular funnel 2½ miles away across the lava. A winding trail takes you over thirty foot deep earthquake cracks lined with ferns, until you reach the lower levels. Then the waves of congealed lava begin, to roll confusedly in every direction until they lap against the rubbly cliffs that skirt the main crater for eight miles around. No matter how you try, you cannot describe the scene except in terms of movement, which is most assuredly not there. The desert is timeless because nothing there indicates change. In Kilauea time is arrested. All this turmoil is merely held in suspension. These lava waves, glistening black at close view, but sooty grey in the distance, once rolled and will roll again. There is no rest, merely immobilization. Nor is there method in their madness. They heap themselves up without design or order and so the trail winds between black billows or across ropy outpourings, signifying all manner of pressure conflicts.

Light clouds of steam drift across from the west wall or puff out of widely scattered cracks or vents in the crater floor, yet there is little suggestion of imprisoned power. Even Halemaumau is nothing but a great hole in the ground into which at intervals avalanches of rock cascade from the crumbling walls. The debris of these rock falls is scattered untidily over the floor of smooth black lava that has welled up through the bottom at intervals in the past twenty years. There are some fume and smoke rising from a heap of talus three hundred feet down, but the stage is empty. The whole scene suggests volcanic force about as much as a steaming kettle resembles a yard full of locomotive engines.

But some day what has happened so often will happen again. What the scientists call harmonic tremor, a mild volcanic *paralysis agitans,* will set in around the pit, signifying an upsurge of lava far below; the fume may get thin and blue, marking increased heat. Then, usually very quietly, the black floor opens to reveal a red eye of fire, the initial welling becomes a fountain, a spatter cone is built, and soon the fiery stuff is cascading down its sides, breaking down and melting into its substance the crust of the old flow, forming pools and lakes that glow and congeal, and glow again.

If the eruption is strong, there may soon be a dozen fountains spouting fire, and separated by slag heaps between which the molten rivers run. The whole great pit comes alive with rumblings and hissings and tossing of fiery fragments a hundred feet in the air. Thus the cauldron may fill for weeks or months, until the volcano's rusty throat, 1,500 feet at its deepest, is ready to brim over into the main crater.

Then the full show for which Halemaumau provided only the dress rehearsals is on. Such was the state of the main crater when the Reverend William Ellis first visited and described the outer pit in 1823. He writes of "a vast flood of liquid fire in a state of terrific ebullition, rolling to and fro its fiery surge of flaming billows." Perhaps you had better hold this description in mind as you walk over the floor of the crater, once the site of this activity. Feeding this burning lake were no less than fifty-one craters in cones of various shapes, twenty-two of them constantly vomiting lava, and the others smoking and intermittently exploding into fiery columns. In those days perdition was pictured in lurid colors for the benefit of the sinner, but no such word-painting of hell itself could have approached Ellis' actual experience. With true missionary zeal he threw at the spectacle every appropriate adjective he could find. Within the space of eight lines of print, he uses brilliant, boiling, raging, flaming, agitated, molten, glowing, tumultuous, dazzling, billowing, to describe the display until, hyperbole exhausted, he descends to the anti-climax "ignited stones." Yet Ellis is regarded as one of the most restrained missionary writers of his time.

In sober fact, molten rock is the term which in its connotation of tremendous heat may bring to the mind of the visitor some realization of what Ellis seeks to describe. At least the author spares us "holocaust" and "inferno"—not that these names are unjustified, but something in the way of language should be left to those who come after, and who wish to make their own attempt to portray the unportrayable.

But if adequate description is impossible, actual narration is within our scope. And for calm—too calm—reporting of the facts, may the writer commend to attention the "Volcano Letter" issued weekly or monthly for many years by Dr. T. A. Jaggar and his staff at the Kilauea Observatory. For a more comprehensive survey of events similarly distinguished by scientific restraint there is his latest book, *Volcanoes Declare War*.

If any scientist has a right to an air of cool detachment as regards burning volcanoes, Jaggar has. He has lived on terms of closer intimacy with active craters than any other man that should not be alive. He, more than anyone else, has justification for refusing to get verbally excited over Pele's pyrotechnics, for he was the first volcanologist to set foot on Martinique in 1902, immediately after a lateral blast of super-scorching fumes had seared the lives out

Photos by R. J. Baker

Upper. The pit fills and overflows into the main crater

Lower. The stick bursts into flame when pushed into a live "lava toe"

Photos by Hawaiian Airlines

Upper. A river of lava flowed down the Koolau Gap into the
cloud-covered ocean

Lower. The cinder-strewn sides of Haleakala crater. The ash
cone at the bottom of the pit (lower left) is 900 feet high

of that city's thirty thousand inhabitants, leaving only one man alive, a prisoner locked away in a dungeon underground. When Jaggar talks about disaster, he means just that, for earthquakes and eruptions are his familiars. It is doubtful if a whole twelve months of his life for forty years has been spent on ground that was not actually shaking.

And so for the benefit of the great mass of visitors to Kilauea who have seen merely the kettle steaming, and are unable to imagine the unimaginable, we might follow Jaggar in his sober attempt to tell what actually happens when a major earth disturbance hits a center of population as it did Napier, New Zealand, in 1931.

"Wherever you are," says Jaggar, "in your car, on the road, standing indoors, standing outdoors, suddenly there comes a tremendous crash like an explosion and down you go. Everything goes down, houses, bridges, gulches, cliffs; fires start, road-fills crack open, automobiles fall into the cracks, wharfs are all down, some of the shipping is grounded, the breakwater has settled out of sight in some places. Rescue parties are organized to dig out the wounded. Explosives must be used to demolish tottering masonry, which is likely to kill more people, with the thousands of shocks that are coming after."

To this picture he adds one last detail. In speaking of precautions against looting, he says, "The contents of the banks are laid wide open as well as many other valuable safes and cash drawers." Then he coldly remarks: "There is no use having hysterics about these things." But, on the other hand, one of these places might be where we bank *our* money.

He then proceeds to outline for these people who live thirty miles away from the largest active crater in the world, and feel quite happy about it, the steps that must be taken after such a happening to establish and purify the water supply, dispose of sewage, put up tents for houses and hospitals, provide free meals—all the things that follow when fifteen hundred people die and another five thousand are left homeless and temporarily starving.

For the encouragement of the timid tourist, we might say that the residents of Hawaii are a tough breed. Other people run away from their volcanic eruptions—we run to them. As to earthquakes, we take them in our stride. But that is an over-statement. We take them sitting down, as you shall later see. Only on two occasions in a hundred and fifty years is there any record of people running away from Kilauea. Some did not run far or fast enough.

The first of these destructive outbursts occurred in 1790[1] when Keoua, one of the high chiefs of the island sent a punitive expedition across from Hilo to Kau. The army with its campfollowers and supply-train of pigs camped near the crater. Perhaps there was confusion of counsels, or possibly for safety's sake, they decided to separate into three groups. That night a vast cloud arose out of the pit and a shower of sand, rocks, and cinders descended upon the country for miles around. The center party was overwhelmed, probably by an outrush of super-heated air, so that they lay as though asleep, men, women, and children, where they had fallen. The rearguard, being possibly out of the line of the prevailing wind, were uninjured.

The story was told to Dibble, the historian, by the survivors, but the volcano kept its own shorthand notes of the occurrence. Tremendous thunder and lightning accompanied the cloud of ashes that billowed out of the pit, and the rain turned the finer deposits into a slime. As the natives of the advance party, who had reached the Kau desert, fled confusedly hither and thither, they left their footprints in this volcanic mud. Then came another shower of ash which filled up the prints and set like cement. The casts thus made have weathered a century and a half of erosion and are still to be seen in the desert seven miles or so from the pit. Through them you can read some of the story. Here the natives stood in confusion or fled in every direction, their terror and haste shown by the sliding tracks and the wide-spread toes. There they converged in panic-stricken groups, only to scatter once again in flight. Rarely have individuals' desperate attempts to escape immediate oblivion

[1] See also Chapter III.

resulted in such a permanent monument to their activities. Motion picture stars have adopted a similar technique in order temporarily to avoid oblivion, but Hawaii has anticipated this Hollywood touch by a hundred and fifty years.

After this dramatic episode, Pele, like the old manic-depressive she is, settled down to a prolonged period of repression, broken at intervals, particularly in 1855, by fits of superactivity. One such outburst was witnessed by William Alanson Bryan in 1909, who adds flaring, gushing, lurid, majestic, churning, seething, and inferno to the list of descriptive terms now available to the tourist. He sums up the following psychological effects common among beholders: "The wonderful and varied spectacle produces in some observers a sense of profound reverence and awe, in others a spirit of wild, child-like glee. However, one and all sooner or later grope as in the presence of the Great Unknown, and ask for an explanation of the wonders before them, so grand, so bewildering, so terrible to contemplate."

The writer's first sight of a similar happening was in 1923 in company with a rather large University party. The lava was then within fifty feet of the rim of Halemaumau, and expected soon to spill over into the main crater. Conical slag heaps seventy-five feet high floated on top of the upwelling lava column and between these cones rushed at intervals fiery rivers from the fountains that were constantly playing. There was a continuous soughing sound like a distant roaring, and a hissing as though the volcano was drawing in its breath. At first the reaction was one of awe; but reverence, we found, like sorrow, endured but for the night, and curiosity came in the morning. Instead of groping in the presence of the Great Unknown, the party one and all next day were running about on the scarcely congealed lava, breaking the crust with rocks, thrusting sticks into the cracks, twirling them around and bringing out masses of live lava. It was a favorite trick at that time to push a dime or nickel into the lump and let it set there. In half an hour the lava was cool enough to carry home. There was scarcely a mantelpiece or cabinet in Hawaii without one of these mementos. Either the depression or the march of time has accounted for their disappearance. In any case, all this points the lesson that man is not fitted to live with wonders. After his initial burst of awe has subsided, all that he can think of to do with one of Nature's greatest marvels is to poke a stick at it. We are certainly children of Nature—with the emphasis on children.

Only when the phenomenon threatens our very existence do we retain our awe, and even then familiarity tends to breed contempt. Except for publicity purposes, even the scientist becomes inured to marvels, and so we find Bryan descending to a characterization of Kilauea as "safe, and as far as volcanoes can be, regarded as perfectly tame, 'docile,' and well-behaved." But in May 1924, Kilauea itself gave the lie to "the general belief that so long as the crater remains open, as it is, there is little or no danger to be expected from it."[2] Reverence and awe—or awe without reverence — seem to be inversely proportionate to the square of the distance from which we view the spectacle—and on this occasion, Pele was so unapproachable that she was truly awful. Three people, who attempted to treat the occurrence in the accepted familiar way, paid for their presumption with their lives. Even the guests of the old Volcano House, "the very personification of hospitality and good cheer" as Bryan puts it, were jolted most inhospitably and cheerlessly into a mad rush for their ash-covered automobiles, and an evacuation to Hilo.

Volcanic phenomena seem to be usually nothing more than a sequence of unusual events so that the happenings leading up to the explosive phase did not occasion particular concern. For some months before, the lava in Halemaumau had behaved exactly like the mercury column does when the doctor takes your blood pressure—a sudden surging up, followed by a long subsidence interrupted by spasmodic rises. In one month fluctuations of as much as 35 feet in an hour were recorded, and by February 21, 1924, the lava lake was nearly 400 feet down. Then it disappeared from sight altogether, the only indication of its presence being a glow from beneath, and the occasional sound of lava splashing.

[2] Bryan, William Alanson. *Natural History of Hawaii.*

Then, in April, occurred what the volcanologists called a prolonged *mild* quaking of the ground in the Kapoho residential district east from the volcano. A block of land sank 8 to 12 feet so that at the seashore a new lagoon was formed, with pandanus and coconut palms standing in 8 feet of salt water 200 feet from the former shore line. Chasms, no doubt inconsequential, opened 20 feet wide and 6 to 14 feet deep, in one place running right through a melon patch so that the owner had to use a ladder to harvest the ripened fruit. In another place the railway line for some distance was left hanging in air—Hawaii's only elevated railway. Some cattle fell into those aforementioned "mild" cracks and were buried alive. Strange to relate, there was even a temporary evacuation of residents, not, as the "Volcano Letter" is careful to state, because of the violence of the quaking but on account of its continuity. Anywhere else but in Hawaii people would hardly have waited until the shaking became continuous.

One observer counted 238 earthquakes on a single evening between 5 and 8 o'clock — more than one a minute. This fact could have been made more impressive if some human interest details had been added to this bald statement. Did the observer sit down with a pencil and paper marking the shocks off in fives, or did he count aloud? Did he have any symptoms of mal-de-terre or whatever volcanologists call land sickness? Did he eat before 5 p.m., or had he lost his appetite? Did company drop in, or did he just stop recording at 8 p.m.?

All these, of course, were minor happenings. At Halemaumau the beginning of May was marked by considerable subsidence until a great funnel 600 feet deep occupied the pit, into which almost continuous avalanches of rock from the no longer sheered-up walls tumbled. Occasionally glowing patches of lava paste were left clinging to the sides of the pit where new fractures tore away the edges of the former lava column.

Then the rockfalls increased tremendously with an immense dust cloud of cauliflower shape rising out of the pit, making what the observer finally admitted was "an impressive spectacle." When the pit was visited on May 10th, unfamiliar fragments of rock up to 400 pounds weight were found scattered over the automobile parking space—evidently blown out during the night.

Here was something unusually unusual; so from then on, a twenty-four-hour watch was set over the pit. Soon the roar of avalanching became continuous, a new ominous undertone was heard, the dust cloud rose to 6,000 feet and the whole sky turned a deep purplish black. Then for ten days ensued a series of explosions, during one of which a rock was seen to be thrown up to a height of 2,500 feet, justifying the observer in terming the blast "violent." There were other accompaniments such as earthquakes, one of which was recorded as having a kind of cradling effect— "a slow swinging motion followed a minute later by one with very rapid motion." The hand that rocked that cradle certainly rules the world.

In between blasts the observatory staff continued to make their regular circuits of the pit, recording such facts as the following: "A rock weighing 300 pounds landed 1,400 feet from the rim and bounced 150 feet from its present position." It is only natural to suspect round numbers such as these. Is it possible that the observations were a little hurried?

A few days later the observers noted "a continuous moaning roar from the pit, sounding like heavy surf." The descriptive terms are somewhat confusing; it was either a moan or a roar—it couldn't be both. At this time the depth of the funnel was estimated at 1,350 feet, the difference between this figure and the original 600 feet representing the rocks and cinders distributed over the countryside, plus whatever fell in from the sides of the pit since the initial explosion. After one blast the noise of rocks falling on the lava floor outside the pit lasted 2½ minutes. There is no need to use triangulation data to show how high those rocks went up if they took 2½ minutes to go up and come down again.

On May 18th there occurred "a great culminating explosion

with a tremendous dust cloud and ejected rocks." It was this blast that caused the death of one man, Truman Taylor, who was struck by a boulder while attempting to take a photo from a spot a third of a mile from the pit. He was rescued but died on the way to the hospital. His camera was, however, retrieved uninjured. Two soldiers staying at the military rest camp also disappeared after this explosion. Apparently residence near a volcano fosters a mood of scientific caution and desire for accuracy. The official military report lists these men as A.W.O.L.

Meanwhile the big show went on. One of the most significant points in the volcanologist's report is well hidden in the following sentence: "Large puffs of steam were rising, and when sitting on the ground, one could feel numerous quakes." What in the name of Pele was one doing sitting on the ground? Why was not one running for one's life, or doing something—anything but sit? Sitting on the ground at such a time cannot be regarded as evidence of presence of mind, but rather of its complete absence. But the report continues:

"At 11:20 a.m. came a rain of mud balls as large as peas (elsewhere called pisolites). The mud rain continued over three quarters of an hour. An intense electrical storm followed about noon and thereafter, so that one received a shock even by touching a motor car. About four miles towards Hilo, twenty-one telephone poles in a line were destroyed by lightning. The thunder and lightning at the volcano, however, were not so strong as on the 17th."

To dwell all the time on these explosive outbursts is to over-emphasize the spectacular in Pele's realm, and thus to give a somewhat terrifying, but false impression of Kilauea. Thirty-three years seems to be the usual span between outbursts of great activity with major crises each 65 years, and explosive eruptions at 130-year intervals. In 1918, Jaggar, considering these cyclic fluctuations, was ready to predict a resumption of violence about 1920. The year after this prediction was marked by the great Alika source flow on Mauna Loa, and the building of a lava hill in the Kau desert, soon to be described, the activity culminating in the great explosive eruption of May 1924.

But in between these manic episodes the area outside the crater remains quietly beautiful. Lava disintegrates quickly, and watered by the frequent showers that drift across the northeastern slopes of the mountain, great fern and ohia forests blanket the country, masking the old craters. Nothing seems so remote from fire and destruction as one of these green pits with the sun glinting on the tops of the trees and the space filled with the calls of native birds as they search for grubs and insects among the moss covered trunks of tree ferns. But down at the bottom, well guarded by tumbled rocks is a dark lateral tunnel, a smooth black gullet through which there once poured a river of molten stone. Not all these subsidiary craters are hidden, for as you pass along the road you find yourself suddenly looking over the edge of Kilauea Iki, an 800-foot pit suggesting, except for its huge size, an ant-lion's trap dug in the sand of the desert. Nor would it take much imagination to believe that hidden beneath the smooth black flow at the bottom there is a dragon waiting.

In volcanic regions almost anything can happen, and Hawaii presents so many surprises that the visitor comes to distrust the face of the country even when it is most expressionless. For example, the area to the east of the crater consists of very ordinary-looking small rises, blighted apparently by hot ash deposits, so that nothing grows except small shrubs and ohelo berry bushes. You may be wandering carelessly, gathering the strange fruit, when suddenly at your feet there opens an empty blast furnace leading down to the depths. The Devil's Throat is well named, scarcely 100 feet across its mouth, 250 feet deep and with sides blackened and red with burnt out fires. How such a sharply defined cavity could open without disrupting the surrounding area is a mystery. It bears all the marks of a deeply punctured wound rather than of an eruption on the earth's epidermis. No doubt the volcanologists, who refuse to admit surprises, have an explanation for it.

For some miles the park road passes by a succession of craters, varying from 200 to 500 feet in depth, which all seem to conform to accepted pattern. Then you come to the last and deepest, the huge double pit of Makaopuhi, "the eye of the eel," whose tumbled walls go down 900 feet. The deeper part of the crater has broken through one side of an older pit whose smooth lava floor stands like a theater stage, with tree-covered slopes as a backdrop. On one wall of the deep crater a small frothy flow of lava appeared some years ago and splashed down into the pit. This same flow broke out along an earthquake crack in the forest, with small gas explosions sending blobs of lava spattering up among the vegetation. It was queer to see such strange fruit clinging to the limbs of the trees.

Even the paved road refuses to be ordinary, for a series of earthquakes have cracked and rumpled its surface. At one place it divides around a traffic island, not because this is a congested area, but passing through a vigorously steaming area obscures vision and necessitates one-way traffic so as to avoid collisions.

If you should become tired of the wonders of destruction, there is a spot within three miles of the Volcano House where you can forget for a time the violent and fantastic. At the Bird Park reservation a little track meanders up a wooded hillside past koa trees of such huge size as to suggest that this has been for centuries nothing but a peaceful, friendly forest. There you can listen to the Hawaiian birds, and pick wild white strawberries and thimble-berries in an atmosphere as quiet and woodsy as you will find in Maine or Pennsylvania. But as the road turns away from the park, it is not long before it ventures out on to the Uwekahuna Bluff overlooking the crater and once again you find yourself surrounded by all the evidences of destruction, the ejecta of the 1790 eruption that overwhelmed the country for miles around.

But for all its billowing cauliflower clouds, its terrific blasts, its showers of ash and boulders, the show that Kilauea puts on once in a hundred years or so is nothing but a temper tantrum compared with the hot rage of Mauna Loa which leaves such utter destruction behind it. Of the great disruptive forces of Nature there is naught that leaves a wake like this. The cyclone may splinter the trees of the forest, the cloudburst may tear away the ground, but here is violence so great that its scars can never, in hundreds of years, be covered. This once-burning river of broken rock that the Kona road limps across is the lava flow of 1868, beyond the memory of any man now living in these parts; yet in places it looks as if it might have flowed the year before last. Even with its rage gone cold, it is still terrifying.

Kilauea in size is, of course, nothing but a pimple on the skin of the earth compared to the bulk of Mauna Loa, whose base, measured in a straight line, is about 60 miles long. This 14,000-foot mountain is but the visible cap of a vast dome rising an additional 18,000 feet from its lowest levels in the depths of the sea. Mauna Loa also has its summit crater, Mokuaweoweo (burning island), which can, if it wishes, put on the same kind of performance as Halemaumau. But the weight of this dome compresses within it a core of molten lava agitated by unimaginably mighty accumulations of the gases of combustion. At intervals of time, very short intervals in this volcano's millions of years of activity, the inside pressure becomes irresistible and the flank of the mountain cracks open. Then a strange flood of molten stone goes spilling down the slopes towards the sea. If the mountainside is steep, the lava is channeled and flows like a river; if the slope is gradual, then the lava flow, called *pahoehoe* if smooth, *aa* if a broken clinker-like mass, feels its way across the surface of older flows, thrusting out tentative toes here and there, dividing and reuniting like a stream on a sandy delta. These flows form one of the most interesting features of the drive around the island.

The road after it leaves the Volcano House skirts the crater of Kilauea and then descends along the edge of a wide depression to the borders of the Kau desert. This is a queer wilderness of slag heaps, with ropy outpourings of *pahoehoe* and thrust-up boulders, amid acres of ash. After a very vigorous period of lava commotion in Halemaumau, the volcano observers saw a line of fume extending down a series of earthquake cracks into the desert. Fifty feet down below the surface a torrent of live lava was escaping through a tunnel leading from the side of the pit. Even where the glow beneath was not visible, the scientists could trace the subterranean flow by the heaving of the ground and the sulphurous fumes and crackling sounds as the rocks beneath melted. Some miles down, where the crack was obstructed, the lava began to well out on the surface. It thrust the sides of the crack apart and welled and welled, until it built a hill called Mauna Iki—little mountain. This is 2½ miles long, 125 feet high, and a half mile wide. Thus the volcanologists were present at the first labor pains of the baby mountain's birth, and watched over its whole delivery to the final culmination. They report that the accouchement was quite normal, without instruments, Nature simply taking its course.

After you have rounded the ankle of the big volcano—its foot is in the sea at Pahala—your road traverses the mountain mass on its weakest side, so that you pass over in succession the flows of 1868, 1887, 1907, 1919, and 1926. Some of the earlier flows branched and you cross their various arms. In some places islands of forest are left untouched in the midst of turmoil. The two most recent flows, the Alika in 1919 and the Hoopuloa in 1926, found steeper slopes and with the weight of a great outflow behind them, raged irresistibly downward to the sea. The Hoopuloa flow wiped out a village of that name built around a small cove at sea level. The broken *aa* formation appeared in the later phases and covered the smooth *pahoehoe* beneath, giving these flows their characteristic broken chocolate fudge appearance. What happens at the rift where the mountain cracks open can be faintly realized by reference to the "Volcano Letter," which reports Jaggar's three expeditions to the source of the Alika flow. He describes the whole show from the preliminary flashing on of the footlights to "lights out" at the end. It was a very typical Mauna Loa performance.

At sunset on September 26, 1919, there was a thin mantle of cloud thrown around the shoulders of the mountain, with a new moon hanging over the summit of Mauna Kea. Someone casting an eye towards the mountain's bulk saw at about the 8,000-foot level the first cauliflower puffs of smoke clouds, lit at their base with the terra-cotta glow that signifies live lava beneath. In a little while these clouds rose to a height of 7,000 feet and quickly turned to orange-red. Having thus flashed this warning signal the footlights died down, and the clouds dispersed. But this was just the pause while the players behind the scenes took their places and awaited their entrance cues. Three days later, the footlights blazed again, and up went the curtain on the big show.

To get a seat close to the stage meant a long rough journey with a pack train over old lava flows and through thick forest. A day's ride brought the party to the 7,000-foot level but still many miles from the flow, and about midday of the third day the party tethered their horses and climbed a high red hill half a mile from the source. From there they could see a solid wall of fountains 1,000 feet long, spouting volcanic material 300 feet in the air, yellow as it went up, red as it came down. There was a roar like an angry surf, made by gas churning its way through the liquid lava which filled a great rift. As these fountains played, they built up a rampart of partly cooled fragments on either side, a wall which dammed back a fiery lake except where a break 40 feet wide carried the main torrent rushing down towards the lower slopes at a speed of about 18 miles an hour.

To have iron in a volcanologist's soul would not avail. It would soon be melted. A good casing of asbestos is what he requires. For like Abednego and his companions in Scripture, he enters the burning fiery furnace and comes out scorched but alive. In front of him is a foaming surging lake of lava a hundred yards wide, at which, in the interests of scientific description, Jaggar must take a look. "The writer," he says, "obtained one glimpse of the lake surface by climbing the rampart at the northeast end where the summit was only 40 feet high and the fountaining less violent than at the south. The heat was intolerable, but by choosing a moment when the falling of fragments was at a minimum, it was possible to scramble to the edge, look in, and then beat a quick retreat." To use only two adjectives—violent and intolerable—in describing such an experience requires considerable asbestos. After dark the show must have been an unforgettable spectacle, but the description is merely factual:

"Flames from the end vents were seen at night to be colored bluish-green to violet. Over the great fountains were banners of nearly colorless transparent flame, 200 to 300 feet higher than the fountains, surmounted by salmon-colored condensing fume. A flutter of yellow-red marked these flames and there was much bright green when the yellow reflection or fume streamers blended with the blue flame of burning gas."

In short, the colors were bluish-green, violet, salmon, yellow-red, green, yellow and blue. Incidentally, the gas was most distressing to the eyes and quite unbreathable, so that at 4 a.m. the situation became intolerable even to Dr. Jaggar, and the party had to leave their bivouac and retreat a third of a mile. But the scene at sunset affected even the somewhat charred soul of a volcanologist and moved him to one short burst of description that became almost lyrical:

"Over the scarlet fountains rose the sheets of red and green flame, topped with lilac fume, against a murky green or blue-grey background. Above rose the great buff-colored volutes of cloud, with individual billows coffee-colored or brown. All of this was backed by an outer sky of deepest cobalt-blue, with normal distant horizon clouds of pearly grey." The reader should remember that this multicolored fire was lit in the clear air of an 8,000-foot elevation, against a dark background of 6,000 feet more of mountain. Surely hell itself could not have been more beautiful—from the outside.

In the meantime what was happening at the other end of the flow? The outbreak occurred at midnight and by 6 p.m. on the same day the fiery river was reported to be 3 miles above the round-the-island highway in the Alika district of Kona. At 9:30 p.m. it heralded its approach to the people waiting on the road by a dull smoky glow as the forest trees and brush in its path burst into flame. Then came a slowly advancing wall of partly incandescent rocks and *aa* blocks which suddenly broke under the pressure and let through a small stream of molten lava. This grew and grew until a stream several hundred feet wide came pouring over the road and plunging down the slopes below. At 4:30 a.m. on the following day it leaped over a 40-foot terminal cliff into the sea. Then for ten days the lava cascaded into the ocean.

With clouds of steam and under-water explosions that sent up showers of rocks and sand, with huge boulders rolling down the lava stream and bobbing up at sea, apparently supported for a time by the gas inflating them, with lightning constantly playing around the steam column, with dead fish floating in the boiling sea, the fiery river came to its end. Most dramatic occurrences were the sudden periodic swellings of the flow when it overlapped its banks, while huge black and red rafts of partly congealed lava rode the flood or rolled over and over, jumping as they hit the bottom, until they either exploded or reached the sea. At one place the river divided, leaving an island of five or six acres on which some cattle were imprisoned. Like everything else in Hawaii, they were taking the eruption as a matter of course and were "quietly brows-ing." Next day the island was considerably smaller and some of the trees burst into flame, causing the animals to bellow in distress. Some days later, a cowboy rode over the partially cooled lava and brought the cattle to safety.

In December 1935 there occurred a most extraordinary event, unparalleled in scientific history — the use of the most modern weapons of destruction for strictly conservative purposes. This was the bombing of lava by the army air force, under the guidance of Dr. Jaggar, the object being to block or divert a flow which was within fifteen miles of destroying Hilo and filling up its harbor. To understand how this could happen, the shape and contour of Hawaii should be kept in mind. In outline the island is like a wolf's head, with one ear cocked at Kohala, the eye at Mauna Kea, the nose at Puna, a swollen throat at the extreme south. A depres-sion above the nose represents Hilo harbor.

But it is a sick wolf, with the swelling wound of Mauna Loa at the angle of the jaw. Sometimes the outflow from this moun-tain breaks out to the south, but often, as in 1843, 1855, 1883, 1899, to the north. The stream, after ponding itself in the saddle between the two 14,000-foot mountains, may elect to turn west, as in 1843, or east towards Hilo.

In November 1935 there was an outburst near Mauna Loa's summit which flowed eight miles, then sealed itself off. Then in December, it broke out 4,000 feet lower down, found its way westward blocked by the 1843 flow, and turned towards Hilo. In four days it had covered five of the twenty miles that separated it from the city, and threatened momentarily to cut off the water supply. Like all flows of this type of lava, its surface in cooling had built a tunnel through which the fiery liquid was pouring. The volcanologist decided that if the roof of the tunnel could be broken in, the gas pressure would be relieved and the lava stream could be diverted so as to spread out in shallow sheets and cool off.

The army was called in to do the job. Ten bombing planes came to Hilo and carried out a pinpoint operation. Several 600-lb. bombs fell directly in the channel not far from its source, and in four days the forward advance of the lava stopped. Here at least was one instance where man triumphed over and controlled one of the great forces of Nature. The usual reports about Pele's vengeance on those who interfered with her were circulated, all the men who participated in the bombing having been supposed to have met violent deaths. But the report was greatly exaggerated, and in any case it was Japs and Germans, not Pele, who were responsible.

In spite of these periodic ebullitions, most of the island is extremely peaceful and nowhere is this calm more evident than when the lava flows of Mauna Loa are left behind and you approach the quiet slopes of Kona. The road winds along at about a 1,500-foot elevation with side-roads down to the shore at such places as Kealakekua Bay where Cook was killed, the city of refuge at Honaunau, and the ancient village of Kailua. The forest is all around you and the houses of the coffee-farmers dot the clearings, the small green plantations filling the pockets of rich soil between the ancient lava outcrops. The whole place drowses peacefully in the warm sunshine, with the silvered expanse of the Pacific rising up at the horizon's level to match your elevation. If you want the ease of the tropics or sunsoaked landscape, the endless break of the waves on black rocks which makes a thin zone of sound between two great quiets, the solitude of the sea and the peace of the land, you will find it at the Kona Inn, almost but not quite in the shadow of Hualalai, 8,000 feet above you.

But this is not all. From eternal sunshine at Kailua you may travel on sixty miles to Waimea. For much of the way you are passing across a very ancient tableland with the old lava flows evidenced only by bulges and hillocks covered with bunch grass. Now, especially when wisps of damp fog curl across the tableland, you have left the tropics and summer behind, and you might be in eastern Oregon during the early autumn. In February with deep snow on Mauna Kea and cold rain squalls sweeping across the bare grassy slopes of the Kohala mountains (the cattle and horses drifting with their backs to the wind and rain), you have been transported to the high moors of Scotland, or, except for the great elevations, to the Panhandle of Texas.

Then back over the gap and down through the forest to Honokaa and you are in still another world. Here are steep gulches, forest-filled, tumbling down to the sea; spidery trestles carrying flume or rail-line hanging hundreds of feet in air; brawling streams; thin, high waterfalls; sugar cane in profusion, and down below the dark blue Pacific, no longer sheltered by the bulk of huge mountains but ruffled by white caps gleaming under the shadows of the low rain clouds, blown up by the incessant trade winds. It is an entirely different ocean from the one that is stretched out below Kona.

Thus, back again at Hilo you have passed, in circling the big island, through six successive stretches of country, each as different from the rest as though degrees of longitude or latitude lay between. There was first of all the subtropical fern forest from Hilo to Kilauea; the desolate but fascinating volcanic desert from the crater through the waste lands of Kau; the alternating ohia forests and lava flows through South Kona; the coffee bush and breadfruit belt of Kona itself; the treeless grassy tundras or moorlands of Kohala and Waimea; and finally the luxuriant river-spaced sugar fields of the Hamakua coast. If you want to go a little distance out of your way, you can see the Kohala district with its wonderful Waipio valley—a little world in itself. But perhaps six different countries are enough to see in 200 miles travel. If anyone should say that he has paid a visit to the island of Hawaii, it is entirely proper to ask—which Hawaii, for there are at least seven.

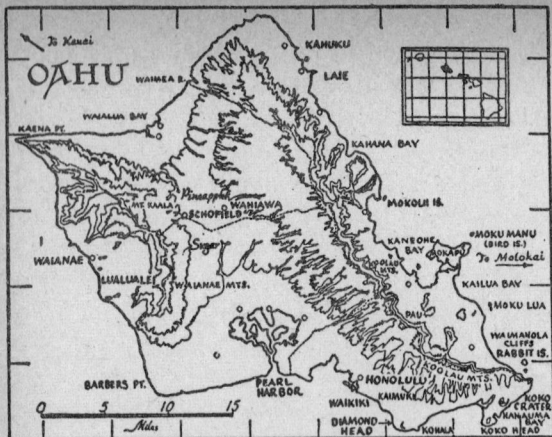

CHAPTER VIII

Oahu

THE GATHERING PLACE

THE VISITOR to the Hawaiian Islands arrives in the middle of the group, or at least a little left of center, which nowadays seems to be the preferred political position also. He lands on Oahu,[1] which is not the highest, the largest, the youngest, the oldest, the wettest, the first discovered, nor even the most beautiful island in the group. The first three superlatives belong to the big island of Hawaii, the next three to Kauai, and the last distinction is still, and always will be, in dispute. As regards date of birth, the chief islands should be introduced in this order: Kauai, Oahu, Molokai, Maui, and Hawaii, for that is probably how they arose along the great crack in the earth that extends the length of the group under the ocean.

[1] Oahu's central position in the group may have given it its Hawaiian name, which means "a place for collecting together."

162

According to geologists, Oahu came up from the depths as two islands, the first formed by the Waianae Range and the second with its center of volcanic activity in the Koolau mountains not far from the Pali. The Waianaes around Mt. Kaala rose higher but the Koolau volcanoes erupted longer, sending successive flows in a northwesterly direction until they filled the strait between, and ponded against the flank of the older island. The road across the island that once ran through Waialua plantation skirted the Kaukonanua Gulch, which represents the meeting point of the two lava outflows.

The terrain that appears in the first view of the hinterland of Honolulu is of more recent volcanic construction. From the sea five ridges run like the outspread fingers of your right hand placed on the table. The little finger represents Alewa Heights, the ring finger Pauoa Ridge, the big finger Round Top and Tantalus, the first finger St. Louis Heights, and the thumb, if greatly elongated, would be Maunalani Heights and Wilhelmina Rise. The knuckles of your hand will then serve to represent the mountain heights of the Koolau Range which notch the horizon at the back of Honolulu Harbor.

Geologists are the soothsayers of science who look at the world as a tea-cup reader and tell you all its past; only their tea leaves are wind-blown sand dunes, so old that they have turned to stone, coral beaches raised far above the sea and left stranded inland, lake and marine deposits in deserts or on mountains, volcanic dykes, cinder cones, and the like. From a study of the superposition and composition of layers of ash and lava, and any shells, tree trunks, and coral fragments imprisoned therein, they have worked out the relative sequence of events which resulted in Oahu appearing as it does. Their reconstruction of its geological story is extremely interesting.

After the twin islands were built and ultimately joined together, immense periods of time passed, which were marked by successive downsettings and uprisings of sea level in the Pacific. These fluctuations are attributed by some to changes in world climate so great that the polar ice-caps were vastly increased, thus imprisoning, in the form of glaciers, tremendous quantities of sea water. At such times the ocean level was lowered. Then in the ensuing warm period, the ice melted, releasing such floods that the sea rose 95 feet above its present level, cutting wave benches and allowing coral reefs to form which are now miles inland. Good examples of these are to be seen from the road which passes by Kahuku on the other side of the island and in a pasture just before reaching Kailua. At this time the valleys which drained the long leeward slopes running down from the Schofield plateau were drowned. Then came another glacial period and another great 155-foot recession, which brought the edge of the shore 60 feet lower than at present. Once again the streams had an opportunity to carve out the contours of the Pearl Harbor lochs and peninsulas. Another rise of 85 feet drowned the valleys, and finally the waters receded to their present level.

These volcanic eruptions and immense floodings and recessions were like the trip hammer blows that molded the general form of the island. But in between there were the countless light taps that smoothed out inequalities or cut the surface design. This was the work of the ocean waves ceaselessly pounding on cliffs and foreshore, and the similar but unending work of the little streams, operating on the cut and carry system. One result was the filling in of the foundations of the plain upon which Honolulu stands. But just as things seemed settled, Pele became a little dissatisfied with the pattern, and decided to put in some finishing touches on the work of island building.

The sequence, according to Mrs. Stearns,[2] whose popular account we are following, seemed to be first of all a sudden explosive eruption on the plain near the foot of the ranges. Lava rose in a crack and overflowed; then, as is its habit, it just as suddenly withdrew, leaving a deep cavity into which the ground water rushed, forming a steam blast chamber, out of which masses of all kinds of foundation material came hurtling into the air. Deep-buried ancient

[2] Stearns, Nora D. *An Island Is Born.* Honolulu Star Bulletin Company, 1935.

coral reefs and old lava flows were shattered by explosions and thrown up in a rough circle so as to form a wall around the vent. The crater in the center filled with live lava, which tossed and fountained and finally broke through the containing wall near where Prospect Street now runs. A spatter cone built up on the rim and forms an eminence upon which, for many years before the war, an Easter cross glowed. Thus Punchbowl, the hill immediately behind the city, was formed.

Diamond Head, we are told, erupted in the same way, tearing through marine deposits and old lava flows and building up its crater walls in a comparatively short time. The ejected material, carried by the prevailing winds, heaped up to the southwest, the highest part of the rim, forming what is now the lookout station, the sharp angle of the diamond in the ring. Like Punchbowl, Diamond Head crater also scattered its ashes for miles around and contributed to the making of the plain between the two craters. Some time later, lava welled out to form the Kaimuki Ridge, much in the same way as Mauna Iki was formed in the Kau desert on Hawaii. The source of the subterranean flow was a volcanic vent in Palolo Valley.

In the meantime, a matter of just a few thousand years, Pele found other weak spots in the island crust. Tantalus seemed to have been one center of activity, sending one stream of lava down Pauoa Valley, driving the stream underground so that it issued in the form of springs near the foreshore. The cold fresh water killed or discouraged the coral polyps, so that a break in the reef resulted, forming the entrance to what is now Honolulu Harbor.

Another flow cascaded down into Manoa Valley and ponded against its far wall, pushing the stream over towards St. Louis Heights. But none of this was done quietly. Gas explosions from the summit cone threw out immense quantities of pulverized rock and disintegrated material of different types, which went landsliding down the slopes. As you drive up Tantalus you can see in the road cuttings all kinds of futurist patterns of black and grey, formed by bands of different colored ash, which filled the little runnels and hollows and thus outlined for us the former contours. Again the prevailing winds carried the lighter ejecta to the southwest, depositing it in layers many feet thick over the Punchbowl crater and on the Honolulu plain.

Your entrance point on Oahu, if you come from the sea, is, of course, the harbor, about the naming of which there seems to be some doubt. It was once called Brown's Harbor after the ship's captain, who, about 1794, warped his ship through the break in the reef and found good anchorage. He called it Fair Haven, though he did not find it such. Kalanikupuli, the king of Oahu, fought for the island with Kaeo, king of Kauai. When the former was being driven back, Brown sent one of his mates with eight English seamen to the battle and they turned the tide. To celebrate the victory, a broadside was fired from Brown's ships, the Butterworth and the Jackal. Somebody, however, forgot to take out the shot from one cannon, which penetrated the Lady Washington lying alongside, killing its captain, John Kendrick. When he was buried ashore with appropriate rites, the natives thought that a death spell was being thrown on his slayers. Then Kalanikapuli and his men turned on Brown, stormed on board the two ships, and killed the captains.

The name Honolulu has been actually translated as "Fair Haven," but this is probably a mistake. The district facing the sea was called Kou and a little fishing settlement on Nuuanu stream was said to have been named Kulolia. *Hono* in Hawaiian means a stitching or joining together, and is applied to a flat surface joining two eminences. It is therefore a descriptive term for the back of the neck and also for the low land between the mountains of East and West Maui. Alexander in his dictionary gives as another meaning "a sheltered spot on the sea." But as the flat space between Diamond Head and Red Hill, it would also be called *hono*. *Lulu,* or *ruru* as it was in its original form, meant "a shelter from the wind." The composite word Honolulu probably should be translated as the flat place joining the hills that is sheltered from the wind, and had, therefore, little to do with the harbor. The accepted translation would actually be "a sheltered shelter," which is certainly painting the *lulu,* if not the lily.

That the naming of Honolulu by the Hawaiians had anything to do with a fair haven for ships is most unlikely. With a bay like Waikiki available for beaching their canoes, the natives were not concerned with any other harbor. At high water any small break in the reef was navigable, even for the big double canoes, and if a storm should come up from the south, they could be easily hauled up on the sand. Consequently, the kings of Oahu had their main residences at Waikiki, close by the best surfboard riding in the islands, and the holua-sledding down the slopes of Diamond Head. Not until King Kamehameha became a shipowner and needed a harbor did the quiet waters off the *hono* become important to him.

After the Russians had begun a fort and been driven out, one was built, under John Young's supervision, at the foot of what is now Fort Street. It mounted 42 guns and was 115 yards long and 100 yards wide, and contained a prison, a powder magazine, a courthouse, and barracks. For fifty years it was a landmark on the waterfront.

After the cession of the islands to Britain in Vancouver's day, Kamehameha flew the British flag, but in the war of 1812, it was pointed out to the king that this might mean trouble. Who designed the new flag nobody knows. Louis Charis published a book in Paris in 1822, containing a plate entitled "Port d'hanarourou" showing the flag floating over the fort. All accounts agree that it had the Union Jack in the corner, but place the number of horizontal stripes variously at from seven to nine. It has been suggested that the stripes were adopted from the American flag. If this is true, Kamehameha made a prudent combination of the ensigns of the two powers. Others say that the stripes represent the number of islands in the group.

In 1828, eight years after the missionaries landed, and nearly a third of a century after Brown's discovery of the harbor, Honolulu was still a town of grass huts without a single frame building. Gradually the town expanded, overflowed the plain, and extended up Nuuanu Valley. It continued to grow to the east, covered the old lava hill of Kaimuki and spread into Manoa. With the building of better roads, and the common use of automobiles, residents discovered the joys of living up above the coastal plain, and soon the finger-like ridges of Alewa, Pacific, St. Louis, and Maunalani Heights were built upon, with the higher, thickly forested ridge of the middle finger, Tantalus, devoted chiefly to week-end residences. When the inter-island ships left at night, you saw the four heights of land strung, as if with jewels, by lines and clusters of electric lights. Whether the valley or the ridge constitutes the better place to live, is a matter of opinion, with loyalties divided according to location. The ridge has the advantage of coolness and views of wide sweeps of sea, but also the discomfort, if your aspect is south-westerly, of an afternoon glare reflected from a mirror-like ocean. On the other hand, the valley dweller has beauty in his back yard. In Manoa, for example, the precipitous eighteen-hundred-foot bluff of Tantalus lines the valley to the left, with just enough naked rock to show off the little ledges where kukuis, koas, pahales, and guavas find a lodgment. Beyond is the back rim of the valley, gapped here and there, the whole upper levels covered with forest. On the eastern side, in Woodlawn, the mountains are so close to the back doors of the houses that residents must step outdoors to see their summits. Though only in a few places is it possible to climb out of this green amphitheater, you have no sense of being shut in. The valley is wide enough to hold more than you need of sunlight so that you may be grateful for the cloud shadows that ceaselessly drift across its floor. Even the waterfalls at the head of the valley, when they run, slide gently down with little fuss or foam. The only drawback is that we who live so intimately with beauty are likely to regard it casually, and take it for granted. The first thrills of possession tend to disappear.

For this reason, I would recommend seeing Oahu slowly. It is like a fine liqueur which should be sipped to be appreciated. Unfortunately, visitors are frequently rushed up Nuuanu Valley to take a quick look at the prize view of the island, the Pali. The scene is indeed breathtaking—a wall of mountain so steep that only grey lichens and crevice-clinging ferns can find a foothold, its rock faces robbed of their sternness by sunlit patches between the cloud shadows. Below you is a broken verdurous bowl into which come flooding all the greens and blues and purples of the Pacific Ocean. It is indeed satisfying, but the visitor comes to other scenes with a sense of anti-climax. Honolulu has an Outdoor Circle, the organization that has crusaded most successfully against the erection of billboards or other wayside disfigurements. It seems a pity that its members could not institute a campaign to induce people to see the Pali last instead of first. We might avoid then the experience of taking visitors around the island and finding them displaying more interest in an old mud-caked carabao bull in a taro patch than the beauties of the Koolau ranges. The carabao is something new, the mountains aren't. Your visitors have drained their liqueur and now you are offering them small beer.

There are some scenes on Oahu that you must catch just at the proper moment, like the hedge of night-blooming cereus at Punahou. On opening night, it is a wonderful show, with all the floral beauties in their most expensive opera cloaks, and adorned with coronets of gold. But the next morning the blooms are withered and the fat and fleshy branches of the cactus-like plant are more suggestive of an assemblage of overfed dowagers. There are some places on Oahu whose beauty is similarly fleeting.

If you continue around the island from the Pali you will miss the "quiet colored end of evening" at Kaaawa. (Some visitors have wished that a few of these Hawaiian place names could be disemvoweled; it takes such a long time to say Ka-ah-ah-va.) But if you should be returning towards the Pali in the early evening, you may catch an authentic fragment of the Polynesian past. It is when the shadows of the mountains are laid down over the lagoon, the quiet water edged by the white turmoil of the reef, its reflections broken only by the wading figures of the Hawaiian women, gathering seaweed for the evening meal. There was no hint of this as you passed in the morning, but now at evening there is a contained beauty about the spot as if you could cup your hands around it and hold it.

A little farther along the coast you may capture another fortunate flash of beauty. It is the habit of our clouds to descend at evening and rest in an unbroken bank along the tops of the Koolau Mountains, the shape of which someone has compared to the bottom of an upturned canoe. But there are holes in the hull, one of the widest where the head of Kalihi Valley makes a gap in the range. At times the sun is framed in this space between cloud and mountain as if it were shining through a window. It sends through, hardly a shaft, but a great column of light, dividing the shadows on either hand and pointing seaward until it is diffused in the sunlight offshore. At Iao Valley on Maui you may get this effect quite often, but nowhere else on Oahu except here.

Another place that is at its best in the evening is the stretch of coastal valleys that flank the Waianae Mountains from Kaena to Nanikuli. This is the leeward side of the island and therefore dry and very warm. The valleys, Lualualei, and the rest, here represent deep cuts into the substance of the ancient volcanic dome that was the beginning of this island of Oahu. The residual ridges that separate the valleys are composed of bisected flows of red and chocolate colored lava, and are cut down very steeply but irregularly, as though they had been chopped out rather than planed down by erosion. Nor was the workman at all careful where the chips flew, for broken boulders cover the bottoms of these deep chasms. The only vegetation that can survive the heat and drought is the *panini,* the prickly pear cactus, some straggly kiawes and sapless lantana. Higher up where nothing grows, the rim-rock is so red and forbidding that little imagination is needed to see it again as hot and glowing with internal fires. But here nightly the setting sun spreads its palette. The rock walls glow again, but softly; purple shadows fill the canyons, cool breezes stray out of their depths, and the harshness of heat and fiery color is allayed. Only in the Sangre de Cristo Mountains in Colorado or in the Krichauff Ranges in

Central Australia are there to be seen such miracles of change, transforming the desert into transient loveliness.

There are very many places where beauty will stand and wait for you. It really doesn't matter when you come around the corner and find Kahana—the curving bay, the river resting between the hau thickets, the green mountains at your side, will all be there. Nor does it make much difference when you cross the Waimea bridge and look down on the beach from the bluffs on the other side. High noon or any other time those long black lava rocks, their backs rounded with a thousand years of ocean buffeting, will still be there, like prehistoric monsters, half submerged, sleeping on the sand. The contrast between yellow beach and black rock will never fail to surprise you. If you will take time to turn aside, three hundred yards upstream will bring you to a little flat strewn with boulders, mossy and fern covered, the whole tented over with the spread of monkeypod trees, a temple of shade.

Of places to visit in the early morning there are so many that there may not be enough mornings during your stay to go around. Honolulu is a sleepy place for visitors, and few except the very earnest and sober wish to get up betimes. But the outlook from the bend on the Tantalus road looking towards Pearl Harbor, with its backdrop of the Waianae Ranges, requires the utmost clarity of Hawaiian air. Whether it be the commotion of traffic, smoke from fires in the cane fields, or the red dust of cultivation, the evening view seems never clear-cut, and the glare from the Pearl Harbor lochs is somewhat distressing to the eyes. But in the morning the sun is behind you, all the ridges are sharp and distinct, the shadows flow gently around your feet, and every detail of Pauoa Ridge stands out, even the old Hawaiian trail that cuts along its summit leading inland to where the sandalwood, so prized for the China trade, used to grow. Pearl Harbor rests in the middle foreground and the green of the intervening sugar cane throws into relief the redness of the Waianaes. It is such a clear picture that the paint seems hardly dry.

If you prefer a near view of Hawaiian mountains, then take a side track on your way back that leads you to the head of Manoa Valley. To get there you walk around a tributary gully, which provides shelter for growth—large koa trees, a fringe of kukuis, clumps of wild bananas, and a few fern trees, with every shrub and small tree covered with the creepers of the *lilikoi,* the purple passion fruit. But neither the forest nor even the depths of Manoa Valley with its taro patches and eucalyptus plantations is the main attraction. What will fascinate you most are the fingers of cloud that continually reach down from the mountain barrier—grey fingers that twist and turn, clasping and unclasping, yet seizing nothing. It is the trade wind topping the ridge and making a sudden downdraft that carries these wisps and tongues of cloud swirling down until they meet the warm air of the valley, when they suddenly dissolve.

It is these clouds ceaselessly banking against the Koolau Range that formed what a naval officer once called God's gift to the Japanese. "Beautiful, yes," said the admiral, "but that cloud blanket is a natural smoke screen that makes Pearl Harbor so vulnerable to attack from the air. Japanese planes loosed from carriers out at sea could come from behind those clouds so quickly that we could not get our defending aircraft off the ground quick enough to meet their challenge." This was in the days before radar, and while the Kaneohe base was still in the planning stage. He little knew how prophetic his words were.

The native people of these islands observed an old custom which had its obvious advantages. Four months in the year, from October to February, were declared a vacation not only from labor, but from all forms of religious observances. The theory was that if you worked and prayed diligently for eight months in the year, you should be able to accumulate enough food and holiness to carry you over the remaining four. This *makahiki* period as it is called covered the coolest months in the year, and was devoted to feasting, sports, and ceremonial visits. But before *makahiki* could begin, the *akua loa,* the god of the long journey, had to be carried all around the island, always with the sea on its left, so that, while it was passing, all the land on that side was tabu, and neither fishing nor cultivation nor movement of people could take place. The symbol of the god was an oblong of tapa fastened to a cross piece and attached to a long pole and was devoted to Lono who brought fertility and abundance. Because the mainsail of Captain Cook's ship was of this shape, the people of Hawaii worshipped him as Lono.

As the *akua loa* was carried around from district to district, it was met at the boundaries of each by the local god, the *akua poko*. This was carried always in the opposite direction, facing the mountains instead of the sea. Where the two met, the local *konohiki,* or tax collector, gathered together the assessed tribute of the district, bird feathers for feather capes, tapa for malos, or loin cloths, pigs, dogs, dried fish, taro, etc. These were then taken away and finally divided by the king among his lesser chiefs and followers. Since no one at the court did any work, by the time the next *makahiki* rolled around, the courtiers were often rather ragged, being reduced to odd remnants to supply them with malos. Only after the gods had passed were the lands *noa* or free from tabu.

Nowadays if you travel from Honolulu following the way of the *akua poko,* the god of the short journey, the sea will be yours. Past Koko Head the cliffs are abrupt, for this coast is exposed to the most restless part of the Molokai channel. At the gap below Makapuu Point where the lighthouse stands, the road followed and destroyed an ancient Hawaiian causeway of flat stones, the only highway which in the days of the kings led to windward Oahu, with the exception of a dangerous foot path which climbed over the Pali. The pavement was no doubt built for the speedy conveyance of food to Honolulu. A runner's fame was often dependent upon the distance between the place where he could take a fish, still flopping, out of the water, and deposit it alive in the king's kitchen.

The one great deficiency in Hawaiian scenery is the absence of lakes. The molten lava, which formed the foundations of these islands, is too porous to provide water-proof lake-beds. So we miss those mirrors of mountain peaks edged with fir and spruce that are so distinctive of the Pacific Northwest and Canada. Sometimes we would like some surcease from the pounding of the surf on the reef, and there are some neurotic souls who find the ceaseless flow of the trade winds mentally disturbing.

Perhaps this stretch of coast between the Waimanalo gap and the other side of Kaneohe Bay has more of the suggestion of lake scenery than any other part of Oahu, for it enjoys the protection of some offshore islands. What that protection means you can realize by contrast as you look down at Kaupo beach at your feet. This narrow sandy stretch is at the top of a funnel of blue "shark water" that is constricted between Rabbit Island and the lighthouse point. This beach is exposed to the Molokai channel and there are always big waves racing far up the sand in front of the low rocky headland of Kaupo.

Beyond Kaupo and flanked by the strange red and black skeleton of Kaohikaipu Island ("held in the middle tide"), there is a shallow bench, a patchwork of yellow and purple coral formations, with black lava heads sticking through, covered by the strait that lies between Rabbit Island and the mainland. The grey bulk of this island, shaped like the head and neck of a dog, provided shelter for the outrigger canoes of the people of the village. On one point a cairn was built for the red god, *Ku-ula,* who watched over the fortunes of fishermen. It was well to carry some flowers or some seashells or coral and lay them on the cairn if you expected good luck and a safe return. The houses of the village were built on the lava flow that points toward Rabbit Island. Even to this day you can see the rock foundations of the houses and the bubbles in the lava that were used to shelter pigs and people.

Rabbit Island was called *Manana* (stretched out), and it really has on it some rabbits, which eke out a scanty living by feeding on the few sparse bents of vegetation which manage to grow in the shelter of the island's crater. Where the rabbits of the island and the people of the village got their fresh water is a mystery, for there are no springs in sight.

Farther along the coast there are the twin islands of Mokulua

and the low coral island of Popoia. Still farther on, flanking Kailua
Bay, you will see the two-hundred-foot cliffs of Moku Manu (bird
island), so named by the Hawaiians because the place has always
been a nesting colony for Man of War birds, boobies or gannets,
and terns of the sooty and other varieties.

Moku Manu, like Honolulu, has an acute housing shortage. Any
bird that can get a few sticks together to call a nest is lucky, but
must keep constant watch lest they be stolen literally from under
its wings. The Man of War birds are the worst offenders. The
booby after a hard day's fishing may return home to find every
stick of furniture misappropriated, and even its eggs stolen by the
piratical Man of War, which is careful never to leave its own nest
unguarded, male and female taking turns to keep house. If a
booby is lucky enough to make a decent nest, the pirates descend on
her in bomb-diving formation. As the first one dives close enough
to make her jump, the next one snatches a stick, with the result that
the young are sometimes hatched on the bare rocks, which perhaps
accounts for the booby's nervous disposition.

As you drive around this part of the island, you will seldom
miss seeing the rakish shape of these piratical frigate birds, as they
are also called. They have rather ridiculous feet, only partially
webbed, and are therefore specialized for flight rather than for
diving and swimming. The wing spread is recorded as being
between six and seven feet, yet the total weight of the bird may
be under five pounds. If it is late afternoon, these sea raiders are
probably sitting up aloft waiting for boobies to come in from
fishing. As soon as one is sighted over the sea, the Man of War
soars over him and makes such a determined attack that the victim
in a spasm of acute nervous indigestion regurgitates its fish, which
its attacker catches before it can hit the water. Bird life, except
for the ubiquitous mynah, is so scarce in Hawaii that any bird at
all is an object of exceptional interest. Those who are really interested in bird life should not go to tropical islands.

But even if we lack birds and lake scenery, we can always come
back to the mountains. It is mountains, mountains all the way

from the time you make the last hairpin turn at the bottom of the Pali and take the *akua loa's* road that curls over and around spurs of the lower slopes of the ranges, past the isolated peak of Olomana, and goes straight as an arrow string across the bent bow of the Koolaus. Nowhere in the world do mountains have that strange fluted appearance, scored as they are by a hundred parallel fissures, each one narrowly separated from its fellows by a ridge running from base to summit. Some of these canyons-stood-up-on-end are so narrow and deep that looking up from the bottom you seem to be in a vertical, nearly closed funnel.

One can readily understand the geology of the valley amphitheater, perhaps a crater to begin with, the walls continually enlarged by converging streams, the side broken away towards the sea, but it is difficult to picture the formation of the organ-pipe structure of these mountains. Why does each little canyon refuse to converge and join with its neighbor? Perhaps the most feasible explanation is that the whole of the range hereabouts represents an intrusive dyke of lava, which after all the softer material has been worn away is left as a vertical wall, so hard that it could only be scored with torrents as you score a surface with parallel strokes of the point of a knife.

In the meantime, the half-bowl around which the bow of the Koolaus is bent is filled with sugar cane up to the point where the string meets the bow. There the vegetation ends and the cliffs march down to the sea. These are no longer fluted, but are quite bare except for a patina of grey lichens, broken only where caves, like black eye-sockets, look out to sea. At the base of a cliff is a scree of fallen fragments, over which a green tide of creepers and lantana struggles. Surely these were once sea cliffs cut into small bays and headlands by the surging Pacific. This was really the case, for what Mrs. Stearns calls the Waimanalo Sea was actually twenty-five feet higher than at present, which would bring the ocean lapping against these cliffs. This is a very dry part of the island, and in twelve miles from the foot of Pali you have passed from a zone with a hundred inches of rainfall to one of less than twenty. Except along one

Photo by R. J. Baker

The Needle, Iao Valley, Maui

The beginning of the Napali coast, Kauai

stretch at the base of the cliffs where a sand dune forms a hollow that holds seepage from the hills, there is no vegetation. The cliffs are stark, precipitous walls, bone dry.

From this point on, so the geologists say, you are passing through a part of the island that represents Pele's last efforts at island building on Oahu before she moved southeast along the under-ocean rift to raise the rest of the Hawaiian chain. Perhaps this corner of the island between Koko Head and Waimanalo was sheered up too steeply and part of it may have slipped and cracked open; in any case, here was Pele's opportunity. To the accompaniment of tremendous quakes that shook the island, molten lava, pressed up by the untold strength of gases underneath, welled out on the surface. Then as the pressure was released, the lava flood subsided again into the depths. Water flooded in and the steam-blast eruptions began. Mud, ocean sand, coral, incandescent lava were hurled high in the air, and with each blast, cauliflower clouds darkened the sky, causing the familiar electric storms that accompany such volcanic outbursts. As the crack opened lengthwise in a northeasterly direction, a chain of craters appeared—Koko Head, Hanauma Bay, Koko Crater, Kalama, the island half-cone of Kaohikaipu, and lastly the crater of Rabbit Island.

Meanwhile from Kalama, west of the lighthouse, came a sluggishly moving flood of lava which reached the sea and extended the land area. You can see the jagged remains of the black *pahoehoe* flow between the Blowhole and Makapuu lighthouse. Back towards Koko Head the lava spills continued, building up the thousand-foot cone seen on your right at the Blowhole. As you pass along the road you may note the ash layers of successive blasts strewn over the slopes. As you take the turn to Hanauma Bay, you pass along a ridge which is built up of plastered mud and ash hardened in layers, in which you can still see strange fragments blown up from the bottom of the sea.

After the build-up came the tearing down. The waves beat their way into Hanauma crater, planed a strange bench all along its northeastern side, and chiseled out an underwater platform on which colonies of coral polyps could spread and thrive. Now the bay lies beneath you, ultramarine in the depths, pale blue over the sandy pools where fresh water springs discourage marine growths, green and brown and yellow where the heads of coral lie. In the meantime, torrential rains eroded the slopes faster than the volcano-baked mud layers disintegrated, leaving at one place just to the left of the Bay a soft clay bank four or five feet deep. Little of this remains, but enough to show that this was once a rookery, for in it you can find eggshells preserved in the loam. This rookery must have existed before man arrived on Oahu or else the birds were formerly more trustful. Seabirds when they select a site for a rookery generally give the *genus homo* a very wide berth.

From the pass between Hanauma Bay and Koko Head Crater you see another view of Diamond Head and the houses that top the lava hill of Kaimuki. If he approaches Honolulu from this direction, the observant visitor will realize the conditions that determine its growth. He will see that the city is tightly squeezed between the mountains and the sea, enforcing a lateral extension in an easterly direction. Scarcely has he descended from the ridge than a residential section begins and continues along the foreshore for about eight miles, except where the Waialae Golf Course fronts the ocean. Twenty-five years ago there were only a few score houses along this stretch, most of them strung along the beach at Kahala. As the city population increased, development to the west was limited by mudflats at the mouth of the Kahili stream, so settlement was squeezed eastward, as you squeeze paste from a tube.

This has made Honolulu a one-street city, with Waialae Avenue, branching into King and Beretania streets, as the main stem. This has become the city's spinal column surmounted by the head which is the down-town business district. A helmet at Hickam Field and a steel umbrella at Pearl Harbor have been added for protection. But to continue the simile you must imagine the figure in profile, one arm pointing up Nuuanu and the other up Manoa Valley. Waikiki represents the shoulder, and Maunalani Heights and Kaimuki a rather corpulent middle section, with the legs extending to Niu and Kuliouou, along the road the visitor is traveling. The feet are yet to develop in the area occupied by the Kamehameha School Farm, but the heel is defined by settlement at Portlock Avenue.

Now the observer will begin to understand some of Honolulu's transportation and travel problems. In the morning all the traffic feeds into this single directional stream and flows back again in the evening. Hence, Honolulu suffers from a rush of blood to the head in the day and an anaemic condition at night. In addition, it is microcephalic—its head is too small for its body. Other cities can expand in all directions, Honolulu in only two. These facts are recommended to the attention of the city planners who are at present considering the location of a civic center. If they place it too far west, it may be civic but may soon cease to be central. The heart of the city, as far as population goes, is probably between Beretania and King streets, about the present position of the Department of Agriculture and Forestry. Waikiki, Kaimuki, Manoa, and Makiki feed into this area. Thomas Square, the proposed site of the civic center, is right in the bottleneck.

Consideration of the city's anatomy of growth will provide an explanation of another point upon which visitors to Honolulu are often critical—namely, the absence of large parks. The combined area of these in the city is small, but many people have the Pacific Ocean in their front yards. Since there is so little room for parks, as much of the foreshore as possible should be conserved for public use. A beginning has been made at Ala Moana Park facing Waikiki Bay, and the Waialae Golf frontage should be similarly pre-empted. Thus Honolulu would avoid the reproach of being a maritime town with the sea shut off from all except the favored few.

Nearly all the Hawaiian traditions center about the sea, and if they could be recovered, there is no stretch of coast but would have its legend involving every landmark. The people of the islands looked seaward and the multitude of names descriptive of the moods of ocean is proof of where their interest lay. They noted the play of sunshine and the constant motion of the sheltered waters near

Waialua and named the bay Kaiaka—laughing sea. There was also Kaihili, lashing sea; Kaihoa, friendly sea; Kaiiki, small sea; Kaiki, squirting sea; Kailaa, sacred sea; Kaimakole, red sea; Kaimu, silent sea; Kainamu, growling sea; Kaiehe, murmuring sea; Kaiwiki, quick sea; Kaiolokea, the white rolling sea; and Waikiki, spurting water. There was both truth and poetry in these designations, for, in the old days, the sailor was never permanently home from the sea. He read its storm signals; he knew the places where it was a hungry enemy, a fierce contender. But he knew also where it was quiet or merely murmuring, where his canoe could float lightly, the wavelets gently slapping its koa hull. He has named these places, and you can take your choice of them, according to your mood.

Honolulu and the island of Oahu have an additional claim to interest. It was there that the initial development of the pineapple industry took place. One of the city's most conspicuous landmarks, a water tower in the form of a huge pineapple, marks the site of the city's cannery district. A drive across the island past Schofield affords a first view of broad acres of pineapples occupying a large part of the Wahiawa plateau.

In what the visitor to Hawaii sees and in almost all that he reads, sugar and its production will inevitably take a very conspicuous place. No matter which of the four chief islands he visits, the roads he travels will cut through miles of growing cane, mills will dot the countryside, irrigation ditches and flumes will be much in evidence, villages or towns of sugar folk will be everywhere. If the observer is not well informed, he may overlook the importance of the Territory's truly home-grown and home-developed industry, the second buttress of our island agricultural and business economy — pineapples. Sugar we all know about, but it may be surprising to learn that Hawaii has done more than any place else to make the public pineapple-conscious. Sugar is a necessity; pineapples and pineapple juice have become an American comfort. They constitute one of the things which fill in the gap between bare and good living.

One of the very interesting things about this industry is that it does not seem to compete with sugar. You will find no marked antagonism between pineapple and sugar men; they do not fight each other either for land or labor. Perhaps the main reason for harmonious relations is that pineapple production is comparatively new in Hawaii and was introduced into a business set-up in which co-operation was not only usual but necessary as the only possible working basis. Another factor is that a great deal of the land devoted to sugar is not suited to pineapples. Then, too, much of the labor used by the pineapple people is seasonal, and in the canning end of the business is urban instead of rural. So the two industries of sugar and pineapples flourish amicably, side by side.

Airplane travel[3] is perhaps the best way, not only to see but to understand these islands' productive life. Perhaps in time to come, when this experience becomes general, human beings may attain wider viewpoints in many matters through accustoming themselves to seeing things as wholes. Flying between Schofield and Wahiawa on Oahu, or over the low end of Molokai, around Haiku on Maui, near Anahola on Kauai, or across the center of the island of Lanai will give the visitor a conception of pineapple production as nothing else can. Spread between low mountain ranges, patterning each plateau in strange designs, there are huge fields, with countless thousands of rows of plants laid down with mathematical precision.

The pattern may be one of squares of light green or grey, tooled in marvelously straight lines, the whole marked off by red strips that converge and cross in exact fashion. These are the roadways necessary in the cultivation and harvesting of the "pines." If contour planting has been done—mainly to counteract erosion—the pattern is even more striking. The lines will sweep around in graceful curves, adapting themselves to the terrain and thus outlining dark intrusions of forests, rocky promontories or deep gorges, too rough for precision planting.

The designs are so clear and striking because the plants at

[3] Flying between the islands is both safe and comfortable. Hawaiian Airlines since 1929 have carried over half a million passengers without a single fatality. Interisland steamers, in normal times, bring the other islands within a night's journey from Honolulu.

maturity are no higher than three to four feet above the surface of the ground and considerations of their culture require a precise or regular lay-out. The pineapple industry is the only one in which the grower wraps up the land instead of the product in paper. Over the fine tilth of soil, sometimes ploughed 20 inches deep, miles of strips of tar paper are carefully laid, row after row. The machine that does this also deposits a ribbon of fertilizer under each strip of paper. Having thus wrapped up acres and acres, the planter makes holes in the paper at regular intervals and puts in a slip culled from the stem of the plant just below the fruit. He covers the land with paper for three reasons: it smothers the weeds, it conserves the moisture, and it helps to control the soil temperature.

In twenty months the pineapple plant will bear its delicious fruit, weather and weeds and mealy bugs permitting. The fields are not irrigated, so that local droughts are the first hazard. Since pineapple growers are farmers and therefore subject to all the climatic kicks, they can be plagued by excessive moisture also. The mulch paper, of course, cannot stand many months of weather, and weeds will make their way. Those that would choke the growing plant must be removed by hand, and the high school students of the Territory, working in squads, have since the war performed yeoman service in the cause of keeping civilian and military population supplied with this healthful fruit.

Next to weather and weeds, the chief hazards are those insect slave-holders, the ants. These clever schemers carry the little white fuzzy-looking mealy bugs in their pincers and spread them through the fields. There they attend them closely, feeding on the sticky sweet substance that the bugs exude while ravaging the plants. When their cows go dry, the ants butcher them for meat. But in the meantime, if the bugs are unchecked, the pineapple plants and their growers wilt most alarmingly. As soon as the pests appear, the pineapple men get out their spraying machines. These spray emulsified oil in a thin mist over the fields to the total discouragement of the "mealies." An iron solution to take the place of the iron "fixed" and unusable in the soil is also spread in a fine spray for the plants' sustenance. The machines in use remind one somewhat of those prehistoric monsters depicted in museums with huge bodies, long necks and ridiculously small heads.

Once the fruit has ripened and been harvested, the cannery takes over. Only a visit to one of these establishments will demonstrate adequately for you the uncanny skill of a pineapple robot such as the Ginaca machine—developed in Hawaii—which cores and peels the fruit, ninety to the minute, and sets it out on the trimming tables. Machines can do everything that human hands can do, but there is no substitute for human eyes and judgment. That is the reason for those long rows of neatly-uniformed, rubber-gloved girls at the tables, carefully inspecting, finally trimming and grading the fruit on its way to being sliced, canned, and cooked. Nothing in the pineapple is wasted except the smell, and a good deal of that is captured in the can.

One would like to say "That is the story of pineapple," and make an end; but there is much more of interest which in itself would fill a book. For pineapple production in Hawaii is not a matter only of plants and ploughs, sprays and sprinklers, girls and Ginacas, cans and candy. It is also a matter of men and how much of human thought and effort went into the business. For example, there was old Captain John Kidwell who started cultivation, canning, and exporting here, and long before him Don Francisco de Paula Marin, Spanish friend of Kamehameha the Great, served sea captains invited to his table with this strange, taste-intriguing fruit. Then there was Jim Dole, founder of the present Hawaiian Pineapple Co., to whose courage and vision the industry owes so much. To tell these men's experiences and those of the men who followed them is to get into the field of adventure stories.

The islanders are naturally proud of an industry that grew up here from infancy to the production of twenty million cases of canned fruit annually, or about ninety-five per cent of the world's supply. It is something that is Hawaii's own. There are now eight companies engaged in the business, and like the sugar firms their continued success is dependent upon the enlistment of brains on their behalf. Not only must the industry rely upon skillful management, excellent field work, and efficient milling practices, but a small army of agronomists, entomologists, chemists, etc., are always standing by, on the alert to deal with its recurring scientific problems.

Perhaps the most spectacular thing that one of the pineapple companies did was to purchase the whole island of Lanai, used formerly merely as ranch holdings running a few head of cattle, and develop 14,000 acres of pineapple land in its center. This involved cutting roads, building landing stages for tugs and barges, and setting up a small, excellently planned city of more than 3,000 inhabitants living in good houses at a most healthful elevation. To take such an island as Lanai with its huge barren gulches, its desiccated slopes, too dry and eroded for anything to grow on but straggling mesquite and scraggy lantana, and turn its interior into a great productive garden required plenty of that unbeatable combination—brains and courage—both of which Jim Dole had at command.

Fifty-five million dollars' worth of pineapples is now produced throughout the islands—a truly remarkable achievement. Perhaps this fact should be called to the attention of the uninformed and foolish phrase-makers who called this Territory "a sugar-coated fortress." It should also be made known to the more sober writers, who persist in calling Hawaii an outpost or a bastion of defense. Gibraltar, Aden, Rabaul, Iwo Jima, Truk, Panama are justly so described, having been developed for purely military reasons; others such as Singapore and Hong Kong serve a dual purpose as trading posts and bastions of defense. But in the case of a richly productive area such as Hawaii the term is most inadequate and wrongly applied.

This statement does not mean that the Territory's military importance is not bringing about the most drastic changes in the life and appearance of these islands. Events have moved at a most dramatic pace on Oahu. As history goes, it is not such a great while since Honolulu was a collection of grass shacks set down on a dusty shadeless plain that stretched from Punchbowl to Manoa Valley, a time when cautious ship captains had their vessels warped in by gangs of hefty Hawaiians pulling on blocks and hawsers until safe anchorage was reached behind the reef. If one of the early missionaries could have revisited here, say in 1940, it would have been an interesting conjecture as to which view would have surprised him most—the city nestling at the foot of Punchbowl or the view from Red Hill showing the miles of sugar cane extending from Pearl Harbor up the broad slot between the Waianaes and the Koolau ranges until they end at the edge of the pineapple fields at Wahiawa.

Now, five years later, the face of the country is again changing. Huge tractors are at work cutting down the hillsides, the cane is visibly shrinking, the forests of algaroba are being cut down and the land is rapidly being reconverted to miles of those flat plains, as bare as your hand, which modern aviation demands for its airfields. Lagoons and basins are being filled in with dredged-up coral until the city·threatens to be continuous with Pearl Harbor. Its 360,000 inhabitants already outnumber the population of all the rest of the islands.

Those of us whose recollections go back a scant twenty years to the time when gracefully leaning palms watched their quiet reflections in the duck ponds and paddy fields where now stand the cheap and noisy apartments of Waikiki, may have some doubts as to whether such quick changes really mean worth-while progress. If the urbanization of Oahu proceeds at the same pace for the next hundred years, there may be little of quiet and beauty left. If this island ever becomes a welter of humanity, visitors like Stevenson may yet thank God for "the antiseptic ocean." Fortunately that time is not yet, and Oahu still possesses many soul-cleansing graces besides the sea.

KAUAI

CHAPTER IX

Kauai

WILDERNESS ISLE

THE RESIDENTS of Kauai like to call this the Garden Isle, but in the sense that a garden is usually laid out on familiar lines, the name is not very suitable. Relative to its size, Kauai has probably a larger area that is wild and untamed than any other island of the group. There are miles of beaches where you will scarcely ever see a soul, not even a solitary fisherman. It has a long stretch of coast almost completely inaccessible either by sea or land. Its interior is dominated by a 5,000-foot mountain whose summit is like a moated castle guarded by an almost impassable swamp. There are valleys on Kauai, once well populated, where no one has lived for a hundred years, and others, rich and fertile enough, where people have never set foot, nor are likely to do so. All of the island has color and charm, but the garden part merely sets off

186

a wilderness of natural beauty, a garden of the menehunes[1] perhaps, but not of man.

The common people of Kauai know that this is so. Back in the mountains there grows a creeper called mokihana whose leaves give off considerable fragrance even when they are dried, and someone has written a song in its honor. Though ungrammatical, it is a sincere tribute of affection.

> "Mokihana lei, with its sweetness
> Bringing happy memories of Kauai
> There is all the valleys, there is all the palis
> Mokihana lei, the lei I love."

One thing which distinguishes Kauai is the multitude of little streams. You never know where you may meet them. You may be strolling along a wide beach like Manini, when suddenly slipping out from under the hau trees, comes a tiny freshwater creek, with no more work to do than to make a little cutbank in the sand where it can wash out black kukui nuts and bits of white coral and an occasional fluted landshell that has somehow got mixed with the playthings of the sea.

Rivers have dignity as they roll along to the sea, or lie in quiet stretches overhung by willows or other trees that like to see their own reflections in the water; but it is the brooks that chatter and dance and are so companionable. There are few of us in whose lives some little stream has not an affectionate place. Creeks are as friendly as a country lane. If this is so, then there must be many happy childhood memories clustering about the creeks of Kauai, for every gulch has its stream and almost every stream its homestead.

You must not expect that these island creeks and little rivers will be very impressive even though Kauai has in its center Mt. Waialeale. *Wai*, of course, means water and *aleale*[2] rippling, and the mountain is well named. The claim has been made that this is the wettest place on earth—at least it has the highest recorded

---

[1] Menehunes, probably the first inhabitants of the islands, have now taken their place in Hawaiian folklore as "the little people"—gnomes or fairies.

[2] Pronounced al-e-al-e.

downpour. This equals Seattle's rainfall multiplied ten times, or if you like addition better, that city's annual precipitation plus fifty feet. The mountain's slopes are indeed perpetually rippling. The creeks that descend have little opportunity to get together before they reach the sea. Most of them, no matter how small, are permanent streams, for the morass on Waialeale's summit is like a giant sponge from which the water is squeezed by each fresh inundation. When it rains heavily, you may count a score or more of cascades, all visible from Hanalei Bay. Many of the creek valleys are inhabited by colonies of landshells, each differing in species from the neighboring colonies in the gulches on either side. Some of the shells are beautifully marked, and several fine collections have been made on Kauai. How these landshells ever reached these volcanic islands is a mystery. Possibly they represented originally sea species that lived in the brackish water at the rivers' mouths, and with the recession of the ocean, they were faced with the alternative of dying out or becoming adapted to fresh water. They chose the latter. Many of them are not unlike some species of seashells in their architecture.

Each stream as it comes from the central morass makes a swift run down the mountain declivity, usually in a series of waterfalls, pausing here and there to scour a pothole in some ancient lava bed. One stream is famous on Kauai for having at one place a smooth channel hollowed out of the rock, which has provided generations of Hawaiians with breath-taking slides into the cool depths of the pool below.

Only when these little rivers reach the narrow coastal plains which they have laid down for themselves in the course of centuries, are they able to slow down and collect into those quiet reaches that help to make a drive along Kauai's foreshore so satisfying. There are no willows to cast reflections but hau and kamani trees make a solid green frame for mirrored clouds and mountain peaks nearby.

Kauai is said to mean "the drying out place," but another interpretation states that the name refers to the things that are dried out, the driftwood and other material cast up by the sea. Because of its northerly position in the Hawaiian islands, tree trunks from the American northwest sometimes come ashore. Hence, the beaches were eagerly watched by the natives. An early account records the discovery of a sixty-foot pine log which was promptly hollowed out into a hull. The chief waited years for its mate to drift in so that he could make a double canoe, but finally he gave up hope and used the log to make a single craft. Pine was valued highly; it was so much easier to work and more buoyant than koa. What acquaintance the natives had with iron before Cook's visit came from the salvage of nails from pieces of wreckage that drifted ashore. A nail or two would buy anything in the islands.

It is the southeast part of the island which is laid out to dry and forms a crescent, like a quarter moon lying somewhat on its back, with one tip at Kekaha and the other at Kilauea. The land is planed down and fertile, and this part indeed deserves to be called a garden, particularly the broad middle of the crescent lying between Waimea on the south, through Koloa and Lihue to Kapaa on the east. This area is divided in two by the worn-down stumps of an old range, of which Mt. Hoary Head, or Haupu, overlooking Lihue, is the highest peak. The drying out of the land is here aided by four streams that almost attain the dignity of rivers, the Waimea, the Hanapepe, the Huleia, and the Wailua. Within their lower watersheds are the fertile lands of Kekaha, Makaweli, Koloa, and Lihue plantations.

Because of its physical form and characteristics, the symbol for Kauai should be the Turkish flag reversed so as to form the star and sickle, with the latter representing the garden part of the island, while within the crescent is the star, its disk the dome of Mt. Waialeale, its rays the streams radiating in all directions.

Back from the extreme northern tip of the sickle at Haena you will pass a succession of little rivers with their dividing headlands, and wonderful beaches curving in between. Some of the indentations are large and open like the half-moon bay at Hanalei, others are small and secluded and quite unexpected. Such are Kalihiwai and Kalihikai, which are just a "whoop and a holler" from headland to headland. On the one hand you have white ocean rollers thundering on the beach in endless succession, on the other the quiet grey water of the little river gently lapping the sand. These contrasts are very characteristic of Kauai. And in all your journeys there you are never far away from the mountain wall out of which the streams issue. The valley floors are usually dark green with hau trees, while their sides show the much lighter vegetation of the kukui, lauhala, and breadfruit. In these small valleys there is not enough flat land to invite settlement—perhaps a Chinese store or an Hawaiian church, surrounded by monkeypods and kamani trees, is all that you may see.

Perhaps the most beautiful beach in the twenty-mile stretch between Kilauea and Haena, and certainly one of the most beautiful in the islands, is called Lumahai, or sometimes Olivene Beach, from the little green semi-precious stones to be found there. The bay is the usual crescent shape except that it is divided in the middle by a black tongue of lava, on either side of which the waves swirl viciously. Flanking this rocky outthrust are two wide sweeps of yellow sand, up which the big Pacific rollers rush. The whole bay is edged with a thick fringe of puhalas, variously known as pandanus or screw palms. This tree is extremely stiff-jointed, the branches going off at unusually wide angles so that each bunch of long ribbon-like leaves gets a maximum of air and sunlight. To compensate for this wide-angled growth, the stems are buttressed by numerous aerial roots. It is from these leaves, stripped of their midribs, that lauhala mats are made. Pandanus palms also cover the bluffs that contain the bay, giving the scene a typical South Seas appearance. If you drive around the headlands too fast, you may miss the view down into Lumahai. No stream seems to empty here, nor is there even a beach-house in sight. You may have the whole place to yourself with not even a footprint on the sand to indicate that anyone has ever been here before you. It is a grand place to idle, but not to swim. The waves are always big, with a dangerous undertow.

A headland or two farther on you come to a river which the Hawaiians called "wild water," Wainiha. A couple of miles upstream it deserves its name, for there is a tumbling mountain stream, in whose cold water the brown trout thrive. But at the place where twin bridges cross, it has become sobered by its first glimpse of the surf. It dawdles and hesitates, takes time to divide around an island jungle of hau; at the very last it avoids the wide beach in front of it, and taking a sudden turn, shelters itself behind a rocky headland, waiting its chance between combers to slip out to sea. It is fascinating to watch this unequal conflict between river and sea, and to note especially the rush of the fresh water as the wave recedes.

There are a few places in the islands where, if you want to add surprise to pleasure, you may ask the visitor to keep his eyes shut until you give him the signal to look around. One is at the approach to the Pali. His last view is of a country road, shaded by eucalyptus, winding between two mountain walls. His next is the wide-open sweep of the Pali view at his feet. It is an unexpected gift of rare beauty. Another place where you can offer him an unusual experience is at the Haena dry cave. Ask your visitor to close his eyes at the creek that crosses the road where it seems just about to swerve around a massive cliff right in front of the car. Then you turn at right angles at the break in the stone wall across the cavern's mouth and drive in eighty yards to the back wall, turning the car to face the entrance. When the visitor opens his eyes he is sitting in a great empty rock-walled theater, looking out through the dark to the sunlit trees framed in the cave's entrance. The illusion is that of a vividly colored scene thrown on a screen. For sound effects you can have the roar of the surf breaking less than two hundred yards from the entrance.

A twenty-five-foot rise would bring the ocean sweeping once again into the cave just as it does into the great sea caverns that are to be seen farther along the Napali coast, the wildest part of

Kauai's shore line. (Napali is the plural form of Kapali—the cliff.) The time to see the play of waters at such a spot is when, at rare intervals, league-long rollers come down from the north, an aftermath of great storms offshore. Mighty hills of sea water, smooth sided, with seventy-five-yard troughs, forty feet deep, hit the cliffs at well-spaced intervals. First comes the thunder of the main assault, then the deep penetration, and many seconds afterwards the muffled roar when the wave hits the back wall of the cave. Then as the piled-up flood rolls back, it may chance to meet the next incoming wave in a vast confusion of waters.

One of the rather saddening features of a trip around Oahu is the feeling that comes to the visitor, rightly or wrongly, that now he has seen it all. For some, the feeling is justified; they have so little capacity for seeing. But you cannot feel like this on Kauai, for there are parts of this island where no human foot has ever trod. A few hundred yards past the Haena Caves you come to the end of the road. From thence there is only a bridle path that swings recklessly around windswept precipices, or descends into sudden gulches, making three or four miles forward for many miles up and down. This track brings you to Kalalau Valley, but beyond this there is no trail, and no travel except by sea.

The reason for these sheer precipices is well illustrated along the Hamakua coast of Hawaii, where island-building and island-cutting run an as yet undecided race. But on Kauai the contest of mountain versus sea is decided; the sea has won. The Pacific seems to resent these solid islands that have been thrust up from its depths, and has marshaled all its assault waves to cut the intruders down. Perhaps because this is the most exposed salient of all the island chain, the northwest shoreline of Kauai has had to withstand not only the bitterest, but the longest continued attacks. Now the enemy has stormed all the outer defenses and is up against the citadel itself. There must be great depths off shore, for sheer cuts of two to three thousand feet appear without hardly a trace of detritus at their base. On some of the headlands ancient lava tubes have been exposed and enlarged into great sea caves. At one place, the combined efforts of stream and sea have drilled a tunnel clear through the headland with a little beach at either end.

In this shearing off of the face of the island, little streams that once ran down to the sea at ordinary levels have been cut off in mid-course. Now they have their mouths in the precipice wall, five hundred or more feet above the sea. They are known as "hanging valleys," and as their sides are also precipitous with palis a thousand feet in height, they are inaccessible from either above or below. Standing off a mile or so from shore you can look partly into them and see that they are filled with trees and, no doubt, with the songs of Hawaiian birds. Waterfalls, like slender ropes whipped to a frazzle with the wind, hang from their outlets. Geologists consider that it has taken the Pacific two million years to cut back these cliffs, and as man has been here a paltry thousand or two, it is true that no human foot has trodden the Napali hanging valleys.

In some other places where the streams are more constant and considerable, the cutting down process has kept pace with the cutback, so that the valley mouths are nearly at sea level. One of these is called Nualolo, the meaning of which is given by Alexander as "layers of young coconut sheaths," but as coconuts are not plentiful hereabouts, this meaning seems strange. Much more fitting would be its meaning if derived from *nu,* a great sound, and *alolo,* a term of derision or triumph over the ills or misfortunes of others; for Nualolo was by its nature a secure refuge for the lawless and those who defied the power of kings or kahunas. Its inhabitants could well afford to laugh at the misfortunes of those who suffered under tyrannical tabus.

There was a strong stream issuing from the mouth of the valley and the only advantage the sea had won was represented by a twenty-foot cliff of slippery rocks, over which the water tumbled. Except in the calmest weather, any canoes would be dashed to splinters, and swimmers could be kept off by a few determined men with stones and spears. There was just one drawback. The valley mouth was constricted between two headlands. There was no view up and down the coast so that the chief element to be guarded against was surprise.

But the people of this hidden valley found a way to escape any sudden invasion fleet of canoes sweeping around the headland and coming on them unawares. On the west side, ledges ran from the side of the valley but ended above a sea cave. There was, however, another ledge some thirty feet below, which led into what is now called Nualolo Flat.

This is merely a horseshoe beach of cobblestones contained within tremendous cliffs. It is noteworthy, however, as being the only place on this coast where the waves have planed off a bench extending out almost a hundred yards beyond the headland. It is barely covered at high tide and is full of deep cracks and pot-holes, alive with fish, lobsters, great eels, and occasional turtles. In this bench there is a wide crack, in the mouth of which a sampan can anchor in calm weather and put off a rowboat for the beach. The cave in the dividing headland is so deep and the waves are sucked into it with such violence that only the strongest swimmers would attempt to swim around to Nualolo Valley, and then only by going well out into deep shark-water.

The Hawaiians, however, are not easily frustrated. They chiseled a hole in a projecting knob of stone and hung from it a sennit rope by which they descended to the lower ledge that leads into Nualolo Flat, where there was a high pinnacle of rock providing an excellent lookout. In canoe weather, which was only during a couple of months in the year, a watch was kept, and at the first alarm, the people climbed the cliff, hauled themselves up on to the next ledge leading around the headland, and then pulled the rope up after them. With the front door into Nualolo easily defended, the side door was thus effectively barred against any invader.

Bingham, in 1821, on his first trip back to Oahu from Kauai, was taken by canoe to Nualolo and has left this description of the place. "At another part of this precipitous coast, we landed where there is a small tract of sterile ground, partly environed by a stupendous precipice, nearly perpendicular, forming at its base a semi-circular curve which meets the ocean at each end. This vast rock rises at the ends of the curve about 300 feet, and in the center nearly 2,500 feet.

"Commencing the ascent by a rude ladder that hangs over the sea, natives sometimes climb for amusement to the summit, to exhibit their simple fire-works, and throw off torches, so constructed that they will reach the sea. Near one end of the curve, the rough face of the rock projects gradually forward some fifty feet, so as to cover a little hamlet built in its shelter, where the frail houses of the poor inhabitants are generally defended from the rain, and always from the direct rays of the sun, till afternoon." It was no wonder that the preacher was reminded of "a great rock in a weary land."

More than a century after Bingham's visit, the writer was taken to Nualolo Flat in a sampan by Hawaiians whose ancestors had lived in this place. The foundations of the houses which Bingham described are still standing, the cliff's overhang providing such excellent protection from the weather that the mouldering grass of the walls and the ashes of the fireplaces were still lying there, though no one had lived in the place for eighty years. It was evidently an ancient habitation, for the deposits left by the natives were in places six feet in thickness.

At the base of the cliff, about in the middle of the horseshoe bend, we found the burial cave of the chiefs. It contained seven complete skeletons and large numbers of detached bones. On a shelf near the entrance were the bones of an Hawaiian dog, possibly the favorite of one of the chiefs, or simply left there for the spirits' sustenance. The discovery was of exceptional scientific interest as the skeleton was of such great age that the dog was undoubtedly pure bred. Dr. Wood Jones, famous comparative anatomist, from a study of this canine skull determined that it was quite distinct from both the Australian dingo and the Red Dog of the Deccan. This indicated that the wandering Polynesian and his dog did not come in contact with Australia, and that if he came originally from Southeast Asia he probably picked up his dog somewhere along the way.

Why the Hawaiians deserted the place we could only conjecture. Perhaps the *pax theologica,* the missionaries' peace, put an end to the tyrannies and cruelty of king and kahuna, and made a place of refuge unnecessary. The whites, as we know, brought measles, influenza, and tuberculosis with them. Smallpox also took a fearful toll so that the total native population in thirty years was cut to one third of its former size. Once an epidemic was introduced to Nualolo, the area was so confined that few could escape infection. Perhaps the women became tired of living where they could see nothing and hear little of this brave new world that was building around them, and insisted on moving away. But for tragic or other reasons, the people deserted the spot completely. These could easily have been valleys of death—in any case they became valleys of silence. From what has been said, it may be judged that Nualolo was not an easy place to land on even by sampan. The wind and surf had to be just right and the channel, being only thirty yards wide at its broadest, required some careful navigation. Nevertheless the Hawaiians took us in on one occasion at night.

There was a three quarter moon just rising over the mountains, and black shadows lay inside the throats of the valleys. The cliffs could be barely discerned but now and then there was a flash of phosphorescence as a big comber hit the rocks at their base. Presently the Hawaiians slowed down the engine and turned the sampan in towards the darkness. Then they shut off the motor and listened to the recurrent roar of the breakers. "That is not the sound of Nualolo," one said, "that is the surf of Milolii." The others agreed, and the sampan's nose was turned while we went slowly chugging along in the direction from which we had come, still in the dark shadows of immense cliffs. Soon our pilots turned the masthead spotlight on the face of the seaward precipice and we nosed our way back a couple of miles to the mouth of the little bay of Nualolo. These Hawaiians knew their coastline like a blind man knows the sounds of his city. By the time we reached our anchorage the edge of the moonlight had come within a hundred yards of the shore but the channel was still in the shadow. Nevertheless, the sampan was surely directed to safe anchorage.

The visitor may never have the pleasure of landing at Nualolo, but the day is coming when plane flights along the Napali coast will be included in the itinerary of the visitor to Kauai. He will be able to recognize Nualolo by the traditional sign, X marks the spot. On the overhanging cliff face mentioned by Bingham is a huge cross made by two narrow intersecting dykes—cracks in the rock through which intrusive lava of a different color and composition has been forced by pressure from below.

This coast, though you will not find a score of people in Honolulu who have visited it, figures at least twice in the literature on Hawaii. Besides Bingham, Jack London writes of the place in his story of Koolau, the leper. This man was a cowboy from Niihau who contracted the disease in one hand and arm, and when the edict went forth that all lepers were to be segregated at Kalaupapa on Molokai, he was supposed to have led a band of fellow sufferers into one of these almost inaccessible regions, the valley of Kalalau. Actually, the cowboy went off alone. The deputy sheriff and a companion went to capture Koolau who took refuge on a ridge. There the leper drew a deadline and warned the sheriff not to cross it. The latter, who had been friendly with Koolau, disregarded the warning and was shot dead. Later the cowboy was besieged by a company of soldiers with a machine gun. He was wounded but escaped. Some weeks after he was found dead. Thus the Napali coast had again become a sanctuary for the hunted.

Just as this part of the coast is exposed, the southern part is sheltered, and for this reason whatever history Kauai possesses was made in or around Waimea. In 1809 the Neva, a Russian ship, arrived at Honolulu and took back to Alaska most favorable reports of the islands as a winter haven for ships in the fur trade. Five years later a vessel with a valuable cargo was wrecked near Waimea, no doubt in one of the infrequent southerly storms. Baranoff, the Russian governor of Alaska, sent a German, Dr. Scheffer, to salvage what he could of the cargo which was being guarded by Kaumualii, the Kauai king. Scheffer was a very ambitious man, and obtained from the king a free grant of the Hanalei Valley, at the mouth of which he built a fort mounting six guns. The king was so taken with this new fortification that he engaged Scheffer to build a substantial fort at the mouth of the Waimea river. In 1815 several Russian ships arrived in quick succession, the fort was built and at one time mounted 52 cannon. At this time Scheffer was reported to be negotiating for the cession of the island to the Russians. Kamehameha, hearing of these plans, ordered the ejection of the Russians, and according to one account, several Russians were killed in a scuffle. However, Scheffer left, and his designs were later disavowed by his Russian employers.

Before the war, a visit to the Russian fort was part of the tourist itinerary. Now, after another full turn of the wheel of fate, it is again a military post. The path to the old fort led through giant prickly pear, along the low cliff beside the river. Labor was free and rocks plentiful, so that the plan was to pile a great stone circle with a number of projections, particularly on the sides facing the river and sea, to serve as embrasures for cannon. On the inner sides of the ring, particularly around the embrasures, walls were constructed, and in the center of the enclosed space was a magazine cellar, built of a soft cement made with what seems to be crushed coral. Lines of stones still mark paths or roadways, but these may have been merely house foundations put in by Hawaiians who for long afterwards occupied the fort. The cliff below the fort is particularly broken, and tradition says that a tunnel once led from the river level into the middle of the fortification. It is entirely possible.

The place had its baptism of blood after Liholiho's death when there was an attempt made to restore the son of the former king who had been deposed by Liholiho. The insurgents attempted to rush the fort but were repulsed, with eleven of them killed. The defenders lost a number of men, including two white men who manned the guns, one of them a man named Trowbridge whom

Bingham had tried to convert. The missionary party were well within the whistle of bullets and were given passage on a brig to Oahu. A young chief, one of the insurgents, was on board and was disposed of by a common method of getting rid of prisoners of war; he was knifed and thrown overboard. Reinforcements were secured on Oahu and the revolutionaries were defeated in a battle near Hanapepe.[3]

Besides the fort there is another work of foreign origin at Waimea, a piece of stone carving which is a great anthropological puzzle. About a mile up the river is the so-called Menehune Ditch, contained behind a low wall of dressed stone. Only a little of this work is left, the rest having been destroyed in the building of a road. The Hawaiians say that they have no record of this wall being constructed, and ascribe it to the menehunes, little people of the mountains, who are supposed to have come down and completed the work in a single night. The stones have undoubtedly been chiseled, with smooth rectangular sides. Stone adzes could have done the work, but it would have been most laborious, and the Hawaiians have done no other dressed stonework like it. Moreover, the stones are keyed, so that each course sets snugly into the one below it, a projection on one stone fitting into a depression in the other, after the style of the stone work of the Incas of Peru. This wall may be proof of the presence of Spaniards, or even of Incas, long ago on these islands, but if so, it is strange they did not leave more traces of their stay. Members of the crew of the Santa Rosa, a ship which turned pirate and looted cities on the Peruvian and Chilean coasts, were living here in 1818, but were later rounded up by a Spanish warship, the Argentina. The first officer was executed on the beach at Waimea. Whether these men had anything to do with the Menehune Ditch is pure conjecture, but so is everything else about the matter. One of the stones has on its side a round cavity that looks suspiciously like a drill hole for blasting.

[3] This was the first battle of Hanapepe. In 1924, about one hundred years later, another fight took place between some striking Filipinos and the deputy sheriff, who had enlisted a posse of Hawaiian cowboys to assist him to rescue two non-strikers from the hands of the mob. In the ensuing battle 5 deputies and 23 Filipinos were killed.

Where there are no records, the memory of man in such things is notoriously short. The Hawaiians may have forgotten the men who chiseled the stones. All that we know is that whoever built the ditch wall, the menehunes didn't.

Along the west side of the rim rock that bounds the east side of the Waimea Valley, there is a strange memento of the past. Arizona and New Mexico have their ancient cliff dwellings, but Waimea used its cliffs as a cemetery, a vertical burying ground. The red lava wall is honeycombed with small caves and these were pre-empted as places of sepulture by Hawaiians who claimed alii rank. High chiefs did very much as they pleased, and old Hawaiian tales were full of situations in which the king on a journey was attracted by some beautiful girl with whom he left his malo so that their child later might come to court and claim a chief's rank. Illegitimacy was no bar to such pretensions. Sometimes the claim could not be fully established, and one way in which a man could assert his right to noble ancestry was to refuse to put his garments on the same rock or ledge with a commoner's possessions. Such people were called "clothes rack chiefs," and as such claimed the honor of cave burial.

Common persons were merely interred in sand dunes. There was one of these burial grounds near the lighthouse that stands on the rocks beyond Koloa, the exposed bones giving rise to the mistaken belief that this was an old battleground. Another large cemetery is near Mokapu on Oahu, some four hundred skeletons having been disinterred by a University anthropological party. The Navy intended in any case to level the dunes.

Bodies of high chiefs, on the other hand, could not be buried so openly. The higher the rank, the more secret the burial. Some ill-disposed person might get possession of the chief's bones and use them for working some evil magic. Hence the actual burial place of Kamehameha I was a most closely guarded secret. That the Waimea cliff face cemetery was in use after the whites came is shown by the fact that a few of the family caves are boarded up with hewn planks, in some cases secured by nails, but the more ancient by wooden pegs.

The Waimea high chiefs had a separate burial place higher up on the cliff face, to which access was gained by a narrow ledge. It was a double cave, an outer chamber being filled with a great miscellany of bones. At the back was a square opening lined with four beams, leading down a steep incline to another deeper cavern. The writer, engaged in a skull hunting expedition, crawled down this narrow passage only to find all headway blocked by fallen rocks. To crawl backward over sharp rubble up a 45-degree inclined plane for some fifty feet, kicking up the dust of decayed tapa, rotted canoes, and dead Hawaiians, did not constitute a very pleasant experience.

Interesting as the surroundings of Waimea are, the visitor will rarely spend much time there, for he will be on his way to Kauai's scenic pride, the Waimea canyon. This is no Grand Canyon of the Colorado, no matter how local pride expands it, but its three thousand feet of colored depth are enough. Three tributary gorges, scored deeply in the flank of the central mountain mass of Waialeale, unite to form the main canyon, and your first view is across one branch and up the length of another. It is even more unexpected than the Pali view. You step off a few yards from the winding motor road that has brought you up, first through cane and then through forest, and suddenly you are on the brink of the gorge. Another step and you could go hurtling down a couple of thousand feet.

Waimea has none of the stark wonder of the Grand Canyon. Its colors are softer, perhaps because of the green shawls of forest that cover the summits and dip down into the valley heads, reminding you that this is no desert setting. Perhaps because Hawaii lacks the clarity of Arizona atmosphere, you need only a few miles of distance here to partially dissolve the harshness of red rock wall and naked promontory into a purple mist.

The quiet of these depths is perhaps their most impressive feature. There is seldom any wind and the only motion you can see is the flight of the white, long-tailed tropic birds, who are true cliff dwellers and ceaselessly scout the canyon crevices. Even the lacy waterfalls are immobilized by distance, so that the place is empty of everything but beauty. And for contrast you may turn your back, and far down below, framed in a vista of koa trees, is the dark bulk of the island of Niihau, set in the gleaming Pacific. No photograph can do justice to the canyon and only one artist, Howard Hitchcock, seems to have captured its colors. But the essence of Waimea hues is that they are not static. They flow, and such motion is difficult to transfer to canvas without blurring the form that lies behind this gentle flux of color.

Whether artist or explorer, you will be more at home with the things of the forest at Kokee, the rolling plateau into which the Waimea streams have cut so deeply. The trees may be strange to you—great koas, ohias, tree lobelias shading a riot of wild nasturtiums, and creeping passion fruit vines—but these things are much nearer man's stature than canyons. This mild mountain climate provides perpetual spring, and is hence most favorable to the growth of all the old-world flowers. Roses, azaleas, fuchsias, and the like go wild without the least provocation, while every little stream is shaded with purple lasiandras.

A forest trail four miles or so in length carries you across the tableland and brings you to the lip of a green precipice stretching down nearly four thousand feet into Kalalau Valley. If you are lucky, the mists may divide and let you look down a grey corridor to see a fragment of the blue sunlit Pacific, and the soundless surf breaking in purest white on tropical sands below.

The road down the mountain brings you again to superheated Kekaha, and from there you may continue to the nether tip of the garden of Kauai until you come to Mana, famous throughout the islands for its barking sands. The dunes, when dry, emit a hollow sound as you stride down them, which, with the aid of some imagination, you may describe as the "whoofing" of a dog. The dunes, however, are really more notable for their strange patterns of sand and creeping vegetation.

Beyond Mana, the dry hills, broken and cactus-covered, close in, until there is no room for any road. You are now turned north and have reached once again the other end of the Napali coast with

Milolii, its first hidden valley, not more than seven miles distant, as the shearwater flies. Once more the big seas and currents from the north sweep in towards the land and cliff cutting begins again. Off the coast hereabouts is an ocean deep that the Hawaiians believed to be the abode of Po, the ruler of the dead. The high cliff opposite provided a diving platform from which the spirits could gain sufficient momentum to carry them down into Po's domain. Because of this, the houses all along the shore were built on an east-west line, with an opening at either end so that the spirits would not be tempted to delay in their passage but would go right through.

The idea of this procession of the souls of all dead people from around the island must have had some terrifying elements. The rustling of the breeze among the dry leaves of the lauhala, the ghostly flapping of the Hawaiian owl across the face of the moon, the splash of a big fish off shore when the sea was quiet must have struck deep into superstitious minds. Hence, the heiau built above the last narrow strip of beach was of particular sacredness.

Its name was Polehale. *Pole* means a depression or hollow, and *hale* is house. Hence, Polehale may well have meant the house that divides the living from the dead, the resting place of the lost souls before they took the rocky trail that led to the summit of the cliff, and the last long plunge down to the underworld. So that ill-disposed persons, who might wish to manufacture lucky fishhooks out of chiefs' legbones, would avoid the spot, it was chosen as a hidden place of sepulture. In among the fallen blocks of stone that form a scree at the base of the cliff is a narrow opening which goes straight down for five or six feet. Then it opens out into a narrow lava tube, as dark and smooth as the inside of a rubber hose. This tube runs straight into the cliff for a couple of hundred feet, and in it, laid end to end, were seven complete skeletons, each having once had a canoe as a coffin, though these were all mouldered into dust.

It did not take much imagination to see again the wall of the heiau lined with horrid grinning idols, the human sacrifices laid face down in front of the altar, the priests chanting before the chief's *akua* or family god. Then came the slow night procession, lit by the wavering light of the split kukui nuts threaded to form a torch, the body borne by a pair of husky commoners, who would never return from this mission to divulge the place of burial. Thus primitive life merged easily with the shadows.

A story goes with the heiau. Years ago Mr. Eric Knudsen, a well-known ranch owner on Kauai, was Speaker of the Territorial Legislature. The Hawaiian members were easy spenders and it was not uncommon for them to vote more appropriations for various worthy projects than there was money in the Treasury. This led to a mad scramble among the heads of government departments, and the one who got to the Treasurer first usually won. After a particularly generous session, Governor Carter decided to call the Legislature together for a short special session in order to straighten out the financial mess. But the legislator is paid by the day, plus his expenses in Honolulu, so that the Governor's hope that the time would not extend to the regular sixty days seemed especially vain. However, he enlisted the Speaker's help in this matter.

Eric's Hawaiian foreman was also a member of the Legislature, and just before the session they were rounding up cattle near Polehale and ate their lunch at the heiau. Presently Eric wandered down to the beach, bringing back a handful of coral and shells, with which he decorated a small cairn of stones that he had built on the altar. Then to his foreman's amazement, he launched into a long Hawaiian incantation, at the end of which he called down the vengeance of the gods of the heiau on any who should obstruct the business of the next Legislature.

"You don't believe that stuff, do you, Mr. Knudsen?" asked the foreman.

"Of course not," was the reply. "This is all in fun. No one believes those old superstitions any more. It's all old women's poppycock."

Nevertheless, on the steamer going to Honolulu and later in the legislative halls there was a great deal of quiet whispering among the Hawaiian members. The whole business of the session was finished in fifteen days, and the legislators went home.

Some years afterwards the story had a sequel. Mr. Knudsen was one of a party who visited a Yellowstone Park geyser just too late to view its performance, which was not due again for a couple of hours.

"Well," said Eric, "we people in Hawaii have a goddess named Pele who is in charge of all these volcanic shows. When she gets temperamental, and refuses to put on a performance, the Hawaiians placate her with offerings. Perhaps the Yellowstone fire-spirit is some relative of Pele's and the same plan may work here. Let's try it!"

So he set to work building a cairn near the geyser's mouth and sent the rest of the tourists to gather flowers and leaves for offerings. Then he recited his Hawaiian incantation, as an invocation to the spirit of fire. Scarcely had he finished than there was a rumble underground, and the whole party had to run for their lives as the geyser blew up almost in their faces.

That night at the big Park Hotel a score of people asked the magician just what he had said that made the geyser go off in that way. It is not only the simple Hawaiians who are possessed by superstitions.

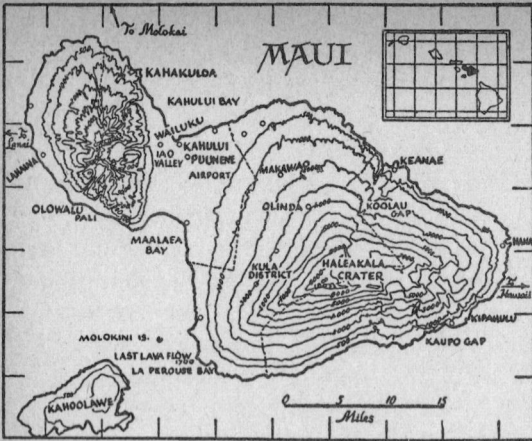

CHAPTER X

Maui

SPREADER OF LIGHT

NOTHING emphasizes so clearly the fact that the Polynesians are men of the sea than the content of their traditions and legends. The canoe voyages that carried migrants from the traditional dispersal point, Havaiki, in the Society Islands, all over the wide Pacific, are justly celebrated in song and story. Hawaii's traditions contain many references to voyages to and from Tahiti or Kahiki, which is the Hawaiian form of the word. A channel between Maui and the island of Kahoolawe is still known as Ke Ala-i-kahiki, the road to Tahiti. Among the voyagers whose names appear in these legends is that of Kahai, who brought the breadfruit from the homeland and planted it on Oahu. The Maoris also have their traditions of a series of migratory voyages southward which peopled New Zealand. Their songs recite the names of these canoes, and to be able to trace one's genealogy back to an ancestor who came over in one of these Polynesian "Mayflowers" was to insure honor and prestige.

Beyond the time of these traditional migrations is a period where myth and history blend. The ancient chants contain the names of Kupe who first visited New Zealand, and Hawaii-loa, the reputed discoverer of Hawaii. The latter is placed in the fifth century, the former in the tenth. Before this is the age of unadulterated myth. Here, as is fitting among a seafaring people, we come upon great tales of legendary fishermen and their magical catch. The most famous deep sea angler of all was Maui, who appears in legends all over Polynesia. Dr. Buck, in his book,[1] gives the Maori version of Maui's fishing. According to this story there were at first four brothers named Maui, represented by the thumb and first three fingers of the narrator's hand. The thumb was Maui-in-front; the middle finger was Maui-in-the-middle; then came Maui-on-the-one-side, and Maui-on-the-other-side. The little finger, Maui-the-last, was thrown into the ocean in an embryonic state by his mother, but was found and reared by Tangaroa, the god of the sea. He was the magic worker, with a spice of the devil, who played all kinds of tricks on his brothers.

It was he who fished up the North Island of New Zealand in the likeness of a sting ray, the tail being the peninsula of Auckland. While Maui went to get a priest to utter the incantations that would preserve the new land, his brothers proceeded to carve it up. Its painful writhings formed the valleys and mountains that wrinkled the island's surface. In Hawaii, Maui's place as a fisher of islands is taken by Kapu-he-e-ua-nui, who hooked a piece of coral on the bottom of the sea and hauled it up to form the island of Hawaii. Then followed Maui and the rest of the group.

Another myth relates that Hawaii and Maui were the offspring of Wakea, Sky-space, and Papa, the Earth-mother. When the latter left for Tahiti, Wakea played around with other women to whom Lanai and Molokai were born. The golden plover carried the news

[1] Buck, Peter. *Vikings of the Sunrise.* Stokes Co.

of these goings-on to Papa and she made haste to return. In revenge she had an affair of her own and gave birth to Oahu. Then she and Wakea were reconciled and the rest of the islands were begotten. The significance of these marital complications is not apparent, but we suspect that they were added to the legend to make the tale more worth telling.

In Hawaii, though Maui is not the fisher of islands, he is credited with the discovery of fire-making by rubbing a hard stick in a groove made in a softer wood, thus inventing the so-called Polynesian fire plow. Most spectacular of Maui's exploits was his journey to the pit of night where Ra, the sun, slept, and as the light giver came out he snared him with a noose fashioned out of hair. Once Maui had captured the sun, he made him promise to go slowly across the heavens so as to make more daylight for fishing and getting food. Thus, though Maui was a rather impish and uncertain deity, he remained for Polynesia the great educator, the spreader of light, the original daylight saver.

The Hawaiians were keen observers when it came to conferring place-names, as witness the wealth of descriptive terms applied to localities because of the behavior of the sea nearby. There must, therefore, have been special reasons for giving to the island of Maui the name of the almost universal culture-hero of Polynesia. It is possible that the situation and appearance of the great extinct or quiescent volcano that so dominates the whole island landscape explains this signal honor.

The sweep of the island of Maui is impressive. No other island of the group is so conveniently divided that you can see its two halves at once. For here you can stand on the lower slopes of either the East or West Maui mountains and see the whole width of the island spread out from sea to sea. From West Maui particularly it is a wide expanse filled in by the great bulk of Haleakala. In the minds of those who lived in the more populous part of the island, the volcano, standing directly in the path of the sun, may well have been connected with Maui, the spreader of light.

In the very early morning the mountain may be clear of clouds

Lumahae Beach on Kauai has never been written about

Olokele Canyon, Kauai

The Pacific declares war. Island carving on Molokai

Surf riding class at Waikiki

and then the long curving line of the summit is sharp against a topaz sky which gradually, as the sun rises, changes to the lightest blue. Because the ten-thousand-foot massif lies right in the path of the sun, the summit is still in shadow, while the green of the lower slopes is slowly emerging as an authentic foreground, checkered here and there by rectangles that retain their darkness of before the dawn. These are the eucalyptus groves.

No wonder the Hawaiians called it Hale-a-ka-la, house of the sun, La, or Ra, being the opposite of Po, the abode of darkness or night. Those who have watched dawn across the black crater of the mountain can almost believe the ancient legend of Maui waiting with his noose at the edge of the pit. Every clear morning the people of Wailuku see the sun come out of his house and stretch himself from Paia to Kula. Had these islanders been Navajo Indians, Haleakala would have dominated their religion and colored all their imagery. No sunrise would ever have gone by without prayers and hymns to its beauty and the scattering of sacred pollen dust to the god of the mountain. But calling it "House of the Sun" was as far as the poetic and religious imagination of the Hawaiians could go. For it must be remembered that this was a nation of voyagers to whom land was a resting place between sailings. For beauty they had the emerald fringe beside the shore, the dark blue and purple of the deep water beyond. These and the white of the bursting surges were always before them, a beauty perhaps more intense than that of the land. Had it not been for this, the Hawaiians would no doubt have been mountain-worshippers like the Navajos.

Isak Dinersen in her *Out of Africa* describes the view from the Ngong Hills near her farm. She says, "It was Africa distilled up through six thousand feet like the strong and refined essence of a continent. The colors were dry and burnt, like the colors in pottery." So too, if you will stand on the Kula road and look across the deep gulf that lies between you and the West Maui mountains, you will get the same effect. The colors are brown and terra cotta, and through the morning air the essence of the island comes up to meet you. In the afternoon and evening there is usually some haze, and occasionally a mouldering mist of blue rain sweeps in from Kahului. Then the colors are no longer burnt, but soft and moist. Later, the sun's rays lie lengthwise across the folds in the hills and every gulch is picked out in purple shadow. Some day there will be a city strung out along the three to four thousand foot belt around this side of Haleakala. People seeking its particular elixir of life cannot fail to find it out; but when this happens, one of the charms of Kula will be dissipated.

For what you will appreciate most is the calm of the place. The mountain barrier at your back restrains all the winds except for an occasional kona or southerly wind that sweeps up from Maalaea Bay. Down below, the hot red dust may be flying off the fields of Puunene, but here is a great stillness, one that can be felt. But you must stop to enjoy it. Half a mile up from where the crater road turns off the main highway is a little rocky gully filled with Australian wattles and blue gums. Perhaps there may be some English skylarks overhead, but otherwise there is a great calm, unless it be for the faintest breeze which is merely the earth breathing. English skylarks, Australian trees, Hawaiian atmosphere, all contribute their quota of charm to this bit of America. Perhaps this is the quiet center of the Pacific.

There is no climate in the world like that of Kula. California has its fogs, Washington State its rainy seasons, Florida its hurricanes, Australia its scorching northwinds—brickfielders they call them—and a damp chill in winter. The high veldt of South Africa is cool in summer, but raw and wind-swept in the winter. Go farther north to escape the cold and you must have great elevation to temper the heat. Nairobi, for example, which boasts of its climate, needs five thousand feet of altitude to make its summer bearable. Mexico City is still higher. Even the Mediterranean basin has its very disagreeable periods. There is surely no place in the world where you can have all through the year such comfort as at Kula—moderate elevation, yet cold enough at night so that an open fire is a comfort but not a necessity, rains infrequent yet heavy enough so that they are soon over and done with, and sunshine almost every day. All the flowers of the temperate zone will grow for you, and along the roads the scent of the Australian wattle and gums load the air.

The distinctive quality of Haleakala is remoteness. The narrow road to the summit zigzags back and forth, first through grassland dotted with fat Hereford cattle, then past groves of tall eucalyptus into a wide zone of low brush where the pheasants feed, and finally into a region of volcanic slag and broken lava flows, among which a few bents of tough grass or ragged brush find a precarious footing. When a damp mist shuts off the view of sunlit ocean below, and the cold moisture drips from the scanty brush and blackens the rocks, this is no longer Hawaii but the Scottish highlands "where ever the whaups are crying"; or it might be the Bogong High Plains of Southeast Australia, where among the winter-killed grass and wet rocks the spurwing plover runs and hides. Sometimes the Haleakala clouds gather only in a belt between the five and eight thousand foot levels and above that you are again in the clear Hawaiian sunlight.

Then you will begin to savor fully the remoteness of this Pacific height. Always as you ascend you take with you a sense of withdrawal from bustle and noise and the clutter of humans. Suddenly you make the discovery that it is not only human struggle that is excluded but much of Nature's confusion as well. Here is none of that rapid pulse of growth, of green things struggling with each other for light and sustenance, of animals preying and being preyed upon. This is not Nature, red in tooth and claw as Tennyson saw her, but remote and contemplative, almost austere.

Before the war the only animals you could see around the summit were the wild goats. Once the park officials took over and prohibited shooting, the goats soon became unconcerned. You may even see a patriarchal billy goat, his harem gathered around his feet, surveying your car from a lava rock with what looks like a benignant but might easily be a contemptuous stare. Nowadays, with the army setting up an observation and listening post near the summit, the goats have probably become very ferocious and the soldiers have had to shoot them in self-defense. As an observation post, Haleakala must be superb; there is absolutely nothing in the world to do but listen and observe.

If your imagination has a whimsical bent, you might believe that the mountain is so quiet because at one time it used up most of the noise that was available around these parts. It looks as if Pluto, supreme god of the underworld, was jealous of Pele's orchestra, and with one mighty blow he smashed the bass drum, so that it fell forever silent. There the instrument lies, with its empty crater and jagged walls, still eloquent of that last crashing crescendo of sound. When Haleakala blew up, the noise must have been as great as Krakatoa's explosion, which was heard 1,200 miles away and threw such quantities of dust into the stratosphere that it took three years to clear away.

The tourist literature will tell you that the crater is 27 miles around, and that the city of Philadelphia could rest comfortably within its bounds, but as Philadelphia could rest comfortably anywhere, that statement may not help the visitor to realize its magnitude. The highest buildings in New York would look like anthills if placed on the crater floor, but they are like nothing but anthills in New York also. As a matter of fact, the cinder cones that you see below are from six to nine hundred feet in height, and the crater itself is 3,000 feet at its deepest point. In the mountain's clear air it looks no more than 500 feet to the bottom, but if you should try the experience of going down the cinder trail either afoot or on horseback, it will seem as if it were actually miles deep.

No one who ascends Haleakala fails to be impressed by the cloud effects. As the crater falls into shadow and becomes cooler than the surrounding air, clouds occasionally break away from the outside and drift in, one at a time, through the Koolau gap, until they unite into a fleecy mass that fills the whole enclosed space. Then in the morning, when the sun's heat begins to beat on the cauldron of cloud, the mists swirl and divide until a procession of clouds drifts out again through the gap and the whole crater clears.

It is on the rim of Haleakala that one discovers a little understanding of the modern artist who seems determined to throw perspective out of the window in his endeavor to reproduce, not a photographic copy of a scene, but its emotional effect upon the beholder. No photograph can give you any feeling of the magnitude of the place. The crater is not round but quite unsymmetrical, with a wide open lip called Koolau Gap to the northeast. This looks as though some giant bull-dozer had ploughed its way through the rim and then plunged off seven thousand feet into the sea. Along its furrow has flowed a slow black tide of lava, issuing from between two volcanic ash cones each close to nine hundred feet high but looking in a photograph like insignificant sand piles built by children on the shore. At the left of the observation house, precipices of two to three thousand feet descend to the floor, making irregular headlands that jut out into space. Only to the right is the rim of the drum clear and unbroken; elsewhere, the jagged parchment still clings to the edge. In front of you lies another extension of the cavity stretching away to the narrow Kaupo Gap, ten miles across the crater floor.

Only those who have journeyed through this burnt-out silent cauldron can realize its essence. If some modern artist were able to mix devils' throats and towering naked cliffs with twisted black lava and the heaped-up broken chocolate fudge of *aa* flows, and place among them all the symbols of drought and loneliness and a sense of overwhelmingness, then we should have some grateful understanding of what the contemporary painter tries to do. But I suspect that all he would succeed in producing would be the appearance of seismic confusion. Haleakala has that, and much besides.

It is, no doubt, impossible for us to imagine great waves of sound by looking at a broken drum. Realization can come only in one way—if you have seen furnace blasts that are volcanic cones in action, mushrooming cauliflower clouds of dust and steam rushing up thousands of feet in air, lava throats ejecting rocks and ash and spattering melt, black crags suddenly splitting asunder and spilling forth a fiery torrent, fluid and glowing in its central channel, push-

ing up a slow tumbling slag heap on its edges. You must also have
stood within a few feet of viscous lava spreading its black swollen
toes over the surface of a former flow before you can realize that
this is the first attempt of molten rock to flow, and that unlike
water, its efforts to find its own level are slow and tentative. If you
have any imagination left, you may visualize that vast tide of lava
moving off slowly towards the Koolau Gap, urged on by spurting
fountains cascading hundreds of feet in air, the flood ponding
itself against the crater wall until it gathered sufficient strength to
lip the edge of the gap and go streaming down the mountain to
the sea.

There are lost rivers in the crater, but they are rivers of stone.
Some of them wandered around helplessly looking for an exit. On
the way to Kaupo there are two flows that approached and par-
alleled one another for a couple of miles, curve for curve, but never
met. Hence, you ride down a narrow grassy ribbon edged by an
occasional algaroba tree, the bulk of *aa* stone threatening you on
either hand. Some day, no doubt, there will be a motor road
through the crater, enabling the hurrying tourist to compress into
an hour's experience all that impression of turmoil and violence that
Haleakala took a thousand years to create.

Before the road up the mountain was built, the visitor used one
of the oldest instead of the newest modes of travel. Those were
the days when you took horses at Olinda and rode for eight hours,
angling the flows and threading the gulches until you stopped to
gather fuel for the night just at timber line at eight thousand feet,
or two thousand feet below the summit. On such a trip you had
leisure to watch the sunset, and the clouds drifting in through the
gap to fill the air-cooled crater or arranging themselves in new
patterns of color and form over the dark Pacific. If it were moonlight, it was worth while to brave the cold and, wrapped in one of
the community blankets, to stand on the crater's rim and look across
to the snow-covered summits of Mauna Kea and Mauna Loa ninety
miles away. There were the three great mountains of the Hawaiian
group, united in a community of silence.

It was by horseback that most of the early ascents of the mountain were made, and there is no traveler who has not attempted, even if it is only by comment in the old guest book at the summit, to convey some idea of his impressions or feelings. Perhaps the low water mark was reached by the Reverend Henry Cheever, who rode up the mountain in 1849 and told what he saw in his book *Sandwich Islands, The Heart of the Pacific*. He speaks of the crater "vomiting from a score of mouths its igneous bowels"—a rather complete emetic job if ever there was one.

The motor road to the summit is a great convenience to those who want to take a hurried glance at one of the most impressive sights of all Pacific lands, but the minor discomforts attendant upon staying the night are worth suffering if it is clear weather. The road has brought Haleakala within reach of every visitor to Maui, but I do not care how long the building of a road into the crater is delayed.

As you turn your back on the mountain to begin your descent, you might find it strange to consider what a reversal of conditions has taken place. Quiet has taken possession of the crater, once the mouthpiece of sound and fury; now all the noise and bustle and confusion are centered outside. For as you come down through the clouds the plain that occupies the waist of Maui will be alive with tractors and jeeps, the air with planes shuttling across the isthmus or getting into the air from the two great air fields. A hundred years ago the wide curve of Maalaea Bay might have been black with invasion fleets of war canoes, for this plain was the traditional battleground for the possession of the island. Whoever established himself across the isthmus effectively cut off the men of Lahaina from Maui's eastern defenders. The strategy of war has not changed radically. This is still the focal point in the defense of the island. Battles have been so often fought here that the plain of Kahului gave its name to a particular order of battle in which the two opposing forces were drawn up facing each other in crescent formation.

Those who believe the Spanish discovered the Hawaiian Islands rely largely on a chart found by Lord Anson in a galleon captured after a bloody sea fight in 1743. They identify Maui on this chart as an island called La Desgraciada. The name means "the unfortunate," and Maui being in the middle, may well have deserved the description, subject as she was to attacks from both Hawaii and Oahu. One of the greatest conflicts was the Battle of the Sandhills, fought near Wailuku between the warriors of Kalaniopuu, the king of Hawaii at the time of Cook's visit, and Kahakili, leader of the Maui men. The Hawaii army was soundly defeated and almost destroyed. Kahakili, by the way, was a very tough character, who to confuse and terrify his enemies had one side of his body tattooed until it was quite black. It was he who afterwards invaded Oahu and made such a slaughter that a house in Moanalua was surrounded by a double fence of the legbones of the slain. *Maui no ka oi*—Maui over all, was no empty boast in Kahakili's time.

Even the names of the streams that are disgorged from the West Maui mountains are reminders of savage battles. There is Wai-ka-pu, the water of the blowing of the conch shell that calls the warriors; next is Wai-ehu, the water red with the dust of battle; then comes Wai-luku, the water of havoc, of exceeding great slaughter; last is Wai-hee, the water of utter rout and headlong flight. Thus these streams commemorate the stages of some great battle, tragic in the annals of Maui.

But Kahului has reason to remember invasions other than human, for being flat and directly in the path of what was once a sea-way between East and West Maui, it has suffered at intervals from tidal waves. A most remarkable one is recorded in 1837, an aftermath of a great earthquake on the coast of Chile. These great hills of water travel over the open ocean at about 450 miles an hour and a fifteen minute interval between them, which gives them a distance of 112 miles from crest to crest. Where the wave is constricted within bays such as those at Hilo and Kahului, the water is heaped up as in a bottleneck and great damage may ensue.

On this occasion the sea retired from the shore for a distance of about 120 yards, much to the delight of the Hawaiians, many of

The Royal Palm

Photos by R. J. Baker

Upper. The Rainbow Shower tree blazes with color

Lower. Hedge of Night Blooming Cereus

whom rushed out to the reef to secure the stranded fish. Others with more experience knew what would come next and fled inland. Suddenly the astonished fishers saw the sea rising up like a wall and sweeping down upon them. The wave rushed inland carrying away a whole village of thatched houses. Canoes, calabashes, house frames, chickens, pigs, dogs, and people were picked up and carried some hundreds of yards and deposited in the swamp at the back of Kahului foreshore. Others near the harbor were carried out to sea, then swept in again on the next huge wave. Any other community of people would have been overwhelmed and drowned, but not the Hawaiians. They grabbed whatever promised support and paddled with gleeful shouts or swam to safety. Only two lives were lost. In 1923 an earthquake near Alaska caused considerable disturbance in the seas around Hawaii. At Honolulu the water off Waikiki fell eight feet but returned quietly. This ebb and flow took place about seven times within a two-hour interval, much to the delight of all the boys along the beach who had great fun chasing fish in the shallows and catching them by hand. At Kahului, however, the harbor almost emptied, and then a huge wave swept over the piers. No lives were lost though one man was caught near the foreshore. The wave lifted his car and deposited it over a fence; the damage, a broken leg. As long as tidal waves do not occur at more than forty year intervals, the residents of Kahului do not seem inclined to worry.

Maui people call their island the Valley Isle because of its famous Iao Valley. Iao means "towards the dawn," and it is well named because it has no sunsets. It is a gash in the West Maui Mountains, so narrow and deep that the sun is gone behind the mountain wall long before it is sunset at Wailuku just a mile away. Time has its ups and downs on this part of the island. It is night in Iao when it is sundown at Wailuku, while the sun will still be shining for fifteen minutes longer on Haleakala across the plain. On a clear evening you can watch the zone of sunlight gradually contracting until only the summit is caught in a crimson noose of light. But by then the grey-green river of kukuis which flows down the floor of Iao Valley is almost lost in darkness.

Spread the first two fingers of your right hand, keeping the others doubled up with your thumb; then the space between is almost exactly Iao Valley; on the left a steeply sloping wall with a bulge opposite the knuckle. The right side of the valley is so steep that from some places below it appears almost concave. Above the bulge on the left hand wall a few trees find lodgment, but otherwise the valley's sides are steeply bare, yet green with moss and small ferns. Nowhere will you find mountain sides that so well deserve the term that Robert Louis Stevenson used—viridescent. And when it catches the sunlight the green of Iao Valley actually glows.

One wonders how high the canyon walls really are. That odd monolith, with a lei of kukuis around its shoulders, that they call the Needle and which stands near the fork of the valley is 1,200 feet. The West Maui mountains go up over 6,000 feet, the crater Eke being at that elevation. Certainly the valley cannot be less than between two and three thousand feet deep—how deep you can best realize if you look up a tributary canyon whose topmost rim is leveled off by clouds. A strange feature about Iao is the way in which it opens up soon after its stream divides, and becomes one of those amphitheaters characteristic of island scenery. The valley's sides are mostly unscalable, not because of sheer rock faces, for there are none, but simply because of their smooth greenness which offers no foothold. Climbing in the upper reaches is possible, but precarious. Difficult rescues after nights of exposure have been the experience of several people who have tried hiking in these mountains.

If you are lucky enough to have a good moon well overhead, you should see Iao by moonlight. Though you feel as though the walls of the valley are so close that you might touch them with outstretched arms, there is no sense of apprehension. The gurgle and splash of the stream seems reassuring and there are always the lights of Kahului shining in the distance. The Hawaiians must have felt at home in this place or they would never have called it Iao, "facing the dawn."

Like Kauai, Maui has no round-the-island road. Few people drive beyond Kula, though the road to Ulupalakua is interesting. Down below in blue Maalaea Bay is the half circle of Molokini, part of the rim of a submerged crater. It is bright pink in color as though someone had painted it on the sea's surface. It is odd to think of the big fish, hundred-pound ulua and the like, nosing about in watery caverns that were once lava bubbles or fountains of fire. A few miles farther on and you look down upon two converging tongues of black lava that were the latest flows from Haleakala. Tradition places these about three hundred years ago. Between the lava outflows is a bay named for La Perouse, the famous French navigator who helped the Americans fight the British in 1782 and three years later explored around the Pacific basin, especially on the Asiatic side. He spent a couple of days in Maalaea Bay and his ships were last reported in Botany Bay in 1788. Then they disappeared wholly from sight, without a trace of their discovery since that time. They were probably victims of a hurricane, or some hidden Pacific reef.

In the other direction lies Hana, one of the most remote and therefore most interesting spots in the islands. The road, like all roads around the windward sides of the islands, has many gulches to contend with. Some it elects to cross high up on the mountain, others near sea level. Hence, the road has the roller coaster habit, but high or low the sea on one side and the forest on the other make the way interesting. Hana itself retains some of the old-time Hawaiian charm, probably on account of its extreme isolation. However, on the seaward side, there is only a twenty-mile strait separating this part of Maui from Hawaii. Like the white cliffs of Dover, the black cliffs of Hana saw the approach of many an invasion fleet. Overlooking the little town is an old volcanic cone which abuts on the coast, and the seizure of this was a first objective. It has consequently figured largely in Hana's history, having withstood several sieges and being on one occasion the scene of a bloody massacre of an enemy force which was starved into surrender there.

About a mile from the little settlement a side road leads down
through a kamani and kukui forest to the sea. The coast there is
particularly rough, with great jagged spires of blackest lava, detached
from the mainland and exposed to the full fury of the sea, there
being no protecting reef on this side. This is a region of lava tubes
which form caves and blowholes. A hundred yards from the shore
there is a deep pit, and as you peer into its depths you may be
surprised by a sudden spurt of sea water which has rushed inland
along a subterranean tunnel in the lava. How much farther these
caves extend no one seems to know, but in the days of savage warfare, they no doubt afforded a secret refuge that the enemy would
hardly dare to explore.

Just on the fringe of the kamani trees are to be seen a dozen rough
cement slabs covering the graves of Hawaiians. These have no
finely chiseled epitaphs, but someone has taken a stick and while
the cement was still wet, has scratched names and dates of birth and
death on the slabs.

One inscription, however, carries a note of poignancy. Written
at the top of the slab are two names and ages—Antone 10 years,
Virginia 9 years. Then below in the roughest script is scribbled "The
poor children." What tragedy these words concealed there is no
telling. It is a wild spot and to reach the graves you pick your way
carefully over jagged points of rock. Down below, the great rollers
come sweeping into the little bay, dashing themselves to foam against
black lava crags. And there, at the edge of all this turmoil, lie the
poor children. Perhaps they were part of a fisherman's family and
at home near the sea; otherwise one might wish them a more
peaceful resting place.

Inland some distance is a cave which the writer once visited in
company with an Hawaiian deputy sheriff who acted as guide.
It had a very peculiar formation and was partially filled with fresh
water, fed by springs. There was a very low entrance with about
three feet of clearance above the water, though inside the opening
the roof rose to form a fair-sized cavern. You could either swim in,
or gain an entrance by crawling through a small tunnel at the side.

This ended at a little platform, ten or twelve feet above the water. If you waited until your eyes became dark-adapted, there was enough light reflected from the entrance to enable you to discern, very dimly, objects in the interior of the cavern. Seated on this platform our guide told us the story of the place.

The king's sister had fled with her serving maid in order to escape an unwelcome elderly suitor to whom her royal brother had promised her in marriage. The fugitives entered the cave and the princess sat on the rocks at one side, her attendant on the other, the latter keeping the kahili, the royal feather fly-whisk, waving in the air over the princess's head. The king searched everywhere and finally gave his sister up for lost. As he stood brooding at the entrance of the cave, he saw the moving shadow of the kahili dimly reflected in the water. Diving in, he caught the serving maid by the heels and swinging her round dashed her head against the roof. After that his anger evaporated, and he allowed his sister to marry the man of her choice. As the light filtered in from the front of the cave, the sheriff pointed to a folded red core in the black lava. "There," said he, "are the girl's brains." Perhaps more interesting than the tale itself was the manner of its telling. It was full of Biblical phrases—Hawaiian legend strained through a fine missionary mesh.

If Kailua, Hawaii, with its palace, was the Washington of the islands, and Honolulu its New York, then Lahaina was its Philadelphia. Without figuring as the scene of great battles or other very startling events, Lahaina managed to make history. To get to the town from Wailuku you take a road of whose scenic features Maui people are quite proud. It follows the bay just where a number of palis or cliffs plunge down to the sea. The contrast between the dark red and chocolate-brown of the dry headlands and the extraordinary color of the deep water is striking. So blue is that water that you almost expect some of its color to be left on the rocks over which it washes. Before the war this was a fine place to watch for whales and giant devil rays, called by the Hawaiians *hihimanu,* the spread out shark, fourteen feet and more in width, which feed near the surface, their flat bodies and long whip-like tails looking quite black from above. Since the war these sea monsters have had a bad time. They could, with the aid of an aviator's sporting imagination, be mistaken for submarines and were often bombed to make sure.

Along a few miles of such a road there are, of course, numerous and unexpected turns. Filipino laborers have three passions, one for fine raiment, another for cars, and the third for big words. A resident of Wailuku drove around a sharp curve and there, by the side of the road were gathered about eight Filipinos looking at their new car, its radiator smashed against a big rock.

"How did it happen?" inquired my friend.

"Well, sir," the driver explained, "I am driving my automobile and I come to this turn in the road. So I turn my wheel, and I turn my wheel, and I turn my wheel, and finally I become discouraged and run into this rock. And now my automobile is completely decomposed." There have been quite a number of discouraged drivers on the road to Lahaina.

It is little wonder that the Hawaiians had a great affection for Lahaina. The mountains, hardly more than a mile from the sea, are bare and sunsmitten except where they are gashed by deep gulches whose shadows and streams offer relief if the constant warmth of the beach becomes oppressive. The bulk of the mountains keeps the wind down to a gentle breeze except when the southerlies blow, and even then the roadstead is partially protected by the island of Kahoolawe, from whose desiccated slopes you can often see the red dust blowing in clouds out to sea. The warm equable climate, with a sea breeze gathering itself in the daytime off the bay and a gentle land breeze at night; the fertile black soil so ready to be laid out in taro patches; the fine groves of coconuts, breadfruit, and kou trees[2] for shade—what more could the people of Lahaina want?

Its very accessibility broadened the people's interests. In the old days the double canoes came and went, when kings and regents and lesser chiefs visited from the other islands. The land was rich

[2] The kou tree was once one of the finest shade trees in the islands until the groves were killed by the ravages of a pest called "red spider."

and entertainment easy. Lahaina folk built up a reputation for hospitality. The sight of canoes across the bay was the signal for putting fire in the *imus* or dirt ovens, and the killing of the fatted pig. The fur and whaling fleets found this an ideal winter haven and early observers record as many as four hundred ships anchored there in the one season. Much money was put in circulation, *hapahas* and *hapaluas* (quarters and half dollars) and many a Spanish *real* besides. Intemperance and prostitution were rife until the chiefs, under missionary influence, declared a state of prohibition for Lahaina. Thereafter the place was not so popular, but the seeds of depopulation had been sown.

In return for hospitality, Lahaina got the news, and no doubt this circumstance affected the people's receptivity to new ideas. The early missionaries, Stewart and Richards, received a very warm welcome. While their church and residences were being built, they lived with a Mr. Butler in a place that Stewart describes enthusiastically: "The thick shade of the breadfruit trees which surround his cottage, the rustling of the breeze through the bananas and sugar cane, the murmur of the mountain streams surrounding the yard, and the coolness and verdure of every spot around us seemed in contrast with our situation during a six months' voyage, and four weeks' residence in Honolulu, like the delights of an Eden." It must be remembered that Honolulu was at that time in the center of a dusty treeless plain.

The receptive character of the inhabitants and its climate no doubt determined the choice of Lahaina as the site of a seminary for the training of teachers, the first institution of higher learning west of the Rocky Mountains. The visitor can still see Lahainaluna, as it was called, situated at several hundred feet elevation a couple of miles behind the town. It was founded in September 1831.

By the year's end, sixty-seven students, who had passed an entrance examination in reading, writing, mental arithmetic, and geography, were selected and exposed to a curriculum including arithmetic, trigonometry, geometry, algebra, surveying, navigation, history, natural and moral philosophy, chemistry, church history, and languages "for a select class." "Carpentry, turnery and mason work, all received some attention, at least from individuals, connected with needful exercise and profitable labors."

Such practical pursuits were entirely necessary, for here was a seminary with teachers, students, and campus, but no buildings. Most of the pupils were married, with families, and had to build their own houses and prepare plots of ground for their dependents' sustenance. They themselves were fed at a cost of two cents a day by the school and though often hungry did not relax their studious efforts. Bingham was close to the scene and his description of the work involved is worth quoting.

"The walls and roof of the schoolhouse being erected by their own hands, the pupils, in the summer of 1832, went to the mountains for planks and timber for writing tables. There was no sawmill in the island, and the pupils had no team to aid them in their work, nor capital to procure its accomplishment. They must cut down trees, and hew them away to the thickness of the plank needed; then bring them on their shoulders, or drag them on the grounds, by hand, for miles. . . . . The pupils collected stones for a floor, hewed them a little, laid them down, and painted them with lime-mortar. Then they collected coral for lime and went to the mountains for fuel to burn it, and brought it on their shoulders, made a kiln and burned it, then plastered the walls of the house, outside and in, and made their writing tables, seats, window-shutters, doors, etc."

Lahainaluna is a monument, among other things, to the warmth of feeling that grew up between the missionaries and the Hawaiians. On the one hand was devotion to a great cause, on the other courage and determination to acquire the new knowledge. The influence of Lahainaluna, with its pupils drawn from and returning to every island, was undoubtedly a great factor in Hawaii's educational and social progress. The school for the past 95 years has been supported by government funds, and is still a fine educational influence throughout the Territory.

But Maui's breadth of vision is expressed even more clearly in a very unique social organization. Here we have an island with an entirely rural community, except for three or four small towns. That community is composed of Japanese, Chinese, Koreans, Filipinos, Portuguese, Anglo-Saxons, Hawaiians, and every combination of these original stocks. There are people living in small groups in the most remote localities. Maui has a few wealthy individuals; it has very many people, who, if not actually poverty-stricken, can make ends meet with a minimum of overlap. By all the rules of social circumstance Maui should be one of the most backward and neglected communities. Instead it is the very reverse, largely through the vision and effort that stand behind an excellent social agency.

Wisely recognizing that the Hawaiian tradition is one of interest and adventure, the Alexander House Community Association has for many years centered its program around activities that appeal to youth. It has fifteen hundred volunteer workers organized into well over a hundred committees, representing all classes and kinds of people. Its operations extend to the neighboring islands of Molokai and Lanai, whose inhabitants are included in the county's fifty-odd thousand permanent residents. These recreational and club activities extend to every small community, however remote. The Association's work is enmeshed with every kind of social activity—boy and girl scouts, health, relief, juvenile delinquency prevention, kindergarten work. Fifteen thousand individuals participated in these activities in a single year.

As an instance of what recreational organization can achieve, the Maui Alexander House swimming team, for three years in succession before the war, won the National Outdoors A.A.U. championship against the whole U.S. These swimmers were coached by a Japanese who for fifteen years had devoted four hours daily of unpaid labor to developing swimming among Maui's children.[8]

For the untiring spirit and effort of its workers; for the vision

[8] In such an island-wide effort only the leaders can be named—C. S. Childs (director), E. L. Damkroger (athletics), and Harold Stein (Boy Scout and kindred activities). The swimming instructor is Seichi Sakamoto.

that has inspired its whole program; for the generosity of its financial supporters and advisors, this island organization is worthy of far wider notice. It has demonstrated for the world—if the world only knew—that there is a level on which the youth of all peoples can not only meet, but live together on terms of the friendliest rivalry. It is a wonderful example of internationalism. Perhaps Maui is not inaptly named for the spreader of light.

CHAPTER XI

Home in Hawaii

TREES do what they can to cover the face of the land they inhabit. They do not determine the character of the country—only the mountains can do that—but they set the scenic mood. Think what the juniper and piñon do for the Southwest, the cottonwoods and live oaks for the Wichita Hills, the saguaro for the Arizona deserts. How different would be the lake scenery of Western Canada if it were not for those orderly arrays of spruce, hemlock, and jackpine that press down to the water's edge and stand so still and straight as though inviting the settler's axe to turn them into cabin and corral. Elsewhere it is birches, beeches, pines, maples, or cypresses that identify the country, that make the terrain authentic.

Of other continents this is equally true. The camelthorns looking like ragged umbrellas blown inside out by the wind are of the essence of Africa. In Central Australia it is the desert oak standing alone on a wide expanse of arid plain, the fringe of mulga around the base of the broken-down sandstone residual, or the painted gums that line the dry watercourses. In Southeast Australia it is the patriarchal gum tree in the clearing giving shade to a bunch of horses standing head to tail swishing away the flies. Wherever you have been happiest, no matter what place you call home, the trees come instantly to mind.

In the South Seas it is of course the palms that give the unforgettable touch. It could hardly be a Pacific isle without a beach curving towards a tiny headland, with a quiet stretch of water inside the reef, and across the level strip of sand the coconuts leaning. Back of them are the thick dark shadows and above them again the fronds and crowns of spindly palms. Trees, no less than white surf and blue ocean, are of the real charm of the South Seas.

But whether it was because Hawaii is new geologically, or because the islands were too isolated or out of the drift of the currents, much of their landscape was bare and treeless; how bare, it is hard to realize unless you look at old pictures or photographs showing, for example, the plain on which Honolulu now stands. There is a group of coconut palms near the shore, a few now uncommon native trees, such as the wiliwili and the kou, and the rest is a dry and dusty plain stretching away to the foothills which are themselves treeless. Only when the mountains at the back of Punchbowl attained considerable elevation were there any trees to be seen. Towards the Pali you could travel almost to the present level of the water reservoir or the eucalyptus plantations before the forest of koas and kukuis was much in evidence. Quite possibly the needs of the inhabitants for fuel and timber assisted in the deforestation of the lower levels. In any case, they were almost entirely treeless.

Whole areas of coastal plain and lower foothills on the other islands were also as bare as your hand. If the Roman Catholic missionaries did nothing more for this Territory than to import the algaroba tree, which is the Mexican mesquite, they would deserve the gratitude of Hawaii. For the kiawe, to give it its native name, has changed the face of the country entirely. Looking down on the low end of Molokai, for example, it is hard to imagine what the land would be like without this cover of forest, sparse though it is. The soil surface is cut and eroded by dry crumbling runnels and gullies which are red rivulets in heavy rain. Without the kiawes there would be a constant race between the weathering of the lava and the wind which blows the decomposed rock out to sea in red dust storms. Ultimately the perpetual wind, because it never lets up, aided by occasional heavy rains would win, and thus part of the island become nothing but a bare windswept rock. Now the kiawes have come to the rescue, although the battle is still critical.

But in Honolulu, trees are everywhere, with the result that there is probably no place on earth which has had its appearance so enhanced through man's occupancy. Probably everyone has read the poem which adjures the woodsman to spare the tree. Honolulu, it seems, must be the place where all repentant woodsmen have come to expiate their crimes against nature. There are some who think that the city is overplanted and that some of its trees could well be spared. Looking down from Punchbowl, the visitor might wonder whether he is viewing a city or a rain forest. The telephone and electric light companies keep hard at work cutting leafy tunnels for their overhead wires, while the city shade tree commission must sometimes wish that their business were a little less shady. To cut a tree down in Honolulu is almost a crime, so that it is little wonder that most of the tree-felling is done by a prison gang.

Considering that this was once a treeless plain, it appears strange that trees should thrive so mightily here. Many of them, such as certain species of eucalyptus, grow more rapidly here than in their native soil. The great bulbous-stemmed baobabs or bottle trees, which are so characteristic of the scenery of Northwest Australian plains, of Madagascar and South Africa, and are reported to be a thousand years old, put on girth so rapidly here that they promise in a short time to rival their bulkiest fellows elsewhere. Like the Hawaiian people, trees in Hawaii grow to generous proportions. One of these bottle trees can be seen near the offices of the Department of Agriculture and Forestry on King Street.

We probably have such a remarkable wealth of flowering trees because seeds are so easily transported. Some natives in Central Australia gave the writer beans of the beanwood tree (*Erethryna vespertilio*), which were brought home to Hawaii. The seedlings flourished and grew into fine trees, but unfortunately the transposition of this tree from the Southern to the Northern hemisphere has thrown its blossoming schedule out completely. After fourteen years of splendid growth the beanwood tree has not yet found out which is springtime in Hawaii, with the result that it has never flowered. When it does make up its mind, there will be another fine flowering tree added to our permanent tree population, which must already outnumber Honolulu's human inhabitants.

The result of this arboreal profusion is complete mental confusion when it comes to becoming really acquainted with our tree neighbors. Most of us have no more than a bowing acquaintance with them. Honolulu and its environs resemble a huge botanical garden, but some careless person has thrown away all the labels. Elsewhere in America almost any old-timer can name for you most of the trees common to his locality; here, no one but a botanist can identify ten per cent of our arboreal residents.

Moreover, the botanist is not a very simple or direct informant when you want him to straighten out the tree community for you. He is usually the kind of man who would rather say sessile for stalkless, selose, pilose or even hispid for hairy, sinuate for wavy, and porrect for projecting. Not content with multiplying words, he uses some common words in special meanings. For example, to a botanist's idea, only a bisexual flower is perfect. How perfectly ridiculous!

Nor do these scientists help matters much, when they casually give us a common name, which is often so uncommon that no one uses it. Take for example, our golden shower, that from March to October is so full of armfuls of yellow blossoms that it well deserves to be called the Midas tree, since all that it has, turns to gold. Two lady botanists who have written a fine book on Honolulu gardens go on to describe the fruit of *Cassia fistula* as "a straight, black, smooth, cylindrical pod reaching a yard in length and an inch in diameter," adding that these pods give it the name of "pudding-pipe tree." But what in the name of the tree creation is a *pudding pipe?* Then they go on to say that the sticky pulp that surrounds the seed-pod divisions has such a strong medicinal effect that the tree is called "the purging cassia." But no one wants to look at a golden shower and be reminded of purgatives.

It was Oliver Wendell Holmes who married his trees with a tape measure and boasted of this polygamous practice: "I call all trees mine that I have put my wedding ring on," he wrote, "and

I have as many tree wives as Brigham Young has human ones."
It is as well that Holmes did not have a tree honeymoon in Hawaii,
for then he would have had to compare himself with King Solomon,
though even with Solomon's wisdom it is doubtful if he could have
remembered the names of all his spouses.

In this vegetative miscellany you will find no consistent pattern
of growth, no similarity of either flowers, fruit, or foliage, for the
trees have come from every clime and country, many of them
showing the results of their age-long development under conditions
different from ours. They are pilgrims from far places, an arboreal
convocation, a calling together of all trees. So they form a motley
assemblage, dressed in every conceivable habit and fashion, as if
this were the Mecca of trees. It may help the observer a little to
call the roll by country of origin of some of our distinguished
delegates.

One at least carries its own geographical label. This is the
African tulip tree with its clusters of orange-red flowers, arranged
like the finger tips of your two hands bunched together. The
stranger will recognize it by its grey trunk on which its main root
outgrowth is matched by prominent ridges near the base, giving the
tree a deeply fluted appearance. One of these trees growing in
Kamanele Park has a niche in it deep enough to accommodate the
statue of a saint. It no doubt has been used for other purposes.

Small boys love to play with its unopened buds, for if you
squeeze them they emit a fine jet of water. The lady botanists say
this gives the tree its popular name, the fountain tree. The small
boys have a different word for it, which is impolite, but more
descriptive.

Africa also has sent us its most brilliant representative—the
poinciana, which hails from Madagascar but has now ringed the
Pacific basin. It wears its crimson to light red masses of bloom
most ostentatiously, sometimes hiding all the green of its foliage.
These are the painted ladies of forest society, who plaster their
rouge on every available surface. Wilder and Kamehameha avenues
have perhaps the best display. In the flowering season the fallen

petals literally cover the ground with a crimson carpet, though it may more aptly remind you of the morning after an old-fashioned Fourth of July. Flamboyant is the name for the poinciana. There is nothing modest about its display.

But talking of African floral carpets reminds us of the jacaranda. This tree came originally from South America but has also girdled the sub-tropical earth. In South Africa jacarandas are planted in avenues and every guide book raves about the manner in which their pale blue to light purple flowers cover the ground. In Hawaii there are so many flowering trees that the jacaranda, delicately beautiful though it is, merely takes its place among the jostling variegated crowd. In its season it finds space enough, however, to give you some hint of what the South Africans are so enthusiastic about.

Asia has a many-hued representation in the shower trees, the pink and white, and the golden cassias. Yellow, cream, orange, pink, and red—you can have any combination or gradation you choose. Possibly the so-called rainbow shower, a cross between *Cassia nodosa* and *Cassia fistula,* deserves more than any other the name flame tree, for it literally blazes. Flames, as you well know, are not always red or crimson. They are just as often yellow, orange, pink, and sometimes blue. Most of these colors you will see in this tree which in its season is a seething, flaming mass of color from its lowest to its topmost branches.

Australia has made a notable contribution as regards shade, but not so much to our floral adornment. Prominent among its native trees are the eucalyptus, although the best of the flowering gums from Western Australia have yet to find their way hither. Strangely enough, the black wattle, the quietest of the acacias, managed to get itself elected to the Australian delegation, leaving at home the golden wattle or the still more beautiful Cootamundra wattle, whose yellow bursts of tiny golden balls make their appearance in the early spring in the florists' shops of California where they call it "the acacia," as distinctive a name as Smith, there being many hundreds of acacias.

There is a fine forest group of eucalyptus on Tantalus and still finer ones on Haleakala on Maui. Nature in Australia had little in the way of variety to work with, so she took the eucalyptus and proceeded to ring all the changes she could express in difference of appearance. The bark will vary all the way from the smoothest possible to a most unnecessary roughness, with white gum at one end of the scale, the ironbark at the other.

The blue gum *(Eucalyptus globulus)* is perhaps the commonest in Hawaii, and the least useful of its kind. But you cannot always combine utility with beauty. The leaves of the blue gum are so slenderly hung that they let most of the Hawaiian sunlight filter through. If you want sylvan tracery, then plant blue gum saplings against a white wall. The planners of the landscape gardening at the San Francisco Fair made full use of this effect. Like puppies, gums are most appealing when young. Some of them have remarkable courage. One of the bravest sights I have seen was a white gum sapling growing on a ledge in the red walls of a gorge in Central Australia, a young thing still green and graceful, standing in the face of a six years' drought.

Another Australian importation is the *Grevillia robusta,* or silky oak, popularly miscalled the "silver oak." As its name implies, it is a little too robust for city planting, but on the lower windward slopes of the Pali it is a thing of beauty. It does not respond well to urbanization.

Possibly second in point of usefulness is another hardy Australian, the Queensland ironwood, one of the family of casuarinas. Its long grey needles droop rather sadly and the Hawaiian wind that blows through them is pitched to a minor key. Some of the botanists call it the "she-oak," a name which should be reserved for a much longer-needled casuarina whose wailing in the wind has a more feminine quality. Our debt to the ironwoods is that they provide an excellent windbreak and may be planted very near to the sea, thus sheltering the cane fields inland. Apparently the ironwoods do not mind the salt rheum blowing in their faces; it fits well with their sad air.

A tree destined to be very widely known because of its excellent nuts is the Queensland macadamia, a plantation of which covers one of the Makiki slopes of Roundtop. It is noteworthy because it appears to be the only plant or tree from its native continent that has added to the white man's larder. Even then it is definitely in the luxury class.

Thus every part of the world has contributed to this remarkable tree congress that has met in Hawaii. The marvel is that such widely separated plants have found the place congenial. Side by side with the cypress or the pomegranate from Europe you may find the Norfolk Island pine from the other side of the globe. The kiawe, a desert tree, may grow beside the India rubber tree which prefers damp tropical forests. The pepper tree from Peru may have as its neighbor the Litchi nut from China. The mahogany from Central America is equally at home with a bauhinea from Siam.

How did these trees and plants come here? One explanation is that the people of Hawaii have always been interested in flowers and trees and being great travelers have brought seeds back with them from everywhere. In the early days Dr. Hillebrand[1] was responsible for bringing in many of the trees that are now common in Hawaii. The Forestry and Agriculture Department has not been idle, but probably the most credit for tree importing must go to the H.S.P.A. which has for many years kept up an arboretum in Manoa Valley, from which has come a steady augmentation of shade and flowering trees. The sugar planters have, of course, a practical interest in importing trees useful for timber or shelter, but they have kept an eye open for beauty as well.

To the visitor, the great variety of trees is overwhelming unless he gets a book such as *In Honolulu Gardens,* and goes on a still-hunt for identification purposes. If he is a tourist he will, of course, be taken to see the sausage tree on the University campus. In the opinion of local taxi-drivers, it is the most noteworthy thing about the University. Even more remarkable than its crop of huge sausage-

---

[1] Hillebrand, noted botanist, competent physician, and Commissioner of Immigration (1865-66) lived here 20 years, explored the islands, and in his many travels was an assiduous collector of trees and plants for Hawaii.

like fruits are the blossoms that hang down like old-fashioned pipes with curved stems. This and many other strange trees will come under your notice, but identification will be difficult. Perhaps a brief reference to the various forms of tree architecture may cause the visitor to look a little more closely at some of our prominent tree residents, and it may assist him to keep their names in mind.

Most of the trees are built on the umbrella plan, the cypress being the most tightly closed. The araucarias, or Norfolk Island pines, are partly opened with their branches evenly spaced in whorls, the broadest at the base. An avenue of these trees such as the one that leads to Kipu, the Rice family's ranch and plantation on Kauai, has a most unusual appearance. The broad lower branches meet overhead to form a tunnel of shade and then the trees on either side taper off, leaving up above a triangle of air and sunshine. Another araucaria is less regular in shape and was named after Captain Cook. Still another is the monkey puzzle, or bunya tree, whose nuts are enjoyed by the Australian aborigines. As there are no monkeys in Queensland, it is hard to see how this tree could provide a test of a monkey's I.Q. The branches are set spirally on the trunk so that an imaginary monkey might be puzzled by this entirely imaginary problem. It is like the man who carried home a mongoose to kill the snakes his brother saw when he had D.T.'s. The mongoose was imaginary, too.

The full umbrella-shaped trees are the real monopolists of sun and air and keep at limbs' length all other forms of plant life. The most ruthless of the lot is the monkeypod. This immigrant from Central America achieves its great breadth by thrusting out its major limbs within a few feet of the ground just like the ribs of an umbrella. The secondary limbs into which these divide are widely spaced and as the terminal branches also spread widely, the final effect is that of a blown up cupola. The monkeypod is the Rockefeller among trees. Once it has stifled all competitors, it affects an air of pious humility and each evening folds its leaves together like hands clasped in prayer. With all this magnificence of limbs and foliage the monkeypod achieves a little flower like a pink shaving brush.

The banyan, of which there are several kinds, is a whole capitalist combine. Its aerial roots are the subsidiaries of the main holding company with all kinds of interlocking directorates. It, too, through its broad fleshy leaves achieves a monopoly of shade.

Incidentally, the two species last described give the lie to the dictionary definition of a tree. Webster insists that a tree is "a woody perennial plant having a *single* main stem." It would be a difficult matter to decide which of the banyan's many trunks is the main stem and they are certainly not single. The Oxford dictionary also is no better than Webster, for it remarks that the single woody stem must be *self-supporting*. If the lexicographer could take a ride up the Pali Road he would see a tree that *is* a tree but whose trunk or trunks are by no means self-supporting. The hau tree has a multitude of twisted, almost tortured trunks that all support each other so that one tree constitutes in itself a whole jungle. It is useless to call the hau a creeper. It is a sprawler, perhaps the greatest of all sprawlers, but not a creeper.

You may not know, perhaps, that this too is an hibiscus, *Hibiscus tiliaceus,* to be exact, and Webster calls it "a small tropical tree." I wonder what Mr. Webster would call a large tree if a hau that may cover a couple of acres is small!

Conspicuous among the arboreal Big Five in Honolulu is the elephant's ear, or if you care about such labels, *Enterolobrium cyclocarpum.* The size of the tree matches its name. If the botanists are right, and this is really a specimen of the bean family, it must surely be the original sprout of Jack and the Bean Stalk. It gets its common name from the shape of its flattened ear-shaped pods, like the aural appendages of a baby elephant that has never had its ears washed. Its habit is also to dispose of its limbs like the ribs of a huge umbrella. Then having pre-empted more space than it can use, the elephant's ear gets a change of heart and puts out a fine feathery foliage which lets plenty of sunlight filter through. In its display of bare limbs the tree is hardly modest.

No such accusation can be leveled against our mango tree, which like the women of its native land goes closely veiled from head to foot at all seasons. The mango is more secretive than inaccessible, for more boys' legs and arms are broken falling out of mango trees than out of any other tree in the Territory. Hawaiians, with reason, call it the bellyache tree because the green fruit is irresistible to children. Could it be that the mango with its forbidden fruit and all its afterpains was the original tree of knowledge? In the spring, if such a season could be recognized in Hawaii, the mango puts forth a striking display of new leaves, the color of burnished bronze.

Among the other forest giants to be seen in Honolulu gardens is the silk cotton tree or kapok which is distinguished by the huge buttresses which surround its trunk.

If there is one family of trees that may be said to dominate the scene in Honolulu, it is the palms. Down at the seaside by Waikiki, towering above the monkeypods at Moanalua gardens, bristling at you around the corners of buildings, grouped in clusters or standing in ragged lines, the palms are everywhere. Some, like the Royal palms from the West Indies, specialize in elevation. On almost every street you can see their cylindrical grey trunks, pillars of deportment supporting a crown of foliage. The Royal palms, as their name denotes, are rather pompous, and are at their best as they stand stiffly on guard around the Royal mausoleum in Nuuanu Valley.

William Alanson Bryan, who wrote the first book on the natural history of Hawaii, speaks of these palm tops as "fitting capitols for such splendid stately pillars," and thinks they gladden and enrich the landscape, but they hardly enrich a small garden. It seems odd that this palm should erect such a great column to support such a feather-duster of foliage.

The coconut palms, or at least the common species, specialize also in height, the trunks sometimes growing 80 feet to push up their feathery crowns. These palms illustrate the saying that two is company, three a crowd, for wherever three palms are planted together they will usually grow away from each other. But a group of coconuts provide a lesson in easy deportment. They incline to one another in conversational groups. What they say is surely nothing weighty or serious, merely that polite inconsequential small talk that connotes no more than a gracious recognition of each other's presence. Even those of the party that look slightly inebriated sway, but never stagger.

In other Pacific lands, such as Samoa, this tree is extremely useful. Its fruit is both food and drink, its plaited fronds form roof coverings, its trunks serve as house pillars, each post having its degree of honor when assigned as a backrest to visitors of rank. Its husk is a drinking cup, while the fiber from the nut when plaited into sennit braid is the standard lashing, without which Polynesian industry would literally fall apart. But the coconut palms which reached Hawaii came to retire from industry and live the life of Reilly. No one puts them to work. They can drop their nuts or keep them—nobody cares; and sennit braid is out of fashion as material for lashing. The breadfruit tree, which grows here luxuriantly, is comparatively neglected as an article of food, yet in other Pacific islands its custardy fruit is the staff of life.

The difficulties which botanists get into in trying to describe a coconut are quite amusing. They call it "a fibrous, thick, smooth, oval, three-angled husk, surrounding a round nut with a bone-like shell and three hollows near the base; within is a thick layer of white, solid, compact, oily pulp, edible, sweet, containing a hollow with sweet, clouded water." What a dither of description over a husky nut with a drink in it!

We have growing here also the date palm but, strangely enough, it bears a rather small fruit edible only to hookey-players, golf caddies, and mynah birds. It has a very ugly trunk due to its habit of keeping tabs on every leaf it ever bore by retaining a little stump of the broken midrib, giving its trunk a very untidy appearance. But most ragged of all is the Washington palm, which will not give up any of its ragged leaves but keeps them hanging around its trunk in a dry bedraggled mass that, no doubt, harbors all the centipedes in the neighborhood.

Some person, not an Hawaiian I'm sure, has called this the hula palm, perhaps because of this ungraceful drapery of dead fronds. Anything less like a hula skirt could hardly be imagined. Not even a drunken sailor would look twice at a hula if performed in such a costume.

Of all strange habits of growth the Traveler's Palm literally takes the palm. It arranges its huge green blades in a fan shape, each packed neatly side by side with its fellows. Botanists say that it gets its name from the little hoard of water stored at the base of the leaves, from which the thirsty traveler may drink—that is, if he does not object to the distilled essence of dead flies, beetles, drowned ants, and mosquito wrigglers which it commonly contains. The palm usually grows in wet places where the traveler is probably doing his best to avoid water, not find it. Besides that, the botanists say it is not a palm at all, but a kind of banana.

If you take into consideration all the flowering plants of Hawaii, then this will appear a real Pacific treasure island. But none of this treasure is hidden; it is all on display for every one but red-green color-blind people to see. These unfortunate persons are the only ones who should not visit Hawaii, for most of the floral gold that has been pirated from all over the world is red gold.

In any bus ride through the residential sections of Honolulu, the observer may take an interest in arranging on a mental scale all the different hues of red he sees. He will have little difficulty with the extremes of color. At one end he may place the very light pink of the monkeypod blossoms or some of the hibiscus; at the other end he will find the poincianas or the poinsettias competing for top place in brilliance. In between he may place the Mexican creeper, the pink, red or torch ginger, the plumeria, the oleander, the Christmas berry clusters, the red ornamental ti plants, the African tulip, and some kinds of bougainvillea. He may have the fun of arranging these on his own scale and the interesting thing is that he may count all these gradations of pink and red within the limits of a single block. Some species, like the hibiscus, may run the whole gamut of color in its many varieties.

If flowers have a language, then this must be the tower of Babel. Loudest of all is the bougainvillea, named after the French navigator, which fairly shouts at you from wayside gardens. I'm afraid this plant has none of the modesty of the shrinking violet and when its different varieties, with their clouds of purple, magenta, salmon, brick-red, and scarlet or cerise colors are grouped together, they swear at each other in flower language that the worst Billingsgate could not rival.

Unless you have grown up in Hawaii, you may find its floral wealth bewildering. If the trees of the Territory match the league of nations, then our flowers are like its assembly, in which even the colonies are represented by numerous delegations. Among the orchids, for example, you will find specimens from Mexico, Central America, Brazil, Malaya, New Guinea, Queensland, and even Guadalcanal.

Not only color but form is extraordinary. The gold-filled night-blooming cereus, the odd-shaped birds of paradise, the anthuriums with their brilliant red patent-leather finish, the billbergias, out of the leaf spathe of which comes an almost unbelievable flower—the only word for Hawaiian florescence is extravagant. Nothing as serious as a league of nations convocation will do for comparison; perhaps a fashion show, in which all the impressionist designers vie with one another to create the richest dresses on the most outrageously exhibitionist models, is nearer the mark. And some at least that are not remarkable for form or color scent the air so heavily that they would give Araby with all its spices a headache. Try sleeping at night with your window open to a nearby *cestrum nocturnum;* it will take a strong trade wind to dilute its almost overpowering sweetness. Yet the tiny flowers which open only at dusk are so inconspicuous they can hardly be seen.

Living in the midst of such a floral extravaganza becomes at times somewhat disturbing. There are times when one wishes to return to more respectable if less exciting floral society, to the old-fashioned garden world of roses and violets, hollyhocks, petunias, daffodils—yes, and even stocks and honesty. These are more restful than orchids and have a quieter ring to their names than, say, homescioldia, though to some people that may sound domestic enough; or, as another example, we have that huge leafed creeper that swamps some of the tree trunks—the *Monstera deliciosa,* which sounds as whimsical as "reluctant dragon." Unfortunately, the common English flowers, though they may grow for you, hardly compete in form or color with the painted ladies of the Hawaiian harem. They flourish only in the purity and serenity of our higher elevations, such as Kokee or Kula.

*   *   *   *   *

When you consider the marvelous miscellany of our flowers you may well wonder why the birds that ought to match them in variety and beauty are so pitifully represented in Hawaii. One reason is that some of the most attractive native birds have become extinct; another seems to be that the agricultural experts have been afraid to destroy the balance of nature by importing too many fruit-eating or insectivorous birds. Possibly they have been far too cautious.

In great numbers we have the monotonously noisy Indian mynah. In moderation the mynah birds are tolerably interesting, if only for their quarrels. Half a dozen or more will stage a violent debate on your back lawn and then one will be singled out and attacked by the rest for some obscure bird reason and sometimes pecked to death. At nightfall hundreds of mynahs will congregate from a wide area and hold a screeching contest in a banyan tree, where all the news of the day, seed by seed, is vociferously described, all the mynah birds talking at once. With all the wonderful bird life of Australia and Africa available as companions, why must we stay married to mynahs? The only birds that can abide their proximity seem to be cardinals, doves, and sparrows. The modest Chinese thrush has withdrawn from mynah competition to the mountains. We need a few Australian kookaburras, or laughing jackasses, to teach the mynahs their place, while a few of their forest thrushes, warblers, whistlers, finches, and parrots would make these islands an aviary. From Africa, weaver birds, glossy starlings, and egrets would add to the interest immensely.

The native birds of Hawaii are of great importance to ornithologists but of little concern to the visitor, who seldom sees them. There are native crows, hawks, and owls, the first two occasionally to be found on the big island; in the forest uplands there you may also see the *elepaio,* a species of fly-catcher, or the red-feathered *iiwi,* but otherwise the woods are almost birdless. The white tropic bird with its two long tail feathers may also be seen flying around our cliffs and canyons.

*   *   *   *   *

As far as land animals are concerned, the place is biologically barren. The chief indigenous inhabitant appears to be the Hawaiian rat, of which no one would naturally be proud. In far larger numbers we have a most unwelcome immigrant, the plague-bearing Norwegian grey rat. There is also the black rat whose name seems to signify to a layman an astonishing poverty of imagination among scientists. It reminds me of the Englishman who wore two gold watchchains across his vest, occasioning the remark that it was two too many watchchains. I do not mind Rattus as a scientific designation, and Rattus rattus can be tolerated, but when zoologists are reduced to naming another variety Rattus rattus rattus, then their mental processes, in my opinion, seem to be somewhat overratted.

Of the beasts of prey, we have a single specimen; so proudly we hail, for our visitors' benefit, the Indian mongoose, the fluffy-tailed weasel-bodied, rather furtive Rikki-tikki-tavi of Kipling's tale. Like the monkey puzzle tree, which would puzzle our monkeys, if we had any monkeys, the mongooses would eat our snakes if we had any snakes. I believe they were imported to kill the rats in the canefields, but as our most assiduous nature-noter, Major Eddie Bryan, points out, this was done without consulting the habits of either animal. The rat works at night and the mongoose hunts only in the daytime. Hence, they never meet except for a very short period at change of shifts, and as neither animal will give up its way of living, the mongoose is reduced to hunting birds and beetles and such-like things for its sustenance.

*   *   *   *   *

As is to be expected, the parts of these islands that are most populous with wild life are the reefs that fringe their shores. Fish of all kinds and colors which truly match our flowers in strangeness and beauty are there in plenty, along with voracious and occasionally vicious species of eels. Outside the reefs cruise sharks of various kinds, though fortunately the white and grey sharks, the "blue nurse" and the "white nurse," the fierce man-eaters of the South Pacific, are rare. Though there are few instances of sharks attacking people in these waters, there is ample evidence from early writers such as Ellis that they were at one time much feared by the Hawaiians.

Whole books have been written about our fishes and other marine life, to which I would add but a single note. The humu-humunukunukuapua'a is a very little fish with its eyes set far back

HUMUHUMU NUKUNUKU-APUA'A

(After Bryan)

in its head, its cheeks drawn forward and its small round mouth pursed up in a perpetual whistle of astonishment, as though for the first time in its life it had heard its name. The writer does not like dead fish, but if your interest runs in that direction, you can take Spencer Tinker's handbook down to the fishmarket and have a grand time. The rest of us will be satisfied with the gorgeous display of tropical fish at the aquarium.

*   *   *   *   *

Perhaps this is a sufficient listing of the things that are Hawaii. All that remains is to attempt to give some partial answer to the question that people who do not know the place are sure to ask. What is the appeal of Hawaii? Why is it that those who stay long enough become such a part of its life that when away they long to return? Why do the South Seas confer on wandering humans that deep sense of contentment, as if something reached out and laid a gently restraining hand on your sleeve, saying—this is your home, stay here? It affects all kinds and conditions of men. It called equally to Don Francisco de Paula Marin, Spanish gentleman, who made his home in Hawaii in Kamehameha's time, to the missionary from New England, to Stephen Reynolds the sailor, to Culman the blacklisted mechanic, to Robert Louis Stevenson the poet. For R. L. S. loved Samoa for the things it has in common with Hawaii, the things that he had in mind when he penned that poignantly beautiful epitaph for his grave in Vailima:

> This be the verse you grave for me;
> Here he lies where he longed to be,
> Home is the sailor, home from the sea,
> And the hunter home from the hill.

Is there not something strange in the fact that a land so exotic in its beauty, so unlike all that we were accustomed to in childhood, should displace our early ties and come to mean home to so many different types of people?

It cannot be beauty alone, for other places have that. I am inclined to believe that it is Hawaii's evenness, its equability of spirit, as much as its beauty. Softness, mildness, the very insensitiveness of the place to seasonal change, the ease with which all living things seem to adapt themselves to their new surroundings, the nervous relaxation, combine to contribute that sense of well-being which is one of the foundations of happiness.

I would hazard the opinion that the reactions of man to his physical environment are more deep-seated than we have ever realized. For all the ages that man has been on earth he has had to battle with the natural elements. Flood and tempest, heat and cold, have been his enemies from the beginning. The satisfaction that most of us experience under our own rooftree is due to a sense of security not only from foes of our own kind but also from all the physical hardships and dangers of exposure. On the other hand, we have developed a sense of nervous tension and anxiety in the face of dangers, which causes us to avoid by all means in our power that which threatens our continued existence.

Conversely, we are at ease, and have a sense of well-being and security in a place where nothing threatens. I believe that still waters, the calm of the evening, or peaceful pastures appeal to all of us because they suggest that security which man, ever since he began to wander on earth, has always sought. In fact, we must be assured of our own security before we can enjoy any of the great upheavals of nature. A storm at sea is a wonderful sight—from dry land—and we can all enjoy the howling blizzard best from our own firesides.

I suggest, then, that the psychological basis of the home-feeling that Hawaii develops is as deep as human nature itself, and that it is due to the subconcious sense of security that is engendered by equability of climatic conditions. Of course it can rain in Hawaii, and rain hard; but there is no time when a patch of blue sky does not promise the sunshine that so soon follows. It can be unpleasantly warm at times; but even in the dog days of September and October, the clouds hang softly around the mountain tops, hinting that cool trade winds and cleansing showers are only at most a day or two away. There is no perfect climate anywhere on earth, but here at least the sun never stands "all in a hot and copper sky at noon" or any other time; nor is there a place in the islands where thunderheads gather or storm signals fly. Day follows day in peaceful procession, and if you will only let Hawaii have its way with you, that nervous, feverish, hurrying spirit that is the bane of modern existence, will be exorcised and disappear.